The Korean War

D0647777

SEMINAR STUDIES   IN HISTORY

The Korean War

STEVEN HUGH LEE

An imprint of **Pearson Education**

Harlow, England · London · New York · Reading, Massachusetts · San Francisco · Toronto · Don Mills, Ontario · Sydney
Tokyo · Singapore · Hong Kong · Seoul · Taipei · Cape Town · Madrid · Mexico City · Amsterdam · Munich · Paris · Milan

PEARSON EDUCATION LIMITED

Head Office:
Edinburgh Gate
Harlow
Essex CM20 2JE
Tel: +44 (0)1279 623623
Fax +44 (0)1279 431059

London Office:
128 Long Acre
London WC2E 9AN
Tel: +44 (0)20 7447 2000
Fax: +44 (0)20 77240 5771
Website: www.history-minds.com

First published in Great Britain in 2001

© Pearson Education Limited 2001

The right of Steven Hugh Lee to be identified as author
of this work has been asserted by him in accordance
with the Copyright, Designs and Patents Act 1988.

ISBN 0-582-31988-9

British Library Cataloguing-in-Publication Data
A CIP catalogue record for this book can be obtained from the British Library

All rights reserved; no part of this publication may be reproduced, stored
in a retrieval system, or transmitted in any form or by any means, electronic,
mechanical, photocopying, recording, or otherwise without either the prior
written permission of the Publishers or a licence permitting restricted copying
in the United Kingdom issued by the Copyright Licensing Agency Ltd.,
90 Tottenham Court Road, London, W1P 0LP. This book may not be lent,
resold, hired out or otherwise disposed of by way of trade in any form
of binding or cover other than that in which it is published, with the
prior consent of the Publishers.

10 9 8 7 6 5 4 3 2 1

Typeset by 7 in 10/12 Sabon Roman
Printed in Malaysia,LSP

The Publishers' policy is to use paper manufactured from sustainable forests.

CONTENTS

INTRODUCTION TO THE SERIES

Such is the pace of historical enquiry in the modern world that there is an ever-widening gap between the specialist article or monograph, incorporating the results of current research, and general surveys, which inevitably become out of date. *Seminar Studies in History* is designed to bridge this gap. The series was founded by Patrick Richardson in 1966 and his aim was to cover major themes in British, European and World history. Between 1980 and 1996 Roger Lockyer continued his work, before handing the editorship over to Clive Emsley and Gordon Martel. Clive Emsley is Professor of History at the Open University, while Gordon Martel is Professor of International History at the University of Northern British Columbia, Canada, and Senior Research Fellow at De Montfort University.

All the books are written by experts in their field who are not only familiar with the latest research but have often contributed to it. They are frequently revised, in order to take account of new information and interpretations. They provide a selection of documents to illustrate major themes and provoke discussion, and also a guide to further reading. The aim of *Seminar Studies in History* is to clarify complex issues without over-simplifying them, and to stimulate readers into deepening their knowledge and understanding of major themes and topics.

NOTE ON TRANSLITERATION

Chinese names, with the exception of Chiang Kai-shek, are written in Pinyin. Chinese, Korean and Japanese names, except Syngman Rhee, are written with the last name first.

NOTE ON REFERENCING SYSTEM

A number in square brackets preceded by *Doc.* [*Doc. 5*] refers readers to the corresponding item in the Documents section which follows the main text.

PREFACE

This book is meant for teachers and students interested in a concise international history of the Korean War. It differs from traditional studies of the war in several significant ways. The analysis traces the origins and dynamics of the war to the interplay between modern Korean history and twentieth-century world history. The narrative also examines the social history of the conflict, an important theme which is neglected in many surveys of the fighting. Most accounts of the war end their discussions in 1953, with the signing of the armistice. This study carries the story through 1954, with an examination of the often-forgotten Geneva Conference on Korea. The meetings in Switzerland that spring were the last major international effort before recent years to negotiate a permanent peace for the Korean peninsula. A selection of primary material has also been included to highlight the analysis and to add depth to students' understanding of the events.

I would like to thank a number of people who helped me write this monograph. At the University of British Columbia, Don Baker, Yunshik Chang, George Egerton and Chris Friedrichs read the manuscript and offered excellent suggestions for its improvement. My stimulating discussions with them over the years are reflected in the book's pages. Insun Lee has been a strong source of support and encouragement. Emeritus Professor Ivan Avacumovic imparted his many years of learned experience and knowledge about Soviet foreign policy and the Cold War. Two readers outside the university – Michael Hunt of the University of North Carolina at Chapel Hill and Peter Lowe of the University of Manchester – made very valuable contributions to the final product. In Korea, I would like to thank Professor Lew Young Ick and Lee Myoung-Soon for their support. The editor of the Longman Seminar Study series, Gordon Martel, responded promptly and professionally to queries and suggestions. Sarah Bury copy-edited the manuscript with a delicate and precise hand. A number of granting agencies were also instrumental in getting the project completed. Language study in Seoul was made possible by a grant from the Korea Foundation. This book has been published with the support of grants from the Social Sciences and Humanities Research Council of Canada and the Centre for Korean Research, UBC. It is dedicated to my parents, whose love made it possible.

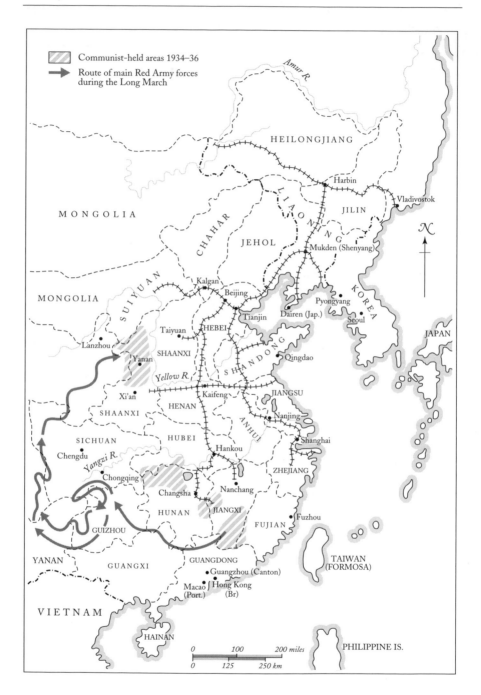

Map 1   China and Korea

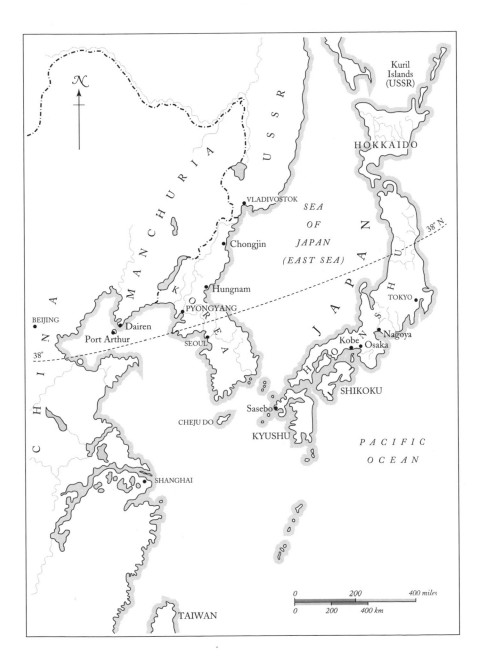

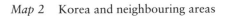

Map 2   Korea and neighbouring areas

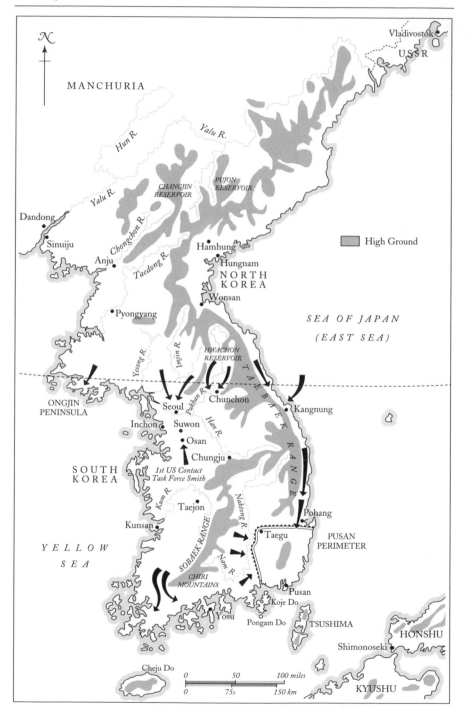

Map 3   North Korean People's Army offensive, 25 June–15 September 1950

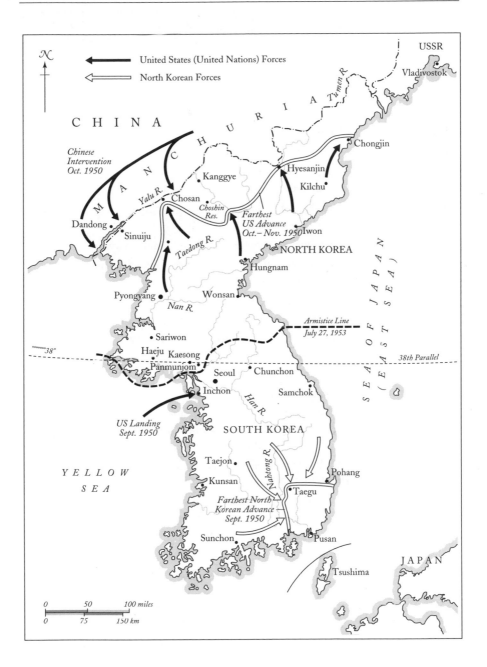

Map 4   The Korean War, 1950–53

CHRONOLOGY

1875	Syngman Rhee born.
1876	Korea's first modern (unequal) treaty signed with Japan.
1879	Joseph Stalin born.
1884	Harry Truman born.
1890	Dwight D. Eisenhower born.
1893	Mao Zedong born.
1894–95	First Sino-Japanese war ends in Japanese victory.
1896–98	Nationalist activities of the Korean Independence Club.
1902	Anglo-Japanese Alliance formed.
1904–5	Russo-Japanese War ends in Japanese victory.
1905	Korea becomes a protectorate of the Japanese Empire.
1910	Korea becomes a formal Japanese colony.
1912	Kim Il Sung born.
1914–18	First World War.
1917	Russian Revolution.
1918	Wilson's Fourteen-Point Speech to the US Congress.
1919	March First Movement: nationwide protests in Korea against Japanese colonial rule.
1922	Anglo-Japanese alliance is replaced by a series of naval arms limitations and great power agreements.
1931	Japan invades Manchuria.
1934–35	Long March of Chinese communists.
1936–41	Northeast Anti-Japanese United Army active in Manchuria.
1937–45	Second Sino-Japanese War.
1941	
August	Atlantic Charter drawn up by President Franklin Roosevelt and Prime Minister Winston Churchill.
December	American entry into the Pacific War.
1943	Cairo Declaration: Korea to receive independence 'in due course'.

1945

February	Stalin and Roosevelt agree to four-power trusteeship for Korea.
August	United States proposes 38th parallel as temporary dividing line between Soviet and American armies in Korea.
	Local people's committees established across Korea.
September	Korean People's Republic established.
December	Moscow Conference between the United States and Soviet Union establishes a Joint Soviet-American Commission to oversee process leading to Korean independence.

1946

February	Conservative-dominated Representative Democratic Council established in Seoul (chaired by Syngman Rhee); Interim People's Committee established in northern Korea, led by Kim Il Sung.
June	Civil war begins in China.
July	North Korean Workers' Party established.
October	Elections for South Korean Interim Assembly held.

1947

March	Truman Doctrine announced by the President.
June	George Marshall launches a plan for the economic rehabilitation of Europe.
September	George Marshall tells the UN General Assembly of his intention to discuss the issue of the independence of Korea at the United Nations.
November	United Nations Temporary Commission On Korea (UNTCOK) established to oversee elections in all of Korea.

1948

8 February	North Korean People's Army (KPA) established.
1 March	US Occupation Commander John Hodge announces elections for South Korea by early May.
10 May	South Korean elections.
15 August	Republic of Korea (ROK) established with Syngman Rhee as President.
9 September	Democratic People's Republic of Korea (DPRK) established.
19 October	Yosu Rebellion begins.

1949

3–5 March	Kim Il Sung visits Moscow and meets Stalin for the first time.
4 April 1949	NATO Treaty signed in Washington.
1 October	People's Republic of China established.

1950

12 January	Secretary of State Dean Acheson's Press Club speech.
28 January	First indication that Stalin was ready to help Kim Il Sung prepare an offensive against South Korea.
14 February	Sino-Soviet Treaty Alliance signed in Moscow.
March–April	Kim Il Sung visits Moscow and obtains Stalin's formal support for an offensive.
12 April	Harry Truman informally approves draft of NSC 68.
13–16 May	Kim Il Sung visits Beijing to obtain Mao's support.
25 June	North Korean offensive begins.
30 June	Harry Truman orders US ground troops stationed in Japan to South Korea.
7 July	General Douglas MacArthur becomes UN Commander.
15 September	X Corps lands at Inchon.
30 September	ROK troops cross the 38th parallel.
	President Truman formally approves NSC 68.
1 October	MacArthur issues final ultimatum to the DPRK to surrender.
7 October	US troops cross 38th parallel.
	Mao informs Stalin of his decision to send nine divisions of troops to Korea after 'some time' has passed.
25 October	First UN Command (UNC) military engagement with PRC 'Volunteers'.
26 November	Major Chinese offensive against UN troops begins.
4–8 December	Truman–Attlee meetings in Washington.
16 December	President Truman declares a state of national emergency.
19 December	Truman appoints General Dwight D. Eisenhower Supreme Commander of NATO troops in Europe.

1951

1 February	UN General Assembly adopts a resolution declaring that China is engaging in aggression.
7 March	Seoul changes hands for the last time during the war.
11 April	President Truman relieves MacArthur of his command.
10 July	Armistice negotiations begin at Kaesong.
28 July	First Commonwealth Division created.

25 October	After a two-month period when the armistice negotiations were suspended, they resume again in Panmunjom.
26 November	The communist side accepts the UNC proposal that the cease-fire line would be along the existing battle line.
27 November	Both sides agree to a four-kilometer-wide demilitarized zone.

1952

2 January	Admiral C. Turner Joy of the UNC informs the communist side that only those POWs who wanted to be repatriated would be sent home.
19 February	Agreement is reached at Panmunjom to hold a political conference within 90 days of signing an armistice.
19 April	The UNC informs the communists that only 70,000 of 132,000 POWs want to be repatriated.
2 May	Both sides agree to appoint four representatives to a Neutral Nations Supervisory Commission which would oversee the implementation of an armistice.
7 May	The UNC and communist negotiators admit that they have been unable to reach agreement on the POW repatriation issue.
May–July	Political crisis in Seoul between the Korean National Assembly and President Rhee.
23 June	UNC launches bombing raids against hydroelectric power dams along the Yalu river.
24 October	Republican Nominee for President, General Dwight D. Eisenhower, makes a speech saying he would go to Korea if elected President.
3 December	The 'Indian Resolution' passes in the General Assembly. It is rejected by the communist side.

1953

2 February	President Eisenhower announces that the Seventh Fleet will no longer protect the mainland, implying that there might be an escalation of Nationalist raids against the People's Republic of China.
5 March	Stalin dies in Moscow.
30 March	Chinese Foreign Minister Zhou Enlai announces that he wants to act on an earlier UNC proposal to exchange sick and wounded POWs.
7 May	General Nam Il tables an eight-point compromise proposal to resolve the POW deadlock.
13 May	The UNC makes a counter-proposal which demands the release of all North Korean non-repatriates once an armistice is signed.

20 May	US National Security Council agrees that an expansion of the war would require the use of atomic weapons. They agree to expand the war beyond Korea 'if conditions arise requiring more positive action'.
25 May	The UNC presents its final negotiating terms.
4 June	The communist side accepts UNC terms.
17 June	President Rhee releases the North Korean non-repatriates.
27 July	The armistice agreement is signed.
1 October	US–ROK Mutual Defense Treaty is signed in Washington.

1954

26 January	Senate ratification of the US–ROK Mutual Defense Treaty, with additional understanding that the United States would only come to the aid of the ROK if it came under attack.
18 February	Big powers agree to convene two conferences, one for Korea and another for Indochina, to discuss a peaceful settlement of the East Asian conflicts.
26 April	Geneva Conference on Korea begins.
15 June	Geneva Conference on Korea concludes without reaching agreement.

CHAPTER ONE

INTERPRETING THE HISTORICAL CONTEXT

HISTORY AND MEMORY: THE KOREAN WAR

Historical memory is a powerful source of state legitimacy. Over the past five decades the two Koreas have vigorously debated the events associated with the Korean War. Both sides continue to shape the public memory of the conflict as a means of legitimizing their respective world views. North and South Koreans may interpret the war differently, but all agree that it was a formative event in their recent past. Simply put, the struggle is central to the way Koreans define themselves in the contemporary world. By contrast, other nations which sent troops to Korea have retained little historical memory of the conflict. In the West, for example, relatively limited attention is paid to the Korean War compared to the sustained popular interest in the two twentieth-century world wars.

The reasons for public and official ignorance about the Korean War are partly a function of cultural orientation, original intentions, and the war's outcome. United Nations troops were sent to fight in Korea not so much to defeat Korean communism *per se* as to provide tangible support for foreign policies designed to contain Soviet influence around the world and to get the Western public to support a vast expansion of the military power of the North Atlantic Treaty Organization (NATO). The Korean conflict also ended in stalemate, without a victory for either side; this has made the war an ambiguous and painful event to remember. Those in the West and in South Korea who fervently believed in the righteousness of the moral crusade against communism were not appeased by the tenuous peace that emerged from the fighting. But after 1953 the United States was not prepared to continue the battle against North Korea and the People's Republic of China. A thaw in the Cold War in the mid-1950s was welcomed by American liberals who sought to forget the repressive period of history linked with the rise of McCarthyism. A decade later, the Vietnam conflict overshadowed the earlier struggle over Korea. By the 1970s the Korean War came to be associated with the television series 'MASH'. Ostensibly set during the Korean armistice negotiations, 'MASH' reflected feelings of alienation connected with the fighting in Vietnam, not Korea. As a consequence of these developments, the Korean War has been poorly understood and misrepresented in the West.

KOREAN HISTORY AND WORLD HISTORY

The relationship between history and memory is a useful way to approach the Korean War, but the focus of this book is not how societies have remembered or portrayed the conflict; neither is it simply a study of battles won and struggles lost. Rather, this monograph examines, in an introductory way, the genesis, international diplomacy, social history, and legacies of the war. These topics are intimately associated with the broad currents of twentieth-century history. Indeed, studying the Korean War leads one into a journey which illuminates some of the major themes and episodes of modern world history. For although the Korean conflict was not a watershed event like the Russian and Chinese Revolutions or the First and Second World Wars, it was shaped by many of the principal historical forces of the past 100 years. The history of Korean communism – part of the larger story of the ideological origins of the Korean struggle – sheds light on the global impact of the Russian Revolution; similarly, the division of Korea into Soviet and American spheres of influence in 1945 is inseparable from the momentous events and 'superpower' diplomacy surrounding the termination of the Second World War in Asia and the decolonization of the Japanese empire; China's intervention in the Korean conflict in 1950 cannot be understood without reference to the broader relationship between North Korea and the Chinese Revolution; and America's experiences in Korea exerted a significant influence over its later involvement in the Vietnam quagmire.

On its own terms, the Korean War was a major event in the twentieth century. It marked an important turning point in the postwar rivalry between the United States and the Soviet Union, and accelerated Cold War trends already present in the international system. In its wake, military and diplomatic alliances crystallized on both sides of the Iron Curtain, the United States affirmed its global hegemony, previous centres of military and economic power were rebuilt in Japan and Germany, and new states in the developing world manifested a more mature historical consciousness as 'neutralist' powers. In the two Koreas, the fighting consolidated the political power of the two rival regimes and hastened the transformation of centuries-old socio-economic and class relations.

The war's social impact on the world beyond Korea was less powerful. Its influence on public opinion was limited, especially when compared to the consequences of the First World War or the Vietnam conflict. After an initial surge of support for outside intervention, the war became unpopular or was conveniently ignored, particularly in the West. Still, the struggle was a crucial psychological turning point which separated the early Cold War from the more intense global competition between the two superpowers after 1950.

Historians, social scientists and policymakers have interpreted the Korean War in numerous and sometimes contradictory ways. Since 1950 the fighting has been described as a civil war, an exercise in collective security, a forgotten war, an international conflict, a necessary war, a police action, a proxy war, and a revolutionary struggle. This diversity has arisen in part because commentators have emphasized different aspects of the war's character, evolution, and origins.

For example, those who stress the rivalry between the United States and the Soviet Union as the context for the conflict within the Korean peninsula have highlighted the international setting of the war. For many social scientists the clash was the first post-1945 proxy war in the developing world, fought at the behest of the dueling superpowers by their South and North Korean allies. Others have located the origins of the war in the dynamics of local events occurring on the Korean peninsula itself. In this interpretation, Koreans were the primary actors in the road to war, and the battle was primarily civil in character. Another influential way of looking at the war has been to contrast it with other major conflicts of the twentieth century, particularly the First and Second World Wars. Seen in this light, the Korean conflict, though fought with great intensity, was more limited in its scope and geographical boundaries [*Doc. 1*].

Western and allied nations initially described their decision to send troops to contain the June 1950 North Korean offensive as a 'police action' and they attempted to legitimize their diplomacy by saying it was part of a wider UN effort to impose 'collective security' on a chaotic postwar world and to contain perceived Soviet aggressiveness. When President Harry Truman (plate 1) ordered the use of US troops in Korea, he did so with the events leading to the Second World War in mind, and he contended that a policy of 'appeasing' the Soviet-backed North Koreans would lead to another world war [*Doc. 2*]. Critics of this interpretation have pointed out that the UN effort was largely led and paid for by the United States, which pursued its own global containment objectives in the context of the hostilities, and that the UN was neither a neutral nor objective agency in the fighting. Thus while historical experience partly informed Truman's thinking about what to do in face of the perceived global communist challenge in Korea, rearming America and its Western allies was at the forefront of the US military effort.

If President Truman tried to legitimize US involvement in the conflict by claiming that sending troops to fight in Korea would prevent another world war, more recently historians William Stueck (1996) and Kathryn

Weathersby (1998) have argued that the Korean War served as a substitute for a Third World War. Stueck's work implies that Korea was a 'necessary' war and that it staved off a third global conflict. In reality, however, neither the Soviet Union nor the United States wanted or was prepared for a global war, and for the most part both sides were careful not unduly to provoke the other. There was nothing inevitable about another world war and neither superpower wanted such a conflict, though the Chinese communists and Americans came close to moving towards full-scale war with each other. By the spring of 1951 the acceptance and recognition of a military stalemate on the Korean battlefield brought the Chinese and Americans to the bargaining table.

Although the notion that the Korean War was at its roots a civil war among Koreans became more widespread in the 1980s, the idea that the origins of the conflict lay in the domestic competition of opposing Korean forces can be traced back at least to the summer of 1945, when one of Korea's conservative leaders-in-exile, Syngman Rhee (plate 2), wrote a letter to President Truman from Washington DC warning him of the possibility of a civil war developing between the 'communist' and 'nationalist' factions in Korea (US Department of State, 1969: 1031).

After 1950 Soviet and North Korean officials publicly condemned South Korea for instigating a civil war between the two Korean states. For many decades the origin of the war was vigorously contested and debated, as a living legacy of the Cold War itself. The issue was drawn into the vortex of superpower attempts to justify their respective positions in their international rivalry. The communists blamed the West for its intervention in Korea's 'civil' war, arguing that the conflict was started by South Korea, at the instigation of the United States, and that North Korea's offensive in June 1950 was simply a response to an unprovoked aggressive attack [*Doc. 3*]. By contrast, the Western alliance placed responsibility for the war on the communists, particularly the Soviet Union, for ordering the North Korean offensive. In this version of history, presented to posterity by, for example, American Secretary of State Dean Acheson, the North Koreans were simple pawns or proxies of Soviet global expansionism [*Doc. 4*].

From the perspective of the new millennium, both interpretations have serious flaws. Documents released from Russian and Chinese archives in the 1990s have shown conclusively that North Korea and the Soviet Union were primarily responsible for the planning and execution of the 1950 offensive. However, they also show that Sino-North Korean cooperation played a critical role in the events leading to the conflict and that the North was not a simple pawn of Soviet great power intrigues. North Korean leader Kim Il Sung campaigned very hard to get Soviet Premier Joseph Stalin to support his offensive across the border with South Korea, which at the time ran along the entire length of the 38th parallel.

Unlike the unidimensional analyses of the Korean War which emerged out of Cold War political calculations on both sides of the Iron Curtain, this book takes the view that the Korean conflict was multidimensional, and argues that in order to unlock a more complete meaning of the events the local and international aspects of the struggle must be seen as an integral unity. The fighting arose not simply out of the machinations of the great powers; nor was it the product of the two Koreas deciding their fates independently of outside interference. Both sides – Korean and superpower – shaped the other's perspective and the options that each attempted to pursue; the interplay of domestic and international factors must be understood together as a fundamental part of the larger process which led to the war and which then underpinned its dynamic.

The very distinction between civil war and international war is somewhat arbitrary and misleading, since the Korean 'civil war' was intimately associated with the decisions the two superpowers made about Korea from 1945 onwards. The fate of the 'international war' was also shaped in fundamental ways by the actions of Koreans. In short, our effort to understand the history, significance, and meaning of the Korean War must first come to grips with the symbiotic nature of the interrelationship between the domestic and international dimensions of this bloody confrontation.

This book interprets the battle in and over Korea after 1945 within the framework of a series of decisions to escalate a growing dispute between rival Korean political factions and their superpower protectors. This conflict had its roots in the pre-1945 era, but the division of the Korean peninsula at the 38th parallel in 1945 by the Soviet Union and the United States established the structural framework in which the violent rivalry was played out. The division of Korea set the stage for the emergence of two mutually antagonistic Korean regimes by late 1948.

Civil conflict in the two Koreas was escalated by Premier Joseph Stalin's decision in 1950 to back Premier Kim Il Sung's pleas to unify the country through an armed attack. The entry of the United Nations into the fighting in the summer of 1950 constituted the next stage in the escalation, of which there were two phases: the first, represented by President Truman's decision to order a counter-offensive and to send US troops into the battle, was given formal UN blessing, and various member states provided limited military contributions. Without US and UN support South Korea would have been incorporated into the northern regime's political system, and the war would have ended in 1950.

The second phase of escalation began when the Western allies unwisely decided in the late summer to move beyond the 38th parallel with an offensive of their own, into North Korean territory. This was soon followed by a critical event which added to the intensity of the war and which portended to lead to global war: the entry of Chinese communist 'volunteers' –

in reality Chinese armies – into the fighting in the late fall of 1950. This chaotic stage of the war was characterized by misperception and misunderstanding by both sides; neither side understood the objectives of its enemy and neither had a clear sense of where its decisions might ultimately lead.

After China's intervention, the South Korean government, led by President Syngman Rhee, attempted to get the United States to back a further escalation of the war, but unlike Stalin's calculations in early 1950, US Presidents Harry S. Truman and, later, Dwight D. Eisenhower (plate 1), did not believe it was in the global containment interests of the United States or its allies to back a second offensive to unify the country. The main series of great power decisions to escalate the Korean crisis thus ended by the spring of 1951, though a final effort to expand the war occurred in the spring of 1953 when, in the wake of Joseph Stalin's death, the United States threatened the Chinese and North Koreans with nuclear war if its armistice terms were not met.

The turning point in the negotiations came in early June 1953 when the communists accepted US and UN terms for the armistice, which was formally concluded in late July. The momentum for a peaceful settlement carried over into 1954 at the Geneva Conference on Korea, held as part of a larger effort to deal – at the same venue – with the ongoing conflict in Indochina, several thousand miles south of Korea in Southeast Asia. The failure of the Korean conference consolidated the uneasy *status quo* on the Northeast Asian peninsula which has lasted to this day. The war has never formally ended nor has it yet been resolved through a peace treaty.

APPROACHING KOREA

Comparisons are often a useful way to understand major historical events or large processes. We have seen how the concept of 'limited war' – as distinguished from global or world war – has been employed by social scientists to describe and analyze the Korean conflict. However, we must also be sensitive to the unique historical character of the struggle in Korea – the war occurred just five years after Japanese colonial rule came to an abrupt end over the entire peninsula – and to the historical consciousness of the antagonists tangled in the decisions surrounding the conflict.

An indispensable and practical tenet in the study of history is that we should be conscious of how the era in which we live shapes our perspective on the past. We should not evaluate history from the simple viewpoint of the present; rather, the historical project should take into account and assess how past actors viewed their own history. The Korean War influenced the trajectory of twentieth-century history, but the people involved in the conflict were also intimately shaped by the events preceding it, during the first half of the century.

Understanding the twentieth-century historical experience of Koreans is crucial for interpreting the motivations of Koreans themselves, who, ironically, are often the least talked about actors in books on the Korean War but who played a critical role in its origins and who continued to shape, and be shaped by, great power diplomacy before, during and after the conflict.

To understand the Korean War – one of the most devastating of modern conflicts – we will begin by examining how Koreans and the great powers responded to and influenced, in their own historical and cultural contexts, some of the major episodes and ideological movements of twentieth-century history: the emergence of the Japanese colonial empire, the Russian Revolution, and US President Woodrow Wilson's liberal 'open door' diplomacy, often referred to as Wilsonianism. These events and ideas indelibly molded and divided the emerging Korean nationalist movement and helped to lay the ideological foundations under which a divided Korea could take shape after the Second World War; they were formative developments on the road to the Pacific War which eventually destroyed the Japanese empire, weakened the traditional European colonial powers, and established a new framework for international relations after 1945.

THE IDEOLOGICAL ORIGINS OF THE KOREAN WAR

The ideological origins of the Korean War can be traced back to pre-1945 legacies of a divided Korean nationalist movement and Koreans' diverse responses to the challenges posed by Japanese colonial rule. Modern Korean nationalism emerged in the late nineteenth and early twentieth centuries in a political and intellectual context permeated by great power imperialism and repression generated by Japanese colonial rule. In this context, Korean elites who appealed to the 'nation' to legitimize their political doctrines, often pursued the broader objective of ridding the country of the dishonour, ignominy, and disgrace associated with colonial rule. In 1950 conservative South Korean leader Syngman Rhee and his communist northern counterpart, Kim Il Sung, shared only one major common ideological tenet: a predisposition to criticize the Japanese for their imperialist past and to make an effort to ensure that it would not be reborn in the postwar era. But as the wider political beliefs of Rhee and Kim attest, the colonial era witnessed the emergence of plural responses to colonial rule, an understanding of which is crucial to discerning the ideological foundations of the Korean War.

Until very late in the Choson dynasty (1392–1910), Koreans had no concept for what Western nations refer to as state sovereignty. Choson Korea had been a neo-Confucian society; relationships between people were based on strict class distinctions, adherence to filial piety, and formal respect for elders and the king. The ruling aristocracy, known as the *yangban*, had traditionally looked to China, the 'Middle Kingdom', as their protector. Although China increased its influence in Korea in the 1880s and recommended a number of modern 'self-strengthening' reforms such as the appointment of Western advisers to the Korean court, Western and Japanese imperialism in the nineteenth century exacerbated internal decline in China and weakened Korea's traditional relationship with the Middle Kingdom.

From the 1870s, Koreans were exposed to Western concepts of state sovereignty and nationalism from a number of sources, including Western missionaries, foreign officials, and voyages which Koreans were beginning to undertake to the United States and Japan. Although a small group of Korean reformers active in the late nineteenth century saw modernizing Japan as the model to emulate, Korean nationalism, confined initially to a small number of elites, came more and more to be associated with an anti-colonial, and particularly anti-Japanese, tone.

Koreans also tried to align themselves with one foreign power in order to limit the influence of another, a theme which re-emerged in North and South Korea during the Cold War of the 1940s and beyond. In the 1890s, for example, the Korean King fled his palace and took up residence in the Russian embassy in an effort to limit the power of Japan in Korea's internal affairs.

SYNGMAN RHEE AND THE GREAT POWERS BEFORE 1945

Syngman Rhee was the dominant political force in South Korea after 1948 but his career as a conservative political activist dates from the late nineteenth century. Born in 1875 and educated at an elite Methodist missionary school in Seoul, Rhee joined a reform movement in the mid-1890s known as the Independence Club. Led by Korean Christians who wanted to modernize their country along Western lines, club members established a bilingual newspaper with separate English and Korean sections. Slogans such as 'Korea for Koreans' reflected the movement's conservative critique of imperialism, but the club advocated the use of foreign help to develop Korean resources and supported the translation of foreign texts into Korean so that the youth could have access to international learning.

Significantly, this period witnessed Rhee's early concern with Russian penetration of Korea and the preservation of Korean sovereignty. Persistent demands by the Russian minister in Seoul to purchase a coaling station on a small island in southeastern Korea for the Russian navy caused the Independence activists to organize a protest rally in 1898. Rhee and others gave public speeches which challenged Russia's forward policy and criticized the transfer of internal political decision-making powers to Russian military and economic advisers. The protest succeeded and the government used the public demonstrations as a reason to reserve more powers for Korean statesmen.

The club was also successful in bringing its ideas to a larger audience. After 1900, concepts of national self-interest increasingly became the measure that the public used to assess the effectiveness of their government. But the influence of the club on the King and his court diminished in the late 1890s and its members were jailed or forced to flee the country. Rhee spent several years in prison.

In November 1904, after his release from jail, Rhee left for Hawaii and America, where he continued his political activities. Over the next several decades the future President of South Korea developed his ideas about the role America could play in supporting Korean sovereignty, and increasingly he turned to the United States as the great power which he felt could best protect and preserve Korea's independence from Japanese imperialism. But as Rhee would find time and again, the United States had its own great power and imperial objectives which prevented Rhee's vision of a Korean–American partnership in world affairs from taking root.

In 1905 the United States hosted peace talks to end the Russo-Japanese War, a military contest for power and influence over Northeast Asia and Manchuria in which the Japanese came out victorious. The document which emerged from the discussions, the Treaty of Portsmouth, 'removed the last obstacle to Japan's domination of Korea' (Eckert et al., 1990: 239). Soon after the treaty was signed, Korea was incorporated into the Japanese empire as a formal protectorate.

But before these dramatic events took shape, Syngman Rhee co-signed a petition addressed to President Theodore Roosevelt requesting American aid to protect Korean autonomy from further Japanese exploitation. With a Korean colleague, Rhee travelled to the President's country home in Oyster Bay, New York, to present the petition, but Roosevelt rejected the initiative, telling them personally that the petition could only be received through proper diplomatic channels.

President Roosevelt also dismissed advice from his minister in Seoul to limit Japanese aggression in Korea, arguing that Japan would effectively stem the expansion of Russian power in the region. Roosevelt believed that American diplomatic support of Japan's power in Korea would facilitate Japanese recognition of America's new empire in the Philippines, recently acquired by the United States in a brief war with Spain. The President referred to Japan's relationship with Korea as being akin to US power over Cuba, an American protectorate acquired in the same war against Spain (Paterson et al., 1988: 240). President Theodore Roosevelt's policies demonstrated some of the harsh realities of great power politics which limited the freedom of colonial peoples seeking independence prior to 1945.

WILSONIAN LIBERALISM AND KOREAN NATIONALISM

In August 1910 Korea was incorporated into the Japanese empire as a colony. In March 1913 Democratic President Woodrow Wilson came to office. On one level, the new President re-affirmed America's traditional interest in great power diplomacy. For example, during the First World War, in November 1917, with Japan allied against Germany and the Central Powers, the Wilson administration, in an exchange of notes between the US Secretary of State and his Japanese counterpart, upheld Japan's 'special relations' with China in those areas contiguous to Japanese colonial possessions.

But two months after this agreement, which implicitly recognized both Manchuria and Korea within Japan's sphere of influence, Wilson made one of the most famous public declarations in the twentieth century: his fourteen points for the postwar order. In a speech to the US Congress on 8 January 1918 the President spoke of a postwar world characterized by an end to secret diplomacy, freedom of commerce on the seas, reduced armaments, the end of colonial rule, and the creation of an international body – a League of Nations – to mediate conflict and preserve territorial independence.

Coming on the heels of the Russian Revolution, the speech attempted to counter Bolshevik propaganda and to stem revolutionary fervour in Europe. Although Wilson's call for the right of people to decide their own political fates was meant to apply to minority groups in Europe, the speech was taken by colonial peoples around the world as a critique of colonial imperialism, and it provided hope to some that the United States might support colonial independence movements.

Koreans active in America met soon after the speech and agreed to send a petition favouring Korean independence to the President. In December 1918, Korean representatives, including Syngman Rhee, were selected as lobbyists to go to Paris where the great powers were negotiating the postwar peace. The US State Department, however, refused to grant them passports, arguing that Korean independence was not an issue emerging out of the war. As Japanese subjects, the appointed Koreans were told to turn to Japanese authorities for the visas.

In a personal appeal to Wilson on 16 February 1919, Rhee asked that the United States make a declaration in support of Korean independence at the Peace Conference and suggested that the proposed new League of Nations take over the reins of government until Korea was fit for independence. The request was rejected.

In Korea, the death of a former Korean King in January 1919 produced a reaction which catapulted Korean nationalism into a nationwide movement. Plans for the King's funeral became the starting point for a brilliantly arranged, massive, and non-violent public protest against Japanese colonial rule. On 1 March, a million Koreans, many recalling Wilson's fourteen-point speech, demanded prompt independence based on their right to self-determination. Japanese authorities responded with brutal repression; thousands were executed and shot down, and tens of thousands were arrested and injured.

Outside the country, disparate exile nationalist movements in China, the United States and Siberia came together to form a provisional government in Shanghai, China (map 1). Syngman Rhee was elected President of what was known as the Provisional Government of the Republic of Korea. The unity of this group was short-lived; the temporary accommodation between left and right soon disappeared and old divisions and antagonisms reappeared within a few years. Rhee was purged from the government in 1925 and the position of President was abolished soon thereafter. In 1926 another prominent conservative ultra-nationalist leader, Kim Ku, became the Premier of the Korean Provisional Government. Unlike Rhee, Kim believed that organized violence by Korean paramilitary groups was a legitimate means of affecting Korea's colonial status within the Japanese empire.

Although Wilsonianism offered hope to a wide range of Korean nationalists, its long-term influence on the movement was limited. Conservative nationalism had a stronger social base in Korea, which had no middle class to speak of in this era, and the reformist impulse underlying Wilsonianism was too weak to have a real impact on US policy towards Korea until the United States recognized its new-found superpower status towards the end of the Second World War.

In the 1920s and 1930s Rhee continued to press the Americans to support Korean independence. At the Washington Conference in 1922, when the Americans, Japanese, British and others renegotiated security frameworks for the Pacific to replace a now defunct military alliance between Britain and Japan, Rhee again presented his case. After Japan invaded Manchuria in late 1931 in an effort to expand its empire at the expense of China, Rhee travelled to the headquarters of the League of Nations in Geneva, Switzerland, to defend the interests of ethnic Koreans living in northern China and to convince the League to embrace Korean independence and to condemn Japanese imperialism. None of these efforts was fruitful, but by 1945 Syngman Rhee was well known in Korea as a champion of Korean independence. His main competitor was Kim Ku, still the leader of the Korean Provisional Government, now stationed in Chongqing (Chungking), China. Kim had the formal backing of the Chinese Nationalist Party under Chiang Kai-shek. For three years after the war, Rhee, with uncertain US backing, and Kim, with Chinese, competed with each other for leadership of Korea's conservative nationalist movement.

THE RUSSIAN REVOLUTION AND THE KOREAN COMMUNIST MOVEMENT, 1917–45

The moderate 'diplomatic' solution to Japanese colonialism, represented by nationalists' efforts to gain US great power support for Korean independence, and proposed by Syngman Rhee and his supporters in America, was consistently met with silence or derision by the great powers. Rhee represented the Christian and, after 1917, anti-communist response to Japanese colonial rule, but the emerging nationalist movement was divided. Other Koreans believed Japanese colonialism could be defeated only through the realization of a political project which included armed resistance, revolution and guerrilla warfare. This became a possibility in the aftermath of the 1917 Russian Revolution which had a tremendous impact on an influential group of Asian nationalists looking for solutions to their countries' ills.

Koreans who found the precedent of the Russian Revolution appealing believed that the Western powers would give little concrete support for movements of self-determination. Marxism, they thought, offered a viable means of achieving independence. Alignment with the Soviet Union brought immediate tangible benefits. These included training, an ideology which purported to explain history from a rational, even scientific point of view, the backing of a growing industrial power, arms, and financial support.

Inside Korea, however, the communist movement faced tremendous, suffocating persecution from the colonial police. Various efforts to build a covert organization in the 1920s were met by infiltration, imprisonment and death. No viable long-term communist organization proved possible in Korea itself, and leaders often went into hiding or left the colony to join their comrades in China or Soviet Siberia.

The Korean diaspora was spread unevenly throughout the Soviet Caucuses, Siberia and northeastern China. After 1945 Koreans living in these areas returned to northern Korea to help establish the North Korean government. Brief sketches of the lives of several of these Koreans will illustrate our point. Nam Il was an ethnic Korean born to Korean immigrant parents in Russia prior to the Revolution. After serving as an officer in the Soviet army during the Second World War, Nam travelled to Korea with the Russian occupying force and served as Deputy Minister of Education of the North Korean government until the outbreak of the Korean War. In July 1950 he was appointed Deputy Chief of Staff of the North Korean People's Army, and in 1953 he became Foreign Minister. He survived Kim Il Sung's purges and continued to hold high positions in government until his death in 1976.

China was also an active area for Korean communists. In the 1920s and 1930s, tens of thousands of ethnic Koreans joined the Chinese Communist Party (CCP). Mu Chong and Kim Tu-bong were the most prominent figures within the Chinese exile faction. Mu was born in northern Korea, joined the CCP in 1926 and survived the 6,000-mile communist 'Long March' from southeast to northwest China in 1934–35, escaping from military attacks by Chiang Kai-shek's Nationalist forces (map 1). He then helped the Chinese communists establish their base in Yanan in north-western China and commanded a group of ethnically Korean soldiers who made up a force known as the Korean Volunteer Army. Mu was also a member of the Chinese Communist Eighth Route Army and was close to Chinese military leader Zhu De. He returned to northern Korea after the war and briefly commanded the Second Corps of the North Korean Army during the Korean War before being purged.

Kim Tu-bong (plate 3), the other influential Korean figure in the Yanan group, was born in southern Korea and left for China in 1919, after participating in the 1 March Movement against the Japanese. He joined the Chinese communists in Yanan in 1942 and commanded the political wing of Mu Chong's Korean Volunteer Army. After 1945 Kim rose to become the first chairperson of the North Korean Workers' Party and remained at the top of the North Korean government until his purge in 1957.

A Korean-born 'domestic' communist of this era who rose to promin-ence after 1945 was Pak Hon Yong. Pak's life during the colonial period shows how difficult it was to remain an active communist within the Korean peninsula. Pak was born in southern Korea in 1901. In the early 1920s he travelled to Shanghai and Moscow and participated in a major Congress of Asian leaders sponsored by the Soviet government. He re-entered Korea in 1922 and played an important role in the domestic under-ground communist movement. After serving a jail term for his activities, he fled the country; when he returned in 1933 he was again captured and served six more years in jail. In 1939 Pak went into hiding in southwest Korea, posing as a bricklayer. He re-emerged after the war as the most important leader of the southern branch of the Korean Communist Party, but fled to Pyongyang in 1946 after a warrant was put out for his arrest. During the Korean War, Pak served as Vice-Premier and Minister of Foreign Affairs for North Korea until he was purged in 1953. He was later executed on trumped-up charges of being a spy.

The most prominent member of the Korean Communist Party after 1948 was Kim Il Sung (plate 3), but his part in the communist movement before the Second World War has been greatly exaggerated by postwar North Korean authors. Compared to the other Korean communists described here, Kim was a junior revolutionary in 1945. A native of Pyongyang, Kim, whose original name was Kim Song-ju, lost both his parents at an early age. In 1929, when he was seventeen, he joined the South Manchurian Communist Youth Association. After the Japanese army attacked Manchuria in 1931, Kim became a member of a partisan corps of Koreans who fought Japanese expeditionary forces under the leadership of a disparate group of Chinese communist guerrilla forces. The force, which at its peak totalled about 15,000–20,000 troops, came collectively to be known as the Northeast Anti-Japanese United Army. Perhaps the most famous of Kim's exploits occurred in June 1937, when his guerrilla group attacked a town called Pochonbo in northern Korea near the Manchurian border. The Korean press reported the incident and Japanese authorities gave it extended publicity because it had led to the death of Japanese policemen in the colony.

Fluent in Chinese, Kim rose to a senior leadership position in the army's activities in eastern Manchuria by 1938. At the height of his power he commanded about 300 men. Most of his military acts were hit-and-run raids against Japanese officials or Korean collaborators. Often hungry and cold, Kim and his party lived in extremely harsh conditions.

In the late 1930s the Japanese began to direct more military resources against the partisans and Kim's forces dwindled. In 1941, with the United Army virtually defeated by the Japanese, Kim Il Sung fled Manchuria altogether and made his way to the Russian Maritime Province, where it is reported he became a major in the Soviet army. Soviet forces remained quiescent until the American atomic bombing of Hiroshima, after which Kim joined other Russian troops entering Korea. Already a veteran guerrilla activist, Kim returned to Pyongyang in 1945 at the age of thirty-three.

THE GREAT POWERS AND KOREA DURING THE SECOND WORLD WAR

Before the Second World War British and American diplomats sought co-operative mechanisms to deal with the expansion of the Japanese empire. Some concern was expressed after Japan invaded Manchuria in 1931 but it was only in 1940 and 1941, in the context of a war being fought in Europe, and as Japan threatened to expand southwards into the oil and resource-rich region of Southeast Asia, that the Western allies began seriously to plan for a Pacific war.

The Japanese attack on Pearl Harbor galvanized American public opinion and led to America's entry into the global conflict, but Korea was still very distant from the minds of American policymakers, and the planning that did take place for the postwar status of the colony was closely related to America's postwar objectives. In theory, Anglo-American policies were dictated by the famous Atlantic Charter which American President Franklin Roosevelt and British Prime Minister Winston Churchill agreed to on the British ship *Prince of Wales*, anchored off the coast of Newfoundland in August 1941. The Charter echoed Wilson's fourteen points but was purposely left more vague; it enunciated eight war aims, including support for the principle of collective security, freedom of the seas, liberal trading practices, and self-determination. Churchill later qualified Britain's support for the Charter by stating that it applied only to those countries in Europe which were under Nazi occupation, thus leaving him a free hand on colonial questions.

President Roosevelt developed a policy towards colonial areas based on a variation of Woodrow Wilson's League of Nations mandate system. Roosevelt's strategy, known as trusteeship, supported eventual independence for colonial territories, but required a prolonged period of tutelage by the great powers. Aid and advice would be given to the colonies and eventually they would take their place as sovereign states in the postwar system. The President's postwar vision for international order required cooperation with the wartime allies, including the Soviet Union.

He hoped that the cooperative diplomacy of the 'Grand Alliance', as the wartime partnership of Britain, America and Russia was known, could extend into the postwar era, but he also knew that the Soviet Union and China, the two allies most concerned about Northeast Asia, would approach policy towards the Japanese empire and Korea from competing perspectives.

In late 1942 Chinese leader Chiang Kai-shek asked Roosevelt to exclude the Soviets from postwar discussions on Korea. The US President rejected the idea and soon talked to his advisers about the possibility of arranging trusteeships for Vietnam and Korea.

The United States was the strongest global power emerging from the war, and the trusteeship framework clearly favoured American global interests; it was an integral part of America's new liberal imperialism, which downplayed protectionism and emphasized increased access to markets, low tariffs, and an 'open door' economic policy. This was recognized by British officials, who stood to lose much of their international prestige and power from decolonization. In 1943, British Foreign Secretary Anthony Eden perceptively noted that Roosevelt 'hoped that former colonial territories, once free of their masters, would become politically and economically dependent upon the United States and had no fear that others might fill that role' (Cumings, 1981: 105).

Despite the rhetoric of cooperation within the Grand Alliance, Roosevelt and the US State Department remained concerned about Soviet intentions in Northeast Asia. In 1943 American officials predicted that an exclusive Soviet occupation of Korea might have a far-reaching impact on the postwar order for Japan and China. Hoping to promote China as one of the postwar world's regional 'Four Policemen', Roosevelt believed that a joint Sino-American approach to trusteeship would restrict Soviet influence in the region. In this sense, trusteeship was an early means of containing Soviet power in Asia.

At the Cairo Conference in November 1943, China, Britain and America discussed allied intentions towards Asia and the liquidation of Japan's empire. Although Chiang Kai-shek hoped to get US support for the recognition of Kim Ku's Provisional Government in Chongqing, Roosevelt rejected the idea and instead got the Chinese leader to agree to a declaration which announced China's support for Korean independence 'in due course'. This critical phrase was contributed by Churchill, but was substantially in line with Roosevelt's thinking on the issue.

No formal reference to trusteeship was made in the final Cairo Declaration, but Korea would be granted independence only after a long period of supervision by the great powers. In Roosevelt's plan the 'due course' process could take up to forty years. At the end of November 1943 Stalin told Roosevelt at Teheran that he approved of the Cairo Declaration.

Faced with apparent great power unity on the trusteeship issue, Koreans of all political colours reacted strongly against this very qualified independence, but their protests had no impact on allied strategy. The trusteeship policy, ostensibly designed for Korean independence, was formulated without Korean participation.

In early 1945 Franklin Roosevelt and Joseph Stalin verbally agreed at Yalta that China and Great Britain should be included in their trusteeship plan for Korea. Although the new superpowers confirmed that no foreign troops should be stationed on the peninsula during the trusteeship period, an important issue was not discussed: how the various powers would cooperate with each other before the trusteeship came into being.

Even before the war ended, the trusteeship agreement which Roosevelt reached with Stalin at Yalta came under pressure. Roosevelt died in April 1945, leaving in office Vice-President Harry Truman, a man inexperienced in international affairs. In July 1945 Stalin told the Chinese Nationalists that the new American administration was cooperating closely with the British, who viewed trusteeship as a means of perpetuating colonial rule. He also told the Chinese that the Soviets and Americans had made no binding commitments about Korea.

Thus at the time the Soviet Union entered the Far Eastern War a month later, the future of the wartime trusteeship agreement appeared uncertain. Few concrete plans for the occupation of Korea were in place. Unprepared for the rapid Soviet entry into the Pacific War, the Soviets and Americans soon entered into a series of *ad hoc* spheres of influence agreements over Korea. Russians and Americans soon replaced the Japanese as the military overlords of the peninsula.

CHAPTER TWO

THE GREAT POWERS AND THE TWO KOREAS, 1945–50

KOREANS BETWEEN THE SUPERPOWERS

By July 1945 American officials in both the State and War Departments were growing increasingly concerned about the spread of Soviet influence in the Far East. Secretary of War Henry Stimson wrote to the President in mid-July that the absence of a firm occupation agreement with the Soviets over Korea would hurt US interests in the region. He warned that pro-communist Korean troops in Siberia would 'probably gain control, and influence the setting up of a Soviet dominated local government. ... This is the Polish question transplanted to the Far East' (Matray, 1981: 158). Both Truman and his Secretary of State James Byrnes hoped that the use of the atomic bomb against Japan would create a power vacuum in Korea and other parts of Asia which could be filled with the United States' power and unchallenged influence. This assumption was abruptly dispelled on 8 August when the Soviet Union declared war on Japan and ordered its troops to fight Japanese imperial forces stationed in Manchuria.

On 10 August 1945, with Soviet forces moving towards northern Korea, two American army colonels were ordered to draw a line across Korea which would incorporate the maximum amount of territory into an American occupation zone. After glancing at a map of Asia for about thirty minutes they recommended the 38th parallel as the dividing line (map 2). If the Soviet Union accepted this, two-thirds of the country's population and the capital city, Seoul, would be under American administration. The situation seemed urgent, as developments on the mainland were certain to influence the course of the American occupation of Japan. On 11 August America's representative on the Allied Reparations Commission urged the President to send US forces to 'occupy as much of the industrial areas of Korea and Manchuria as we can' (Matray, 1981: 164). He was soon supported by the US Ambassador in Moscow who wrote to Truman that the United States was not under obligation to respect Soviet zones of military occupation. In the event, on 15 August, Stalin accepted the US proposal to divide Korea in two. In agreeing to this, Stalin was probably hoping to maintain postwar cooperation, and possibly even thinking about a role for the Soviet Union in the occupation of Japan.

The division of Korea was one of the most significant events of modern Korean history, for it set in motion the momentum which would lead to war less than five years later. If Korea had not been divided, its postwar history would have been very different; indeed, it is likely that the war would not have occurred. Unaware of the momentous decisions taken in Moscow and Washington, on the day of the Japanese surrender, 15 August, Koreans celebrated with jubilation what they erroneously believed to be their newly won independence.

Amidst the chaos of the surrender process the Japanese colonial administration made a political accommodation with a Korean leftist nationalist, Yo Un-hyong, who proceeded to organize a national movement for the establishment of an indigenous Korean government. By late August a significant number of local 'people's committees' were created in all thirteen provinces, and these in turn established linkages with local workers, peasant unions, and student and youth groups. Many of the active members of the people's committees were on the left of the political spectrum, but they also initially included some landlords, former soldiers, students and Koreans who had worked for the Japanese. On 6 September, just two days before American troops began to arrive, a representative assembly convened in Seoul to establish the Korean People's Republic (KPR) and set a date for elections. The KPR was predominantly leftist in orientation. It included some communists in high positions and, ostensibly at least, members of the political right, including Syngman Rhee, who was elected chairman of the government *in absentia*. The republic's political program included the nationalization of industry, land reform, universal suffrage, fair labour conditions, an eight-hour day, an end to child labour, and a minimum wage.

In the south, the head of the US occupation force, Lieutenant-General John Hodge, was ordered not to recognize the KPR or any other political grouping. American officials believed that Korea was ripe for the spread of communist influence and US occupation policy treated the committees as simple communist front organizations. As Hodge later remarked about his policy towards the KPR, 'Flatly stated, one of our missions was to break down this Communist government outside of any directives and without benefit of backing by the Joint Chiefs of Staff or the State Department' (Cumings, 1981: 194). The General was a tough individual who often showed little respect for the people he governed and his racism sometimes boiled to the surface, as when he remarked upon his arrival on the peninsula that Koreans and Japanese were 'all the same breed of cat' (Cumings, 1981: 138).

Hodge did not have any previous experience with Korea or Asia and he tended to assume that the left and communists were a unified force. But the communists were a minority of the left in postwar Korea. The non-communist left included students, teachers, peasants and workers, and they were an influential political force in Korea in 1945. They sought political and social reforms, including land reform, and a purge of former collaborators – like the Korean police – from positions of power. Land reform was the critical issue in the immediate post-Second World War era as about 70 per cent of the society was engaged in farming activities.

The conservative elite, many of whom had collaborated with the Japanese during the colonial period, were opposed to major reform to Korean society. Those who supported the political right included businessmen, landlords who had invested in industry during the colonial regime, and Koreans who had belonged to the colonial police force. The right was less well organized than the left and was generally a weaker political force in early postwar Korea.

In order to help contain the left, Hodge retained much of the colonial power structure, including the police. By contrast, while the Soviet-occupied north retained some of the colonial legal system, it did a more thorough job of purging colonial collaborators. But as Hodge moved to contain the left and communists in the south, the Americans and Russians attempted to work out a political program for a unified, independent Korea.

The Foreign Ministers of the 'Big Three', as the Soviet Union, the United Kingdom, and the United States were known, met in Moscow in December 1945. Just six months earlier, in the war-devastated city of Potsdam, the United States had rejected a Soviet initiative to work out the details of a trusteeship agreement, believing that the Soviet Union might not be able to mobilize its troops before the Far Eastern War was over. Now, faced with the reality of Soviet power in Northeast Asia, Americans were in Moscow to work out a deal.

Soviet Foreign Minister Vyacheslav Molotov and US Secretary of State James Byrnes agreed to establish a Soviet-American Joint Commission composed of occupation authorities from northern and southern Korea. According to the agreement, the commission would consult with Korean parties and social organizations and make recommendations leading to the establishment of a Korean provisional government. The commission would then negotiate with the provisional government and governmental representatives of the Soviet Union, the United States, China and Great Britain to arrange a four-power trusteeship for a period up to five years, after which Korea would emerge as an independent state in the international community.

But even as the United States and the Soviet Union moved to implement the Moscow Agreement on Korea, the hastily arranged structure for great power cooperation in Northeast Asia was being dismantled. Kim Il Sung arrived in northern Korea on 19 September 1945 and in mid-October he attended a public welcoming celebration, an early sign of Soviet support for this ex-partisan and his few hundred supporters returning from the Soviet Far East. But Koreans had heard about Kim's exploits in the 1930s and, despite his young age, they applauded Kim as a nationalist leader. Kim was initially supported by non-communists as well, such as Cho Man-sik, a Christian who was known as the Gandhi of Korea. In February 1946, even before the Joint Commission met for the first time, the Soviet occupation authorities oversaw the creation of what was in effect a provisional northern administration under an 'Interim People's Committee' led by Kim Il Sung. This strengthened Kim's power and weakened that of the non-communist Koreans in the north. Non-leftist nationalists were soon purged or, like Cho Man-sik, placed under arrest.

SYNGMAN RHEE AND THE AMERICAN OCCUPATION

The two leading southern exile rightists, Syngman Rhee and Kim Ku, returned to Seoul from the United States and China in October and November 1945. Although the Korean People's Republic had tried to incorporate Rhee into its political structure earlier in August, once in Seoul, Rhee quickly denounced its leftist activities and its leader, Yo Un-hyong. Hodge's policies weakened the left, and Yo's influence waned. He was assassinated in mid-1947.

Rhee was a popular figure in Korea, and his political skills have often been underrated. But his position was challenged by the leader of the Korean Provisional Government in China, Kim Ku. Like many Koreans at the time, both Kim and Rhee were critical of the Moscow Agreement. Kim sought recognition of his Provisional Government, denounced the idea of trusteeship and demanded immediate independence for the peninsula. When Kim and his supporters attempted to gain power for themselves and openly challenged the legitimacy of the American Military Government (AMG) in late December 1945, Hodge confronted the rightist and threatened to 'kill him if he double-crossed me again' (Cumings, 1981: 221).

After Kim's failed coup attempt, Rhee rose to greater prominence in the south. Rhee was not liked by Hodge, but early in the year he was viewed as an effective ally against Kim Ku and the left. Hodge initially worked closely with Rhee and with a former deputy director of the organization which later became the Central Intelligence Agency (CIA), Preston Goodfellow, to make Rhee the leader of a Representative Democratic Council (RDC) composed primarily of rightists. The Council, established in February 1946, was designed to act as a consultative organ for the American occupation authorities and to strengthen America's bargaining position in the Soviet-American Joint Commission. The left boycotted the Council.

The first meeting of the Joint Commission opened in Seoul on 20 March 1946. The Commission met until early May, but both sides failed to come to an agreement on terms. The Soviets insisted that in the process of establishing a provisional government only those groups which adhered to the terms of the Moscow Agreement could be consulted. This demand was disingenuous since the left in Korea had earlier been very critical of trusteeship. Now they accepted the Soviet position as a bargaining tactic to prevent the Korean right from having any influence in the negotiations. The Americans refused to accept the Soviet position and argued that they would recognize the RDC, even though its representatives were highly critical of the Moscow Agreement and trusteeship. The Joint Commission was thus effectively stifled: the contradictions evident in the bargaining positions of both sides prevented any possibility of genuine compromise.

In the late spring and summer of 1946, the Americans made an effort temporarily to limit the power of Rhee and the far right, and opened up negotiations between the moderate and right wings of the Korean political spectrum. Rhee expressed his concerns about US policy in a private letter to Preston Goodfellow on 19 June 1946. Writing at a time when the conflict in China between the communists led by Mao Zedong and the Nationalists under Chiang Kai-shek was emerging into civil war, Rhee argued that it was necessary to destroy communist power in Korea before the situation in Korea too developed into a civil conflict. If communist strength grew, he wrote, an 'inevitable civil war and bloodshed amongst the Koreans would follow'. His reaction to the deadlock in the Joint Commission was to advocate the immediate creation of a southern regime. Yet he still hoped to become the political leader of a unified, non-communist country. Realizing that a negotiated solution to eliminate the 38th parallel was unlikely, he wrote to Goodfellow: 'If we were left alone to fight the communists we would put them completely under control'. Rhee believed that the communists were an illegitimate political power in all of Korea, simple pawns of Soviet communism, and that some 'police action' would even prevent a civil war. But the type of political violence that he advocated against the communists only contributed to the underlying civil conflict which was emerging in the divided peninsula. His thinking thus both exacerbated and reflected the escalation of the ideological clash within Korea. (ROK National History Compilation Committee, 1996, vol. 28: 85–6).

American officials could not publicly support Rhee at this time since official US policy was premised on working out a compromise with the Soviets. Any military action against the northern communists would be viewed also as an attack on the Soviet Union. Hodge's advisers believed that Korea was ripe for revolution, and the occupation authorities must have surmised that Rhee's plans threatened to increase social tensions and challenge the legitimacy of the US occupation. Just four days after Rhee had written to Goodfellow, Hodge did the same, remarking to the intelligence operative that Rhee had made 'a lot of unfortunate statements ... he wants to set up [a] separate government now and *drive* [the] Russians out. ... I've had a couple of stormy sessions with the old rascal trying to keep him on the beam' (Lowe, 1997a: 33).

In the fall of 1946, against the backdrop of a major peasant rebellion which peaked in the southernmost provinces of the country, the AMG held elections for an interim assembly. The political right emerged victorious, and prominent leftists such as Yo Un-hyong were not elected. Another important step had been taken towards consolidating a southern government. In his continuing effort to bolster the base of the non-communist alternative in Korea, Hodge appointed half of the new ninety-person legislature.

The AMG also accelerated its crackdown on the southern communists, issuing a warrant for the arrest of their leader, Pak Hon Yong. Pak soon fled the southern zone and joined the northern regime as Foreign Minister and Vice-Premier. After 1947, because of the repressive actions undertaken by the AMG and Korean police and military forces, the power of the communist movement in southern Korea declined [*Doc. 5*].

SOVIET OCCUPATION AND THE EMERGENCE OF KIM IL SUNG

In the north, the process of creating a separate state gained momentum after Kim Il Sung became chairman of a new centre of power for the northern communists, the North Korean Interim People's Committee, in February 1946. Although Kim was no simple puppet of the Soviets, his rise to power was greatly facilitated by members of the Soviet occupation force, particularly Colonel Alexandre Ignatiev of the Soviet Civil Administration and General Terentii Shtykov (plate 3), head of the Soviet delegation to the Joint Commission and later first Soviet Ambassador to the Democratic People's Republic of Korea (DPRK).

The police force, a powerful agency of oppression and enforcer of compliance with state policy, extended its power into the countryside. Communist cadres accelerated their indoctrination of the northern population. By late 1946 all newspapers contained the same news bias. The non-left elements of the original 1945 coalition were purged from power. About one-third of local people's committees were composed of representatives from the Interior Ministry. Christian protest was stifled with violence and moderate and rightist political opposition was silenced with 'a draconian thoroughness'(Cumings, 1997: 231).

The military was a powerful instrument of Kim's rise to power. In 1946 a military academy was established in Pyongyang, and a rudimentary 'national' army soon began taking shape under the direction of Choe Yong-gon, a member of Kim Il Sung's political faction. In 1948 he became the

DPRK's first Minister of National Defence, a position he held at the outbreak of the war in 1950.

Korean communists gained experience in war by fighting alongside the Chinese communists against the Chinese Nationalists in Manchuria. In early 1947, 30,000 were sent from Korea to join Chinese communists operating there. Mu Chong, the Korean who joined forces with the CCP in the 1920s, chaired the committee which oversaw the movement of men and munitions across the Sino-Korean border. This coordination between the Chinese and Korean communist parties was part of a deliberate policy to give northern Koreans training for offensive operations against the south [*Doc. 6*]. In 1949 these veteran soldiers of the CCP returned to North Korea with large numbers of comrades, establishing a base for Kim Il Sung's military offensive in June 1950.

Kim Il Sung moved gradually to consolidate his political power. Even after he became Premier of the Democratic People's Republic of Korea in 1948 and Chairman of the North Korean Workers' Party in 1949, he continued to share power with the Soviet Koreans, the Yanan faction and the 'domestic' Korean communists such as Pak Hon Yong.

KOREA'S COLD WAR IN GLOBAL CONTEXT, 1947–48

Developments in Korea were intimately related to, and affected, a broad range of issues in the international arena after 1945. The most important theme underpinning US-Soviet relations during 1945–47 was the decline of the wartime alliance and the emergence of overt global competition for spheres of influence. Any hope for an internationalist solution to the Korean 'problem' ended by 1947 when Cold War developments precluded Soviet-American cooperation. The principal developments related to Eastern and Western Europe, but developments in China and Japan were also critical in shaping the international strategy of the two superpowers.

The decline in British worldwide power influenced American perceptions, as did the civil war in Greece between communist partisans and royalists. In the late winter of 1947 the Truman administration committed itself to a more globally-oriented containment policy. In a message to both houses of Congress on 12 March 1947 President Truman announced his decision to provide $400 million in economic and military aid to Greece and Turkey; the United States would now 'support free peoples who are resisting attempted subjugation by armed minorities or by outside pressures' (Paterson et al., 1988: 449).

Disagreements over the future of Germany were central to understanding the emerging Cold War between the superpowers. Stalin, in an effort to prevent Germany from ever launching another war against the Soviet Union, called for high reparations and a weak German state. For the

United States, Germany's coal industry was the key to its plans to revitalize Europe's destroyed economy. American and British occupation zones had been 'fused' together into an entity called 'bizonia' since New Year's Day 1947 and in the spring of that year the West moved to incorporate western Germany fully into its plans for European rehabilitation. On 5 June, Secretary of State George Marshall pledged substantial American aid for Europe in a program eventually to be known as the Marshall Plan. This joint American-European effort to consolidate pro-Western governments in Europe eventually succeeded in integrating a revitalized West Germany into the global anti-communist economic nexus. By 1952, at the end of the Plan, the United States had spent over $12 billion, had substantially stemmed Europe's postwar economic woes, and had carried out a fundamental goal of its postwar diplomacy: the creation of a liberal system of international economic exchange which would benefit America's own tremendous global advantage in manufacturing capacity.

The Soviets prevented Eastern European states from participating in the Marshall Plan and offered an alternative rehabilitation program for Eastern Europe. The future of the divided Germanies remained at centre stage throughout this process, and the beginning of war in Korea in June 1950 brought further changes for Germany's role in the Western Alliance.

Momentous events in Asia shaped the structure of great power competition there for the next thirty years. The critical factors were the beginning of civil war in China in mid-1946 and the inability of Chiang Kai-shek's demoralized and corrupt regime to defeat the communists, despite a huge outlay of US military aid and a large advantage in military manpower. By 1947 Chinese communist successes had contributed to a fundamental reorientation of US occupation policy in Japan. Like Germany, Japan was now to be tied into a pro-Western network of power centres across·three continents – America, Europe and Asia – designed to contain the Soviet Union and to support industrial capitalism on a global scale. Earlier occupation directives to limit economic production were done away with and Japan's economy was now rebuilt to integrate Eastern Asia – minus mainland China – into embryonic multilateral world trade patterns. The 'Reverse Course', as the new policy towards Japan was called, was integral to an emerging world strategy to contain communism; the outbreak of the war in Korea guaranteed its success.

The hardening of Soviet and American positions on Korea in 1946–47 and the emergence of two separate Korean regimes contributed to international trends. By 1947, the logic of America's world power, Hodge's occupation policies in southern Korea, and efforts by the rightists to block the internationalist solution offered through trusteeship led to a policy of relying on a pro-Western government in Seoul which would survive on US economic and military aid. Indeed, within weeks of the President's Truman

Doctrine speech, Acting Secretary of State Dean Acheson formulated a plan to reorganize America's administration of Korea, to accelerate the creation of a separate provisional government for the south, to send a group of prominent US businessmen to Korea to make recommendations for financial and corporate rehabilitation, and to obtain from the US Congress over $500 million in aid over the next three years. Acheson's grand design for Korea envisaged the end of US military occupation and the creation of an anti-communist government with a viable economy which could help sustain Japanese capitalism. The blueprint for future American activity in Korea was thus laid down in Washington in late March 1947.

The Soviet-American Joint Commission met again in the summer of 1947 but it remained deadlocked. The decision by the United States to refer the Korean issue to the United Nations in September 1947 was a logical consequence of Acheson's containment strategy for Korea: it reflected the State Department's determination to convince Congressional leaders to commit funds to the southern regime to sanction the establishment of a separate southern government while still appearing to search for a solution to the division of the country.

Though the Soviet Union possessed one of the five 'great power' vetos in the United Nations Security Council, a body designed to advocate the use of force if necessary to resolve international crises, in the 1940s and early 1950s the United States was able to exert a significant influence over the larger and less powerful UN General Assembly. This proved important in passing resolutions which reflected America's global anti-communist interests. On 14 November 1947 the United States successfully manoeuvered its allies to pass a resolution – against Soviet-backed opposition – which established a United Nations Temporary Commission on Korea (UNTCOK). Composed of representatives from Australia, Canada, (Nationalist) China, El Salvador, France, India, the Philippines, and Syria, the Commission was originally set up to observe elections in both northern and southern Korea, even though it was widely recognized that the Soviets and North Koreans would not agree to elections in their area. When the communists prevented the members of UNTCOK from operating in the north in early 1948, the UN changed the mandate of the Commission to oversee elections south of the 38th parallel only. Canada and Australia were concerned that this might lead to the permanent division of the two Koreas – they voted against the resolution which recommended a change in the Commission's mandate but did not withdraw from the Commission. These decisions taken by the UN marked the beginning of a significant commitment to the peninsula, and provided some of the background for UN involvement in the early stages of the Korean conflict. The debates also underlined some of the different opinions within the UN and Western Alliance on how to approach Korean issues.

On the twenty-ninth anniversary of the 1 March Movement, 1 March 1948, General Hodge announced that South Korea's first ever national election would be held in early May. Though UNTCOK later voted to endorse the election, the results were hardly in doubt, as the left, some moderates, and even the rightist Kim Ku refused to participate in them. Given the background to the elections – the great power division of the country, US and Soviet occupations, repression of political opposition in both the north and the south – the elections were held in an atmosphere which significantly circumscribed political freedom.

Further, the non-Korean-speaking UNTCOK members who watched Koreans vote on 10 May observed the events in a cursory manner. Still, in December 1948 a UN General Assembly resolution endorsed UNTCOK's final report and declared the Republic of Korea (ROK) as the lawful government in control of that part of Korea which UNTCOK had access to. Thus began South Korea's baptism in Western-style democracy, largely imposed as a framework for governance from without upon a mainly rural society with no experience of Western processes and ideas. South Korea had been firmly established as a bastion of American prestige on the Northeast Asian continent, but the vast majority of Koreans were given little or no opportunity to define for themselves the terms of the new political system which was to rule over them.

America's global containment strategies brought Rhee, an authoritarian politician who well understood how to manipulate the dynamics of the Cold War, into prominence. He recognized that the 1948 elections were a critical turning point for the occupation; with the left effectively contained as a political force and other members of the right marginalized, he knew he was in the strongest position to become President; and he recognized that the occupation policies of the great powers, combined with the intransigence of the right and left, to which he had made his own major contribution, had destroyed any real possibility for the peaceful emergence of a unified Korea. By 1948, if Korea was to be unified it would be through violence. Rhee and Kim Il Sung had accepted this by 1946.

By contrast, Kim Ku, a man accustomed to using violent means against the Japanese to achieve his ends, did not survive the sea-change in US foreign policy represented by the Truman Doctrine, the Marshall Plan and the Reverse Course. A fundamental turning point occurred when Kim refused to take part in the 1948 elections, preferring instead to work with moderates who continued their now futile search for a diplomatic solution to the divided Koreas. Kim's influence on the domestic Korean scene declined, and he was assassinated, possibly by rival rightist forces, in 1949.

The May elections reinforced the power of the right in Korea. The conservative Korean Democratic Party was victorious in the new National Assembly. The constitution provided for a strong executive checked only by the power of the Assembly to nominate the President and to veto cabinet decisions. The relationship between Rhee and the National Assembly has been portrayed as 'a tempestuous marriage of convenience', and the two sides now began to vie for political power (Cumings, 1997: 216). On 15 July 1948 the Assembly elected Rhee President and the Republic of Korea formally came into being on 15 August 1948, exactly three years after Japan's surrender in the Second World War, the day Koreans annually celebrate as independence day.

In the north, Kim Il Sung, ruthless and adept at political warfare inside his party, rose to prominence with the backing of the Soviets and the northern security forces and army, whose formal being came into existence as the Korean People's Army (KPA) on 8 February 1948. Police repression was harsh: 'The regime organized secret networks on a grand scale to report political statements, including rumours and hearsay, both as a means of checking on citizens' loyalty and of providing the leadership with rudimentary information about public opinion' (Cumings, 1997: 233–4).

The system was used to re-educate, purge or imprison. People became accustomed to express ideas which followed the mass party line. In this way the northern regime was able to penetrate more deeply into the countryside than the southern one, and it laid the base for a more thorough form of authoritarianism than that practised by the ROK. The northern government was given a formal institutional base just weeks after the creation of the republic in Seoul. Elections were held on 25 August and the proclamation of the North Korean state was made on 9 September.

THE KOREAN CONFLICT, 1948–50

By late 1948 the international and domestic structures for the Korean War were in place and a new phase of escalation began: for the next year and a half the conflict between the two Koreas intensified. The southern regime consolidated its power against indigenous and northern-sponsored leftist groups while the north strengthened its economy and readied its superior industrial base for war. It reinforced its internal authority and sent agents south of the parallel to bolster guerrilla operations against the ROK.

Repressive tactics against the southern communists had weakened the party apparatus and it now came under the direction of the northern leadership. Orders were sent from Pyongyang to infiltrate the southern police forces, to supply food to the guerrilla movement and to foment disorder. These events took place against a backdrop in which the two superpowers began to withdraw their military occupation forces. Soviet armies left the north by late December 1948, and six months later the US troops completed their withdrawal.

The southern guerrillas operated in two main areas south of the 38th parallel: in the Chiri mountains in the south central area, and on an island south of the mainland known as Cheju (map 3). The island insurgency emerged out of the island's people's committee which had been established as part of the leftist Korean People's Republic in 1945. A rightist governor of the province ordered reprisals against the island guerrilla force of three to four thousand. The insurgency was effectively defeated by the spring of 1949 but the entire island population suffered. Official ROK figures cite over 27,000 dead islanders, but the island governor said that about 60,000 villagers had died and that another 40,000 had escaped to Japan (Cumings, 1990: 221).

The Cheju rebellion also triggered a clash in the town of Yosu on the southern mainland (map 3). On 19 October 1948 some elements of the ROK army mutinied, refusing to fight against the Cheju islanders. Resurgent people's committees were established and within a week the ROK military, under the direction of US military advisers, suppressed the uprising, at the cost of several thousand lives. In the wake of the revolt against the regime, the National Assembly passed the infamous National Security Law. With its broad definition of sedition the law was used against communists and other opponents of the regime for decades.

After their defeat in Yosu, about 1,000 of the rebels fled to the Chiri mountains, where they joined an active guerrilla force. At the peak of their strength in the fall of 1949 there were between 3,000 and 6,000 guerrilla partisans in the ROK. A series of ROK military offensives reduced this number to less than 500 by March 1950, though the north continued to send reinforcements, especially to areas just south of the parallel. Intelligence sources estimated that about 3,000 guerrillas remained in reserve in North Korea.

SYNGMAN RHEE AND THE ORIGINS OF THE KOREAN WAR

The accelerated civil conflict in the south convinced President Rhee to adopt a more aggressive policy against the northern communists; he viewed his strategies to defeat them as a simple extension of the anti-communist measures his government had taken in the south since the inception of the ROK state.

Rhee also recognized that without US support his regime would not be able to unify the country under his leadership. The ROK was dependent on the United States for military and economic aid and for its state budget. Cut off from the northern industrial base and faced with indigenous and northern-backed insurgencies, the southern government lacked the resources to survive on its own. In early 1949 Rhee actively sought American backing and weapons for a southern military push into North Korea, which would see the ROK absorb the northern regime into its own constitutional structure [*Doc. 7*]. American officials realized that Rhee's plan-would lead to war with North Korea and they refused to back it. Rhee complied and agreed not to launch an offensive without US backing.

In 1948–49 US strategy towards South Korea was in transition. The military argued that Korea was strategically unimportant in a global conflict with the Soviet Union and called for the removal of US troops from the peninsula. Support for Rhee's 'rollback' strategy would draw valuable resources to a peripheral theatre. At a time when elements of US public and Congressional opinion severely criticized America's failing effort to ensure that the Chinese Nationalists retained power and defeated the CCP, the Truman administration had little interest in fighting a land war in continental Asia.

Instead of backing a southern offensive, Americans moved to consolidate the power of the South Korean state through a project of nation-building. US policymakers believed that a failure of the experiment in South Korea would undermine America's prestige and containment efforts, not only in Asia but around the world.

Over the course of 1948–49 the United States organized a programme of economic and military aid which ensured a continued US presence in the fledgling republic. Occupation troops were replaced with the largest number of American civilian and military advisers anywhere in the world: some 2,500 American officials were stationed in the ROK to help maintain internal security and ensure the successful Western orientation of the regime. A Korean Military Advisory Group composed of almost 500 US soldiers trained the Korean military force for its new security functions. Another 2,000 worked for the American embassy in Seoul, the largest in the world. Indeed, the US–Korea power relationship after 1948 has been described variously as a 'client-patron' relationship, 'a highly penetrative American regime' (Cumings, 1990: 469) and an 'informal empire' (Lee, 1995: 4), terms which describe the power imbalance between the United States and the ROK government as well as continued US efforts – sometimes reshaped by the Rhee government – to influence the direction of Korea's economic, political and military development.

The logical consequence of this effort to build a South Korean state compatible with America's global and regional containment strategies was an implicit assumption that it would be defended in the event of an attack. A top-secret State Department memo of 1949 noted that 'since Korea is another area in which United States influence should show results in the social and economic life of the country, it is important that we not let the Republic fail' (Lee, 1995: 31).

This was a defensive position, not a strategy entailing the use of force to 'rollback' the borders of North Korean communism. A speech by Secretary of State Dean Acheson on 12 January 1950 confirmed this: in the event of an attack west of Japan, the Ryukyus and the Philippines, Acheson declared, the initial response would come from local military forces, 'and then upon the commitments of the entire civilized world under the Charter of the United Nations, which so far has not proved a weak reed to lean on by any people who are determined to protect their independence against outside aggression' (Cumings, 1990: 422). This was a warning not heeded by Stalin or the North Korean communists.

KIM IL SUNG AND THE ORIGINS OF THE KOREAN WAR

Although Premier Kim Il Sung sponsored guerrilla activities in the south, he did not place great emphasis on the role of the communist partisan movement there. Foreign Minister Pak Hon Yong, on the other hand, believed that their help could be significant (Hershberg, 1995: 6). Pak's ideas were heavily influenced by his experience as an underground communist leader in the south during the Japanese occupation of Korea. While Pak stressed the importance of supporting subversive activities, Kim underscored the need to obtain Soviet and Chinese backing for a traditional military offensive against the south. This was one of a number of conflicts between the two communists which would eventually lead to Pak's purging and execution by the mid-1950s.

Mao Zedong told a visiting DPRK representative in the spring of 1949 that the Chinese communists were willing to further the cause of the Korean Revolution. At the moment, however, they were preoccupied with their own civil war and could not immediately come to the aid of their Korean comrades; military action in Korea should await the successful outcome of the Chinese Communist Party's military operations. After that, Mao said, in the event more help was needed, 'we can throw in Chinese soldiers for you; all black, no one will notice' (Mastny, 1996: 91). In the meantime, the Chinese communist leader agreed to release to the North Koreans two Chinese army divisions made up of soldiers of Korean ethnicity.

The Soviets were initially less amenable than the Chinese. Stalin reportedly told Kim, probably during the latter's visit to Moscow in March 1949, that though the United States had apparently abandoned China, the same would not be true of Korea: 'The Americans will never agree to be thrown out of there and because of that, to lose their reputation as a great power. The Soviet people would not understand the necessity of a war in Korea, which is a remote place outside the sphere of the USSR's vital interests' (Goncharov et al., 1993: 138).

In September 1949, as the south intensified its offensive against the partisans in the Chiri mountains, Kim Il Sung pressed the Soviets for support for an offensive centred on the strategically important Ongjin peninsula southwest of Pyongyang (map 3). If the two South Korean regiments stationed there succumbed to the offensive, Kim reasoned, it might be possible to open a path to Seoul and the south beyond. The Soviet chargé d'affaires in Pyongyang, who reported Kim's position to Moscow, noted with prescience that such a move would be disadvantageous to the north because it would permit the Americans to provide corresponding aid to the southern regime [Doc. 8].

The Soviet Politburo agreed with his assessment and refused to support Kim's plan. Moscow informed its embassy in Pyongyang on 24 September that the northern army was not prepared for such an attack and that if the offensive turned into a prolonged struggle serious political and economic difficulties would ensue for the regime. This would entail a drain on valuable resources which the Soviet Union was not willing to sacrifice. Much more work needed to be done in the way of supporting the southern partisans: only in conditions of a successful general uprising in the south could a northern invasion be successful. Even a seemingly limited military objective such as the seizure of the Ongjin peninsula would cause a civil war which the northern regime was unprepared to deal with.

Throughout 1949, then, Stalin refused to back a northern offensive against the south. The number of Soviet advisers in the north remained relatively small, a sign that Korea was also peripheral to Soviet interests at this time. The Soviet Union had signed bilateral mutual security pacts with a number of its Eastern European satellites which required the signatories to come to the aid of the party which was attacked. No such treaty was negotiated with North Korea, probably because the Soviets did not want to be drawn into a conflict in Asia initiated by its North Korean allies.

Despite the constraints placed on the two Koreas by their great power allies, the 38th parallel was far from peaceful in 1949. Although neither superpower agreed to back a Korean offensive that year, ROK and DPRK forces were involved in a perilous border war. Numerous skirmishes broke out, involving thousands of troops along the parallel and the Ongjin peninsula. The attacks began in May 1949, apparently at the behest of the southern government, but both sides were involved. On 4 August about 5,000 North Korean soldiers attacked a mountain just north of the parallel which had been occupied by southern forces. The battles remained confined to the parallel, however, and no major offensive took place until after the Soviet Union agreed to back a northern attack. This Soviet decision, confirmed in the early spring of 1950, escalated the 1949 border war into a full-scale war between the two Koreas and internationalized the Korean conflict.

PART THREE   INTERNATIONAL WAR IN KOREA

CHAPTER THREE

KOREA'S GLOBAL WAR, 1950-51

Political scientist Bruce Cumings (1990) has argued that the 1949 border conflict launched the beginning of the Korean War, which itself was the logical culmination of civil conflict within Korea and the consolidation of the two rival regimes. Cumings's thesis is part of a wider historical debate about the relative role of local and international factors in the Korean War. He stresses the peninsular dynamics of the Korean War and argues that Koreans were the prime historical actors shaping the conflict: each hoped to provoke a counter-offensive from the other side so as to enable its own great power backer to enter into the conflict and unify the peninsula. Stalin understood the logic behind this strategy very well [*Doc. 9*]. In September 1949 the Politburo refused to support Kim Il Sung's plans partly out of fear that a North Korean attack would invite American intervention. Similarly, as we have seen, the United States was unprepared to be drawn into a war initiated by Syngman Rhee.

According to Cumings, since the border war began in 1949, the traditional starting date for the war, June 1950, is misleading. However, there is a discontinuity between the 1949 border war and the June 1950 attack which should also be highlighted. The crucial difference was the escalation and internationalization of the war represented by Stalin's decision in early 1950 to back a northern offensive against South Korea. Stalin did not simply 'order' the North Koreans to attack, for Kim Il Sung was no simple pawn; rather, Stalin agreed to an initiative put forward by Kim. Further, Stalin's support was qualified, since he would refuse to draw the Soviet Union into the conflict if the United States entered the war.

We do not yet have the evidence to conclude that Stalin supported Kim out of calculations of *realpolitik* – that is, because he expected the United States to intervene, and he hoped the war would distract the West from the larger strategic prize of Europe. It is possible that Stalin manipulated the logic of Korea's domestic conflict in order to benefit his own global position. But Stalin's support of Kim was a critical step towards full-scale war on the peninsula. Both Rhee and Kim had made clear that they would not initiate a major offensive independent of superpower assistance; each pleaded that material and moral support was needed to gain victory. Here again we see the interdependence of international and local factors: Kim and Stalin together were responsible for the North Korean offensive in 1950, a move which exacerbated the domestic Korean conflict but which also launched Korea's international war.

We thus view the period from late 1948 to June 1950 as a unity – as part of a civil conflict which itself was intimately tied up with great power diplomacy and the alignment of indigenous forces after 1945 – and the era after the northern attack as a continuation of that conflict, but with a very different character. Although Korean objectives in the June war remained the same, Soviet support for Kim introduced a powerful new dynamic: it further internationalized the peninsular struggle, and ignited a global powderkeg. Without great power intervention it is possible that the border fighting would have remained deadlocked, as it has since 1953. Stalin's apparent miscalculation had consequences for the structure of the international system for a quarter–century and more.

KIM IL SUNG, STALIN, MAO AND THE APPROACH OF WAR, 1949–50

Between September 1949 and the late winter of 1950 Stalin changed his mind and decided to support a northern offensive. Why did he alter the Politburo's decision of the previous September? What circumstances provoked the Soviets to provide the military aid and moral stimulus for a northern offensive at a time when the southern partisan movement was weakening?

There is still much more we need to know from communist sources, but Stalin's perceptions may have been influenced by the changing balance of power in China and the Soviet explosion of its first atomic device in August. These events, combined with persistent requests from North Korea, may have influenced Stalin to take a bolder, belligerent approach to the issue of reunifying the two Koreas. As early as the spring of 1949 the Soviet leader confessed to a visiting Chinese diplomat that he had previously underrated China's revolutionary momentum; now, he believed, 'the center of the world revolution is transferring to China and East Asia' (Mastny, 1996: 87).

In December 1949, Mao Zedong, the head of the new People's Republic of China (PRC), travelled to Moscow to discuss a treaty alliance. It was Mao's first trip outside China and he found Stalin in a pensive mood, reluctant to accommodate fully China's national interests. On the international strategic situation, the Soviet Premier seemed to want to encourage the Chinese leader while not making any commitments himself. He told

Mao on the 16th that 'the Americans are afraid of war. The Americans ask other countries to fight the war, but other countries are also afraid to fight a war' (Hershberg, 1996–97: 226). Significantly, he also said that Japan was not yet reconstructed and therefore it too was unprepared for war. Jokingly, he told Mao that there were no powers who wanted to fight China, unless perhaps Kim Il Sung did.

On 22 January 1950 Stalin and Mao outlined the framework for what became the Sino-Soviet alliance. They agreed that the treaty should deter Japanese and jmperialist aggression, that it should contain a clause for consultation, and that Soviet troops could remain in Port Arthur until a peace treaty was signed with Japan. Formal arrangements would be worked out between the Chinese and Soviet Foreign Ministers, Zhou Enlai (plate 4) and Andrei Vyshinsky.

Both Mao and Stalin believed that their new alliance would be a major deterrent to aggressive activity by the United States and its Cold War allies, particularly Japan. The key sentence of the final treaty, signed on 14 February 1950, stated: 'In the event of one of the Contracting Parties being attacked by Japan or any state allied with her and thus being involved in a state of war, the other Contracting Party shall immediately render military and other assistance by all means at its disposal' (Goncharov et al., 1993: 260). For Stalin the alliance was a watershed, perhaps a means of neutralizing the West's newly formed military alliance, the North Atlantic Treaty Organization (NATO), and possibly a means to open the globe to new spheres of communist influence. It may have represented a major step towards his decision to support Kim Il Sung's war against the southern regime (Zubok and Pleshakov, 1996: 62).

In this context Kim Il Sung's request for Stalin's 'order' may have been decisive. On 28 January 1950 Stalin received intelligence information which indicated that South Korea would not be defended by the United States in the event of attack. Two days later – less than a week after he had decided with Mao the broad outlines of the Sino-Soviet Alliance – Stalin wrote to the Soviet Ambassador in Pyongyang that the Soviet Union was now ready to help comrade Kim with his plans for an invasion. The matter needed large-scale preparation, Stalin wrote, and it was important that the risk be minimized [*Doc. 10*]. The brief note did not mention a timetable and lacked specific plans. It also placed the onus for the organization of the offensive on Kim. As historian James Matray has recently argued, it was only later that spring, after a visit to Moscow by Kim Il Sung, Pak Hon Yong and other Korean leaders in late March and April, that Stalin formally agreed to provide the equipment and materiel necessary for the North Korean attack. He then ordered a team of Soviet military officials to formulate and implement an offensive strategy based on Soviet military concepts. According to Matray, Stalin made the decision to support the northern offensive because the Soviet leader wanted to pre-empt a ROK invasion of the north which he thought would be likely in the near future (Matray, 2000).

Although Stalin gave his blessing for the attack, he was careful to place limits on Soviet support for the offensive. In April 1950 Stalin told the visiting North Koreans that they 'should not expect great assistance and support from the Soviet Union, because it had more important challenges to meet than the Korean problem'. The Soviets were preoccupied with issues in Europe and the West. Kim was told to consult the Chinese since Mao had 'a good understanding of Oriental matters'. He told Kim that if the United States did intervene, the Soviets would not come into the war (Goncharov et al., 1993: 144). Despite the significant Soviet material aid which had already been given, Kim must have left these meetings feeling rebuffed.

If Stalin provided the material support for the attack, the Chinese revolutionaries also played a significant role in preparing North Korea for the invasion by facilitating the return of soldiers of Korean ethnicity to the north. In the spring of 1949, the Chinese communists signed an agreement with the DPRK which enabled almost 40,000 volunteers to enter into the North Korean People's Army. In April 1950 tens of thousands more troops of Korean background were released to the KPA – about 50 percent of the 95,000 military force that attacked on 25 June received their first baptism of fire in the Chinese Revolution. Many more thousands of soldiers of Korean ethnicity continued to arrive from China into the fall of 1950.

Kim Il Sung visited Mao in Beijing from 13–16 May 1950 to secure the Chinese leader's consent to his plans. Although the Chinese had been complicit in supporting North Korea's 'liberation war' against the south, up to this point they had not been fully consulted about Kim's planning. In a message to the Chinese after the Korean Premier's arrival, Stalin carefully disengaged the Soviet Union from full responsibility if the adventure turned out badly, noting that the Soviets now supported reunification of the peninsula, but that the issue should ultimately be decided by the Koreans and Chinese communists.

Mao had already encouraged the adventure [*Doc. 11*] and his faith in the Sino-Soviet Alliance seemed to reassure the Chinese leader about the proposed enterprise. During their meetings Mao told Kim Il Sung that the possibility of American intervention could not be excluded entirely. Kim replied that the Americans would not have the time to send their troops because the war would be over in a few weeks. When Mao offered to send several Chinese armies to the Sino-Korean border Kim reportedly refused, saying the Koreans could take care of the situation themselves (Chen, 1994: 112).

PREPARING FOR WAR: AMERICA AND NSC 68

The communists tragically miscalculated the intentions of the Truman administration towards Northeast Asia in early 1950. Plans for Korea included an implicit defence of the south. On the international front, far from moving away from a military solution to the Cold War, American officials now moved to embrace one. The Soviet explosion of the atomic bomb in the fall of 1949 encouraged the administration to accelerate America's capacity to develop its own atom bombs. As Secretary of Defense Louis Johnson explained in October 1949, 'when the USSR attains a stock-pile of atomic weapons, overwhelming superiority of our stockpile and production rate will be necessary if our atomic weapon posture is to continue to act as a deterrent to war' (Leffler, 1992: 327). Early in 1950 the President gave the go-ahead for a new 'super' bomb which eventually led to the development of the much more powerful hydrogen bomb a few years later. At the meeting to decide the issue Truman impatiently remarked: 'What the hell are we waiting for? Let's get on with it' (Rhodes, 1995: 407).

Fears about the West's military vulnerability in Western Europe, the Middle East, and Asia soon prompted officials to produce a momentous Cold War document, known as National Security Council 68 (NSC 68), which championed the militarization of the Western alliance against the Soviet threat. The document called for 'greatly increased general air, ground and sea strength, and increased air defence and civilian defence programs' [*Doc. 12*]. There was significant opposition to the envisaged program in the spring of 1950. Truman himself was cautious and sceptical, hoping to maintain his objective of a balanced budget.

NSC 68 was one of the most portentous of Cold War documents, written in a style of deep fear and foreboding. Produced by the National Security Council, a top-level executive committee created in 1947 to delib-erate America's international security policies, the document has been described by historian Michael Hunt as 'a cataclysmic picture of ideological struggle in the offing' (Hunt, 1996: 126). It laid the groundwork for a rapid build-up of America's armed forces during the Korean War, expanded the bureaucratic base for the military-industrial complex, and extended America's hegemonic reach in the developing world.

The Cold War 'hawks' used NSC 68 and the Korean War to pressure the Truman administration to adopt a fiercely aggressive approach to national security, one which would untie itself from limited military spending. Leading figures in this push included Secretary of State Dean Acheson, Paul Nitze, the main author of NSC 68 and head of an important State Department planning body known as the Policy Planning Staff, and Under Secretary of Defense Robert Lovett. In March 1950 Lovett commented that the Cold War required America to do away with the 'sharp line between democratic principles and immoral actions' (Hogan, 1998: 300).

The North Korean attack on South Korea on 25 June 1950 vastly accelerated the trend towards rearmament which had already started to take shape in the Truman administration. The hawks immediately recognized the significance of the attack for their plans. Completely discounting the role of the North Koreans in launching the war, Dean Acheson told a group of Western diplomats in late July that the Soviet move was 'an absolute godsend' because the United States could now move ahead with their rearmament plans. Fortuitously it appeared, the simplistic predictions of NSC 68 were being borne out by events. Acheson would later comment that the Korean War came along and saved America. For the hawks, then, the war was a key psychological turning point in the Cold War which permitted them to justify an acceleration of their global rearmament program. Over the long term, the Truman administration's response to the Korean War made it a lot easier for the country to plunge itself into a series of major conflicts in Asia and the developing world. But let us now return to Korea and the disastrous events of the early summer of 1950.

NORTH KOREAN OFFENSIVE AND US RESPONSE

All told, the North Korean Army had about 135,000 troops in 1950. At the outbreak of the war the Republic of Korea Army numbered about 100,000 soldiers. Unlike the KPA the southern army had no tanks and few heavy artillery pieces.

North Korean troops crossed the 38th parallel in the early morning hours (Korea time) of Sunday 25 June 1950. The assault began along several fronts: a bombardment of Ongjin was followed by infantry attacks on Ongjin, Kaesong and Chunchon. Amphibious forces then landed on the east coast, near Kangnung (map 3). Even though ROK troops reportedly expected some type of offensive, the KPA, using about 130 tanks, 110 planes and heavy artillery, quickly broke through ROK lines and made its move southwards.

The northern offensive was immediately answered by an escalation of the war by the US government. On the day of the offensive, 24 June in the United States, President Truman was at his home in Missouri; he was abruptly called back to Washington the next day by Secretary Acheson. In his January 1950 'Press Club' speech, Acheson had already warned that the United States would turn to the United Nations to counter aggression if it occurred in Asia west of America's defensive island perimeter. In addition, Korea had been closely associated with the UN since the Truman administration had introduced the Korean question to the General Assembly in 1947. With this background, Acheson and other officials swiftly brought developments in Korea to the attention of the United Nations. On 25 June the Security Council passed a resolution calling for the immediate cessation of hostilities, the withdrawal of North Korean forces south of the 38th parallel, and international assistance to the UN in carrying out the resolution. By the time Truman arrived in Washington that evening he was in a belligerent mood. 'By God I'm going to let them have it', he told a meeting of his advisers (Lowe, 1997a: 187). He then secretly made plans for an atomic strike on Russia should it enter the conflict.

The Truman administration argued that North Korea was a puppet of Soviet global expansionism and that the war was not about the two Koreas but about US prestige and power and the worldwide containment of Soviet communism. Domestic issues, including accusations from right-wing Republican Senator Joseph McCarthy that there was a fifth column of communists in government, and pressure from the so-called 'China lobby' composed of prominent and vociferous anti-communists led by Republican Senator Styles Bridges and Republican Congressman Walter Judd, reinforced Truman's decision to move rapidly to escalate the war and to contain Soviet 'aggression' in Korea. But the war only exacerbated the 'general climate of fear and crisis that gripped the nation' in 1950 (Kaufman, 1997: 35).

On 26 June Truman ordered US air and naval forces stationed in Japan to attack the North Koreans operating south of the parallel. At Acheson's bidding, he agreed to station the US Seventh Fleet in the Formosa Strait in order to prevent the Chinese communists from attacking the island and to discourage Chiang from launching an assault against mainland China. This 'neutralization' of Taiwan rankled PRC leaders who were preparing to mount an offensive against the island. The President also authorized further aid to defeat leftist guerrilla movements in the Philippines and Indochina.

In ordering US forces into action, Truman made no effort to legitimize his decision through the UN or the US Congress; the orders to dispatch forces came solely from his Executive Office. American policy was thus manufactured to limit potential criticism from allies and Congress, and to provide the 'leadership' for the others to follow. Not until the 27 June did the Security Council provide international support for Truman's undertaking, by passing a resolution which recommended UN members 'to furnish such assistance to the Republic of Korea as may be necessary to repel the armed attack and to restore international peace and security in the area' (US Congress, 1953: 37). The further concentration of power in the executive branch was one of the legacies of Korea which set a precedent for America's later involvement in Vietnam.

Legacies of past history also shaped the American administration's responses to Korea. As we have seen, Truman drew simplistic historical parallels between the events in the Cold War and Nazi foreign policy in the

1930s. As the British cabinet recognized, the US executive was now influenced 'by the events preceding the Second World War'. American officials had learned the lesson that 'it would be easier to make such a stand in the earlier rather than in the later stages of imperialist expansion by a totalitarian State' (Lowe, 1997b: 191).

The two Security Council resolutions of 25 and 27 June went unopposed by the Soviet Union because it was boycotting the Council to protest the refusal of the American-led UN coalition to replace the Chinese Nationalist representatives in the UN with members from the newly-formed PRC. Had the Soviet Union been on the Council it would have been able to veto these resolutions. Its absence gave the Western powers a free hand to determine their own military response to the Korean offensive.

On 29 June, because of the deteriorating military situation on the ground, Truman authorized US forces to attack targets north of the parallel; the next day, on the recommendation of an on-the-spot report by a US General that US troops were needed to halt the attack, Truman approved the dispatch of an Eighth Army regimental combat team from Japan to Korea. The Eighth Army, commanded by General Walton H. Walker, became the main US fighting force in Korea.

THE UNITED NATIONS' COUNTER-OFFENSIVE, JUNE–AUGUST 1950

America's allies supported the Security Council resolutions, but remained wary of the wider implications of US actions in Korea and Asia. Above all, they desperately wanted the war to be contained on the peninsula and to avoid direct Soviet involvement. In London, the Foreign Office sought ways to provide the Soviets with a degree of flexibility in their diplomacy with the Western powers. A proposal by Acheson publicly to call the invasion an example of 'centrally directed communist imperialism' was criticized by London and dropped. The allies also viewed with alarm the stationing of the Seventh Fleet around Taiwan, fearing that it would needlessly alienate the Chinese and consolidate the Sino-Soviet alliance. The British were also concerned that it might provoke the Chinese into attacking their colony of Hong Kong. In Ottawa, Canadian Secretary of State for External Affairs Lester Pearson made a distinction between policy directed at Taiwan and military action in Korea. The former was an American initiative and the latter was a UN operation, he told the Canadian cabinet in July. These efforts provided limited comfort, however, as the military situation continued to deteriorate and Secretary Acheson insisted on linking the two theatres.

The British Commonwealth initially made only token military contributions to the war effort; a few days after the conflict began, Australia, Britain, Canada and New Zealand ordered naval support to the US-led forces. Australia also sent an air squadron which had been stationed in Japan as part of the allied occupation force. South Africa sent an air squadron. On 7 July the United Nations Security Council established a United Nations Command (UNC) which henceforth included all South Korean and foreign troops fighting on the UN side. Overall command of these troops lay in the hands of General Douglas MacArthur (plate 2), a veteran of the Pacific War, presently Supreme Commander of the Allied Powers in Japan and Head of America's Far Eastern Command. As the first Commander-in-Chief of the UNC (CINCUNC), America's proconsul in Asia was now at the height of his power.

The allies were reluctant at first to provide ground troops to MacArthur's command, feeling that such a contribution would hurt their regional and global defensive positions and tie down limited resources in a peripheral battle. It soon became apparent, however, that contingents of allied troops would help the Truman administration not so much on the battlefield as in the political arena – in its effort to convince the American Congress to raise defence spending and mobilize the NATO deterrent in Europe. Once this was understood, Western capitals ordered small numbers of their ground troops into action; in this way the allies consciously contributed to the global expansion of American power, which they felt was needed to underpin their own foreign and security policies. Eventually, forces from seventeen different nations – Australia, Belgium, Britain, Canada, Colombia, Ethiopia, France, Greece, Luxembourg, the Netherlands, New Zealand, the Philippines, South Africa, South Korea, Thailand, Turkey, and the United States – operated through the UNC. In addition, India, Italy, Norway and Sweden collectively provided several hundred non-combat medical units.

The first two months of the war witnessed the remarkable advance of the KPA, and by late August only a small area in southeastern Korea, known as the Pusan perimeter, remained under the control of the besieged UNC forces (map 3). But by mid-September UNC forces were able to organize their counter-offensive, and on the 15th, General MacArthur launched a major amphibious offensive involving some 80,000 men (including about 8,600 Koreans) of the newly-created 'X Corps' against the western port city of Inchon, located just below the 38th parallel (map 4). The city was defended by only several thousand North Koreans. The Inchon landing was a brilliant strategic move on the part of MacArthur, and the KPA was soon forced into retreat. On 28 September Seoul was retaken.

ROLLBACK, AMERICAN STYLE: SEPTEMBER 1950

The UNC counter-offensive might have stabilized the situation on the ground and restored the *status quo ante bellum* had orders not been given to move beyond the 38th parallel. The collective allied decision to 'rollback' the borders of communism in 1950 and to obliterate the northern republic escalated the conflict and had catastrophic consequences.

The United States and the West viewed the crossing of the 38th parallel as an opportunity to gain ground in the global Cold War. A memo prepared in the Department of Defense at the end of July argued that the 'free world' should take this first opportunity to displace a communist state from the Soviet orbit (US Department of State, 1976: 506).

From the administration's point of view, an offensive directed against North Korea would counter Republican criticism of a soft Truman administration policy towards communism in Asia and it would bolster the Democrats' chances in the upcoming November Congressional elections. It would also add credence to the new rearmament program, designed to contain global communism. In early September President Truman announced that the United States would more than double its defence expenditure to about $15 billion a year and support a substantial increase in its own military forces stationed on the European continent.

America's allies, though concerned about the reactions of the Chinese, for the most part supported the planned offensive north of the 38th parallel. British Foreign Secretary Ernest Bevin's main objective was to keep the war limited to the peninsula; he did not want to hurt the Anglo-American 'special relationship' by attempting to thwart the United States from unifying the two Koreas. Sir John Slessor, the Marshal of the Royal Air Force, did not agree. He argued that the defeat of the KPA meant there was no military advantage to occupying North Korea: 'after having had her army destroyed and all her industries knocked flat, I find it difficult to envisage North Korea, even with Russian assistance, becoming a menace again for a long time to come' (Lowe, 1997b: 202). In response to concerns about the operation, Bevin recommended that the allies not move ahead too quickly, but his policy proposal was not followed. The British cabinet decided against the recommendations of their top military commanders, the Chiefs of Staff, who feared Chinese intervention in the war, and agreed to support offensive operations beyond the parallel. Ultimately, the cabinet decided that the political benefits of moving north outweighed military considerations, and British policy opportunistically paralleled that of the United States at this stage of the conflict.

South Korean officials were the strongest supporters of the UN offensive, but they hoped to unite the country on their own terms. President Rhee did not want another occupation of northern Korea by foreign powers. On 19 September he told a large group of Koreans at a mass meeting in Pusan that: 'We have to advance as far as the Manchurian border until not a single enemy soldier is left in our country.' Even if UN troops halted at the 38th parallel 'we will not allow ourselves to stop' (Appleman, 1961: 614–15). Later that month South Korean Foreign Minister Ben C. Limb told US officials to demand an unconditional surrender from DPRK forces. He said that the ambiguity which existed in the UN General Assembly resolution of late 1948 should be removed, and the ROK should be recognized as having sole jurisdiction for all parts of reunited Korean territory. The United States did not cross the parallel at the behest of South Korea – Koreans were not so much consulted as told about strategic plans – but the South Korean position added legitimacy to Western objectives to unite the country through military force.

The uncertainty and chaotic thinking accompanying the decision to cross the 38th parallel was encapsulated in the original Western term used to describe the war: a 'police action'. Though the United Nations named North Korea as the party responsible for breaching the peace, and the UN charter mandated its members to get involved in conflicts only where a violation of the territorial integrity of a nation state had occurred, in practice the UN did not recognize North Korea as a state. The irony of the term 'police action' was that it treated the war as if it were an internal conflict – a civil war – not an international war organized and plotted by Stalin, as the public was led to believe. Under this kind of expedient reasoning it was easier to legitimize sending troops northward across the parallel, since there was now deemed to be no border. Collectively, UN forces did not have a clear idea what type of war they were fighting, or where its boundaries lay. More important than the need to protect a nation's sovereignty from aggression was the importance of mobilizing America's global military power. This political logic soon led to military disaster.

The day before Seoul fell to UN forces, President Truman approved a policy (NSC 81) which allowed MacArthur to cross the parallel. According to the President's orders, relayed on 29 September, only Korean forces were to be used near the Soviet and Chinese borders of North Korea. In the event of Soviet intervention MacArthur was told to order his troops to assume a defensive position and to consult Washington; if Chinese troops intervened in the conflict MacArthur could continue the UNC offensive as long as the General believed the action had a reasonable chance of success. The day after MacArthur received his instructions South Korean troops crossed the parallel for the first time.

The United Nations now moved formally to authorize non-Korean UNC ground forces to traverse the parallel. The Soviet representative to the Security Council had returned in August, so to circumvent the Soviet veto the issue was brought to the UN General Assembly which passed a resolution on 7 October calling for the creation of conditions of stability throughout the peninsula and the establishment of a commission – the United Nations Commission for the Unification and Rehabilitation of Korea (UNCURK) – to oversee elections for the entire country and to guide economic reconstruction. On the same day American troops crossed the parallel to pursue retreating North Korean soldiers. Two days later MacArthur issued an ultimatum to the North Koreans to surrender. Kim Il Sung rejected the General's demand during a radio broadcast he made from Pyongyang on 10 October.

In the final week of September MacArthur developed plans for the final destruction of the People's Army. He ordered the X Corps, currently in the Inchon–Seoul area, to make an amphibious landing 100 miles north of the 38th parallel at Wonsan (map 4), an east-coast industrial city that had been the major port for Russian supplies coming from Vladivostok. After landing they were originally supposed to move west towards Pyongyang to cut off fleeing soldiers of the North Korean Army. But the plan took several weeks to execute and South Korean soldiers beat the X Corps to Wonsan by more than two weeks, arriving there by 10 October. This rapid advance in the east was matched in the west by Commonwealth, South Korean and American troops who were now heading towards Pyongyang. By 20 October UN troops held the former North Korean capital. At this stage of the conflict there were about 60,000 soldiers left in the KPA. Most retreated further north, taking the majority of their POWS with them. UN forces did not capture any high-ranking DPRK officials. It was soon reported that the northern government had re-established itself close to the Yalu river at Kanggye (map 4), a place where Korean guerrillas had fought the Japanese during the colonial period. The area also included military installations and tunnels which had been used by the Japanese.

On 24 October, MacArthur commanded all UN soldiers to move to the Yalu river, thus violating the Presidential order to use only Korean troops at northern border areas. Although military authorities in Washington queried MacArthur, they soon approved his new orders. Anticipating a quick conclusion to the war, ROK, Eighth Army, X Corps, and Commonwealth soldiers fought their way towards the Manchurian border.

Five years after the country had been divided by the great powers, it looked as though it would be reunited under the US-led UN flag. When President Truman met with General MacArthur on 15 October on Wake Island in the Pacific Ocean, the General told the President that resistance would be defeated by Thanksgiving and that the Eighth Army would be home for Christmas.

PYONGYANG, BEIJING AND MOSCOW

American hopes for a quick end to the war were illusory and based on faulty intelligence reports. Although the Central Intelligence Agency (CIA) predicted that China would not send in ground troops, over the course of the summer and fall Beijing had become increasingly worried about the course of UN intervention in the conflict. In the initial stages of the war the Chinese did not believe that an American offensive towards Manchuria was likely, but there was apprehension over the movement of the Seventh Fleet. Announcements made during MacArthur's trip to Taiwan in late July also suggested a high degree of military coordination between Chinese Nationalist and US forces. To bolster China's military capability, 90,000 of its most experienced troops were sent into northern Manchuria. Eventually there were about 300,000 troops stationed at the Sino-Korean border, along the Yalu river. In the middle of August, with the North Korean situation looking more desperate, Mao ordered his troops in Manchuria to complete preparations for possible involvement in the conflict by the end of September.

Overwhelmed by the Inchon landing and its aftermath, the North Korean government turned to the Soviets for help. On 29 September Kim wrote to Stalin that enemy aeroplanes dominated the air space and motorized enemy units on the ground inflicted great losses on KPA cadres. Units of the People's Army cut off from northern Korea lacked ammunition and food and were being torn to pieces. If these conditions continued and Americans launched an offensive into the north, the DPRK would lose the war. Desperate, the DPRK began to mobilize the general population and even pressed South Korean troops into its army. Kim appealed directly to Stalin for help in establishing volunteer units from China and the other people's democracies.

Stalin responded to this plea with a letter to Mao on 1 October which asked the Chinese to send five or six divisions of 'volunteers' into Korea in order to give the North Koreans an opportunity to regroup their forces. Mao's initial response to Stalin, written the next day, was negative; it underlined the danger that Chinese intervention might lead to a war with the United States, hinder the PRC's economic reconstruction effort, and result in a full-scale conflict for the Soviet Union.

The Chinese were by now trying to avoid a conflict with the United States and they sent several warnings to the West through the Indian Ambassador in Beijing, Sardar K.M. Panikkar. On 3 October, with South Korean forces racing towards the northern border area, but before American troops crossed the parallel, Chinese Foreign Minister Zhou Enlai told Panikkar that American intervention north of the parallel would encounter resistance from Chinese forces [*Doc. 13*].

Stalin continued to press the Chinese, and in a follow-up to his 1 October letter he explained his reasons for encouraging the Chinese to commit their forces to Korea: the United States was not yet prepared for a global war; Japan was not able to provide military assistance to US forces in Asia; Chinese troops would force the United States to yield on the Korean question and on Taiwan; and the Americans would have to abandon their plans to negotiate a peace treaty with the Japanese and to make Japan into a regional anti-communist partner. Global war now was unlikely, but should it come it was a good time to fight it, since the Sino-Soviet alliance was collectively stronger than the Anglo-American alliance.

Mao deliberated the issue very carefully. His newly established People's Republic was under threat, but the threat might be greater if he committed his 'volunteers'. On 7 October Mao gave his initial agreement to send volunteers, telling Stalin that he would dispatch nine divisions of troops into Korea. After further debate in the Chinese Politburo the Soviet Ambassador in Beijing confirmed this decision on 14 October. Uncertain about America's intentions *vis-à-vis* Chiang in Taiwan, the Chinese leader was now convinced of the necessity of supporting the North Koreans and preventing the Americans from possibly opening a two-front war against China.

EXPANDED WAR: OCTOBER 1950–FEBRUARY 1951

The initial military contact with the Chinese 'volunteer' forces came just south of the Yalu river in late October. On 25 October ROK forces encountered Chinese soldiers for the first time, and over the next few days UN soldiers experienced limited Chinese assaults on their positions in northern Korea. Although the first Chinese prisoners of war were captured on 26 October, ROK, American and other allied armies were unprepared for the offensives that followed. Many officials continued to believe, erroneously, that they had the upper hand – if Mao had been serious about intervening he would have committed troops in July when UN forces were backed up against the Pusan perimeter.

The major UN strategic objective – not to get involved in a major war on continental Asia – affected the way the war was fought at this stage. Orders were sent to MacArthur not to follow Soviet MiG fighters into Chinese airspace, a position forcefully backed by allied governments in London, Ottawa, Paris, the Hague, and Wellington. After initial military clashes in early November the Chinese volunteers drew back and did not press their offensive for several weeks.

In an effort to deter further Chinese intervention, the United States sponsored a resolution in the Security Council on 10 November which implied that it was not the UN intention to cross the Korean–Manchurian border, though the resolution also warned of the 'grave danger' that continued Chinese intervention would mean for the maintenance of that policy. The British were also worried. The Chiefs of Staff, concerned about MacArthur's offensive strategy, recommended that UN forces adopt defensive positions *vis-à-vis* the Chinese. In mid-November Britain formulated a proposal to create a buffer zone, roughly along the 40th parallel, between UN and North Korean and Chinese forces. Foreign Secretary Bevin thought about presenting this proposal to the Security Council but Secretary Acheson dissuaded him from publicly pursuing the idea before the results of MacArthur's planned late November 'end of the war' offensive became known. Acheson, concerned about American power and prestige, remarked that 'giving up the part of Korea we do not yet occupy would at this time undoubtedly be interpreted as a sign of weakness' (Foot, 1985: 92).

MacArthur's attack, launched on 24 November, was forced into retreat when some 300,000 Chinese volunteers launched their counter-offensive on 26 November. On 28 November the American National Security Council met to discuss the situation. The consensus of the meeting was that Korean unification was no longer possible and should be deferred in favour of a holding action on the peninsula. Acheson stressed the global threat of Soviet power and the primary importance of rearming Europe. A few days later Truman asked the US Congress for an additional $16.8 billion to expand the defence program. In mid-December he proclaimed a state of national emergency and began to mobilize the country for a possible global war.

America's NATO allies fully recognized the escalatory potential of the 'new' war in Korea. On 29 November the British cabinet met and reaffirmed its decision to support American foreign policy. As Prime Minister Clement Attlee stressed, a break with America over Asia would threaten US support in Europe. Since Britain's 'ultimate threat' came from the Soviet Union, Britain 'could not afford to break our united front with the United States against our main potential enemy' (Kaufman, 1997: 218).

The Chinese intervention, however, also threatened to embroil the alliance in a major war in Asia. On 30 November President Truman bluntly told a group of stunned reporters that the United States would use every weapon at its disposal, including the atomic bomb, to deal with the situation in Korea; the military commander in the field could authorize its use. America's European and Commonwealth allies were shocked by this public revelation. Attlee urgently organized a trip to Washington to make it clear to US officials that alliance members were unwilling to support a further expansion of the conflict with China.

Before the trip, on 2 December, the Prime Minister and Foreign Secretary Bevin consulted with French Premier René Pleven and Minister of Foreign Affairs Robert Schuman in London. The French confessed their deep-seated anxiety about the military situation in Northeast Asia; recent French reports from the UN indicated that the United States might try to declare China an 'aggressor' in the Security Council and General Assembly as a prelude to escalating the war and bombing Manchuria, possibly with atomic weapons. The French government was particularly concerned about its colony of Vietnam, where the French were engaged in a major guerrilla war of their own, fighting an insurgency led by Vietnamese communist Ho Chi Minh. They feared a full-scale war with the PRC over Korea might bring Chinese soldiers into Indochina.

Prime Minister Attlee met Truman in Washington between 4 and 8 December. In their meetings both leaders expressed agreement about the need to limit the conflict to Korea, to defend Europe as NATO's foremost objective, and to work towards a cease-fire, but disagreements emerged over strategy towards China. Attlee believed that a harsh policy towards the PRC would only solidify the Sino-Soviet alliance. Acheson, on the other hand, wanted to harass the Chinese through covert activities and economic sanctions and to organize a mutual defence system with Asian nations.

On other issues as well, the Truman–Attlee discussions did not produce what the British had hoped. Although the President had initially told Attlee that he would consult with the UK and Canada about the use of the bomb, he refused to put this oral statement in writing, and the British and Canadians later learned that the United States was only willing to inform, not to consult, its allies about the use of the ultimate weapon. As historian Burton Kaufman has remarked, 'the United States still retained the option to use nuclear weapons without consulting its allies' (Kaufman, 1997: 71).

In Beijing, Mao thought the Chinese offensive would compel the United States to accept his regime's regional national security objectives, and he ordered his military commanders to maintain the offensive, to occupy Pyongyang and Seoul, to destroy ROK forces and generally to place the PRC in a better position to drive the Americans from Korea. Both the Soviet Union and North Korea seemed to support this strategy. On 3 December Kim Il Sung visited Beijing with a request to the Chinese leadership to push forward to complete victory; Stalin wrote to the Chinese that the communists should take advantage of the UNC retreat and 'liberate' Seoul. Meanwhile, the communist side could bide its time by asking the other side for its armistice conditions. But the Soviets continued to limit their military involvement to the air war above Korea; the Soviet navy did not interdict the sea lanes around Korea; and neither did the communists attack allied bases in Japan.

On 7 December the Chinese informed UN Secretary General Trygve Lie that the PRC would not consider a cease-fire and armistice until several preconditions had been met: the withdrawal of UN troops from Korea; the removal of the Seventh Fleet and US troops from Formosa; agreement that the Korean conflict be resolved by the Koreans only; a seat for the PRC in the UN and the expulsion of Formosa's UN delegation; and the convening of a conference to prepare a Japanese Peace Treaty. A peace conference with Japan while US and UN forces were in retreat would meet Sino-Soviet goals by weakening the Japanese-American Cold War alliance and the momentum which was building for Japanese rearmament.

In the United States, domestic pressure to take harsher actions against China mounted in December. Supporters of escalating the war against China included Douglas MacArthur; US Senator William Knowland of California, a China Lobbyist and prominent supporter of Joseph McCarthy; Stuart Symington, an important figure in Truman's National Security planning; and a number of high-ranking officials in the Department of Defense, such as General Curtis LeMay, a major proponent of strategic bombing who soon gained the nickname 'Mr. Atom Bomb'.

On 24 December General MacArthur put forward a list of targets in China and Korea which he said required the use of 26 atomic bombs. Six days later he told the Joint Chiefs of Staff that US/UN retaliatory measures should include a blockade of the China coast, the bombardment and destruction of Chinese industry, and the use of Nationalist Chinese troops in Korea and for diversionary raids on the mainland, possibly as a prelude for an invasion of China itself.

While Republicans used the Chinese offensive to attack the 'appeasement' policies of the Truman administration, Senator Joseph McCarthy, the most vicious leader of the Republican right, called for the resignation of Secretaries Acheson and Marshall and threatened to open impeachment hearings against President Truman. Many Americans worried that the Third World War might break out any day; America's Western allies believed that world peace depended on the ability of the Truman administration to resist the impulse to escalate the war against China [*Doc.14*].

The pressures on the administration were exacerbated by a renewed New Year's offensive by the Chinese forces which brought them across the 38th parallel and into Seoul on 4 January. On 17 January Zhou Enlai informed the UN that China had rejected the latest cease-fire proposal of the UN because it called for the arrangement of a cease-fire before the beginning of substantive negotiations. On 19 and 23 January respectively, the US House of Representatives and Senate passed resolutions which urged the UN to call the Chinese 'aggressors'. America's allies were concerned that such a move might escalate the war and hurt their efforts to negotiate a peaceful solution to the conflict with the Chinese.

Despite launching a major US–UN counter-offensive code-named 'Operation Thunderbolt' on 25 January, the United States put pressure on its allies to move forward with a resolution branding China as an 'aggressor', a motion it introduced into the UN General Assembly's First

Committee on 20 January. The allies remained concerned about American tendencies to act unilaterally in the Cold War, and the potential use of the bomb was a significant concern. Vigorous efforts were made by leaders of the British Commonwealth, particularly Indian Prime Minister Jawaharlal Nehru and Canadian Foreign Minister Lester Pearson, to get the Chinese to elaborate on their rejection of the UN cease-fire proposals. On 22 January, in an apparent compromise initiative, Zhou Enlai sent a message pointing out that China could now agree to a temporary cease-fire, perhaps even before the disagreement over Formosa was settled. Based on this news, twenty-seven states, including the UK, France and Canada, agreed to a forty-eight-hour delay in the UN debate on the aggressor resolution, much to the consternation of US policymakers.

Anglo-American relations at this point were at a particularly low ebb. As in other cases during the war, the debate between the two allies occurred over the appropriate policy to pursue in the UN. Britain and other Commonwealth nations believed that the UN could act as a restraining influence on the United States. The degree of tension in the 'special relationship' at this time was reflected in a telegram written by the Deputy Under Secretary of State in the Foreign Office, Sir Pierson Dixon, which was sent to the British Ambassador in Washington, Sir Oliver Franks. Using a phrase associated with President Truman, Dixon wrote that it would be necessary for the Foreign Office to engage in some 'plain speaking' with the Americans. It was important to 'drive home to them that we regard their present tactics towards both China and the United Nations as ill-conceived in the interests of us all' (Great Britain Foreign and Commonwealth Office, 1991: 322).

Allied representations to the United States conflicted with the goals of the South Korean leader, Syngman Rhee, who again pressed the American government for additional arms and demanded that UN forces move to defeat Chinese armies in Korea. In a dramatic letter to President Truman, Rhee wrote: 'To save the situation we must do all we can to defeat and destroy the Chinese invaders now … authorize General MacArthur to use any weapons that will check communist aggression anywhere, even the atom bomb. A few bombs on Moscow alone will shake the communist world.' From the South Korean official perspective, their country, already embroiled in a total war, seemed to have nothing to lose from an expanded war [*Doc. 15*].

On 26 January the Americans made a limited compromise in their proposed resolution by agreeing to delay the consideration of further measures against Chinese intervention. On this basis the resolution condemning China of aggression in the Korean conflict passed the UN General Assembly on 1 February by a vote of forty-four in favour, seven opposed and nine abstentions. The United States won an important propaganda victory, but it also lost the opportunity to begin cease-fire discussions and the process of settling the conflict at a time when many nations sought a negotiated resolution to the war.

MILITARY STALEMATE AND THE DOWNFALL OF MacARTHUR

In December 1950 General Matthew Ridgway, a veteran Second World War Commander, replaced General Walton Walker, who had died in a jeep accident, as commander of the Eighth Army. Under Ridgway's command, the Army succeeded in stemming China's offensive by late January 1951; the soldiers sustained their tortuous advance once again towards Seoul and the 38th parallel. On 7 March, the capital city changed hands for the last time – the fourth since June 1950, when it was first occupied by the North Koreans.

By mid-March, Washington recognized the realities of the newly stalemated war. State Department officials now refused to recommend another major military effort across the 38th parallel to unify the peninsula, and under pressure from America's allies, President Truman privately prepared to undertake a limited peace initiative with the communists. A statement was prepared saying that the United States was ready to enter into cease-fire negotiations, though the United States had no intention of meeting the Chinese on the issue of Formosa or a UN seat.

The proposed announcement was forwarded to MacArthur on 20 March for comment. The UN Commander promptly undermined the initiative by making a unilateral public ultimatum to the Chinese. On 24 March he issued a statement which said that a further expansion of the war into China would doom China to a fate of military collapse. Recognizing this, he said, China should now be prepared to negotiate an end to the conflict on UN terms, and MacArthur proclaimed that he was prepared to negotiate the surrender with Chinese military officials.

America's allies were shocked and dismayed. Lester Pearson had long felt uneasy with the direction of US policy in Korea. He had had reservations about the decision to cross the 38th parallel and to move forward with the aggressor resolution. Now MacArthur seemed to be begging for a war with the Chinese. In a speech on 31 March the Canadian Foreign Minister criticized US military policy in Korea. Although he did not specifically name MacArthur, the context of the speech made his target clear enough. From now on, Pearson proclaimed, there would be no more days 'of relatively easy and automatic political relations' between Canada and the United States (Egerton, 1997: 65, 45).

Truman, who had so far failed to deal directly with MacArthur's power games, was privately outraged. Not only had MacArthur purposely undermined the President's initiative, he had also violated a Presidential directive which required him to consult with Washington about public declarations.

MacArthur might have been fired immediately except the President was concerned about the effect such a move might have on public opinion, and so initially he only reprimanded the General.

Less than two weeks later, the minority Republican leader of the House of Representatives, Joseph Martin, a supporter of using Chiang's troops in Korea, made public a letter written to him by MacArthur which stated that the administration's 'Europe First' strategy was wrong-headed and that if the war in Asia were lost, Europe would fall to communism. 'There is no substitute for victory', MacArthur had written to Martin. The letter, which seemed openly to challenge the existing military strategy of the US administration, was the last straw. In London, the British Chiefs of Staff believed that MacArthur was purposely trying to involve the UN in a war with China; British officials in Washington were told to take a 'strong line' against the General (Lowe, 1997b: 232).

It was only at this time, and with the backing of Secretary of Defense George Marshall, that Truman decided to relieve the General of his command. The decision was made public on 11 April, much to the relief of America's closest allies, but to the consternation of Asian leaders Chiang Kai-shek and Syngman Rhee. Ridgway was soon ordered to replace MacArthur.

The downfall of MacArthur did not prevent a spring Chinese offensive which began on 22 April and lasted until the third week of May. This period witnessed some of the worst fighting of the war, during which there were an estimated 200,000 Chinese casualties alone. Neither did MacArthur's dismissal prevent the President from ordering the transportation of atomic bombs to Okinawa in case they were needed against China. As historian Melvyn Leffler has pointed out, 'the atomic weapons could be relied on to cast diplomatic shadows and to embolden policymakers who were biding time, calculating whether to take additional risks in Korea, and working hard to establish positions of strength around the globe' (Leffler, 1992: 406).

By late May, with the military stalemate confirmed, both sides looked for a way to begin armistice negotiations. In early June, Mao and Zhou Enlai met Kim Il Sung to discuss common strategy. The outcome of their meetings was a consensus to negotiate an armistice and to try to get the 38th parallel as the dividing line between the two Koreas. On 23 June, Jacob Malik, the Soviet representative in the United Nations, delivered a radio speech indicating that the Soviet Union and the communist side were prepared to negotiate. Under instructions from Washington, Ridgway replied that he was ready to appoint a military official to meet with North Korean and Chinese representatives. When the communist side suggested that the talks start on 10 July at the Korean town of Kaesong in communist-held territory just south of the 38th parallel, the UNC Commander was ordered to accept the proposal. Although there were hopes in the summer and fall of 1951 that an armistice might be achieved quickly, the negotiations dragged on for more than two years while the fighting continued. We shall return to the history of the armistice negotiations, but before we do so we will examine the social dimensions of the war in Korea.

CHAPTER FOUR

SOLDIER, CIVILIAN: A SOCIAL HISTORY OF THE KOREAN WAR

WAR AS SOCIAL HISTORY

Historians and social scientists approach the study of warfare from a number of different perspectives. One popular framework examines the history of human conflict from the vantage point of the soldiers, or a particular side engaged in battle. Another approach is to analyze how the fighting influenced the various peoples and nations involved in the battle. It is misleading, however, to assess a war merely on the basis of its impact on a particular country or group of people. A social history of war must treat soldiers and civilians as integral components of the societies from which they come. We also need to look at how societies shape the context in which war was fought, for the cultural, political, and social goals of countries engaged in armed conflict establish the groundwork upon which wars are conducted, experienced, and managed.

In order to come to a fuller understanding of war, then, we should explore not only the origins and political outcomes of conflict, but also the complex social and cultural interchanges between the soldier, his or her society, and the 'enemy'. The history of the Korean War provides us with such an opportunity. The brief North Korean occupation of southern Korea in 1950 is unintelligible without an understanding of the political structures and social goals which were embedded in the pre-1950 northern experience with anti-Japanese guerrilla warfare and social revolution. Significant changes in race relations which were beginning to occur in the United States shaped the lives of US soldiers on the peninsula. And prisoners of war on both sides were subjected to propaganda which reflected dominant cultural and political values and ways of thinking in the countries of their captors. We shall examine these and other themes as a way of illuminating the reciprocal relationship between war and society during the Korean conflict.

WARTIME KOREA, 1950

The Korean War was not a conventional military conflict, fought between professional standing armies in large-scale battles. It was a hybrid struggle which combined massive firepower – especially on the UNC side – with guerrilla warfare. The war's character was apparent from the initial North Korean advance. Although the Soviet Union provided tanks, and Russian military advisers played an important role in formulating North Korea's offensive strategy, a large percentage of the attacking troops were seasoned veterans of unconventional civil warfare in rural China. These battle-hardened soldiers were accompanied by guerrilla forces operating in tandem with the DPRK Army. During the summer of 1950, groups of up to 3,000 guerrillas fought alongside the 'regular' army forces.

As northern armies penetrated deeper into the south in the summer of 1950, North Korean political cadres moved into occupied areas and began to shape local politics in the image of the DPRK regime. Leftist people's committees which had been disbanded by the American Military Government in 1945 and 1946 were reconstituted. North Korean propaganda emphasized the south's 'liberation' from the American-sponsored 'puppet' regime of Syngman Rhee and glorified the role of the Korean People's Army, which was portrayed as a guerrilla organization that had fought valiantly against Japanese imperialism. Significantly, this northern propaganda made few references to the indigenous South Korean communist movement before 1945. The clear leader of Korean communism was now Kim Il Sung, not Pak Hon Yong, and the brand of communism imposed on the south was one borne of the Manchurian guerrilla conflict against Japan in the 1930s.

North Korean political cadres were ordered to confiscate land in the occupied areas and to organize a land redistribution program for the peasantry. Before the war, however, the Syngman Rhee regime had begun to implement significant land reform measures, based on monetary compensation for the landlords. Although the program was interrupted by the fighting, peasants and landlords had made detailed arrangements about the amount of land to be redistributed before the conflict started. As a result, North Koreans sometimes found it difficult to implement their own land reform program. In other cases, the occupation simply confirmed the pre-war land redistribution plan. In this sense, the conflict accelerated changes in social structure which were already under way in the south.

The North Korean occupation attempted to mobilize workers, peasants and women in ways which differed radically from the previous regime. Some Seoul-based politicians collaborated with the new northern government-in-being, as did many students and prominent figures in the labour movement. Regionalism also affected local responses to the North Korean occupation. The southwestern province of South Cholla, for example, had a history of leftist activism: KPA troops were sometimes greeted by the local populace as genuine liberators. Some citizens waved the northern flag upon their entry into towns. At the end of October 1950, several weeks after UN forces pushed the KPA back across the 38th parallel, the CIA reported that between 8,000 and 10,000 pro-northern armed militia had established bases in the southwest. Many were from South Cholla and had joined the communist guerrilla forces during the northern occupation period. American sources estimated that there were some 30,000 guerrillas operating in South Korea after the KPA's retreat.

North Koreans in occupied areas carried out their own retributive summary justice, killing 'collaborators' of the Syngman Rhee 'puppet clique'. In Seoul, this tended to occur in the early days of the occupation. Britain's diplomatic representative in Korea, Henry Raywood Sawbridge, reported to London on 17 August that North Korean policies towards the civilian population tended to be more conciliatory than was assumed. He had received news that 'People's Courts' in Seoul had stopped carrying out executions after their first week of operation and that North Korean cadres had ordered the release of the remaining political prisoners. A South Korean politician who had left Seoul made similar comments [*Doc. 16*]. Even so, injustices abounded. Despite efforts by the northern military command to prevent battlefield executions, KPA soldiers shot many American and Korean prisoners. North Korean troops also participated in mass murders and other atrocities, particularly towards the end of the northern occupation.

For the great majority of Koreans, the northern offensive and the US/UN counter-offensives caused tremendous suffering, grief, dislocation, and separation from family. In the wake of these battles, millions of civilians fled their villages and became refugees (plate 5). Both sides conscripted people from villages and towns under their control, and many former ROK soldiers who were captured were then impressed into the North Korean army.

When US ground troops from Japan arrived in Korea in early July, they were unprepared for the war ahead. Expecting little effective resistance from the KPA, most believed the war would end quickly. As one American participant later recalled, 'morale was good. A spirit of optimism prevailed, and the men were under the impression that they would take part in a two week campaign' (US Army Center of Military History, 1950: reel 1).

Outnumbered and pitted against seasoned troops, US and South Korean forces were consistently forced into retreat throughout July and August. American soldiers could not tell differences between North and South Korean troops, and sometimes did not distinguish the enemy from civilians. Their ignorance was captured in the 1951 American Korean War film, *Steel Helmet*:

OFFICER: They're hiding behind them white pajamas and wearing them women's clothes ... These guys are smart.
SECOND OFFICER: We're wasting our time.
SERGEANT: Look. ... I don't want to turn my back and have some old lady shoot my head off.
SOLDIER SEARCHING A KOREAN: They all look alike to me.
SERGEANT: Don't you know how to tell the difference? ... He's a South Korean when he's running with you and he's a North Korean when he's running after you. (Engelhardt, 1995: 62)

The line between soldier, refugee and civilian – and between enemy and ally – was precariously fluid. Fearful that North Koreans were disguising themselves as civilians among the refugees, as some did, American commanders ordered their troops to treat civilians as the enemy [*Doc. 17*]. At a village called No Gun Ri, southeast of Taejon (map 3), in central southern Korea, US soldiers fired into a group of civilian refugees, killing several hundred. From the air, US planes strafed civilians, and in one case at least US soldiers gave up warning civilians to stop crossing a bridge and simply blew it up while refugees were crossing. The 'blurring' of the relationship between friend and foe did not occur simply because the situation in Korea was inherently 'chaotic'. It was a product of a *purposeful* policy by both sides in the conflict – of decisions taken by the combatants to use civilians for their own expedient political and military purposes, and a function of individuals who had little respect for the lives of the Korean people. The war crimes committed by both sides cannot be excused because they were a simple product of a confused military situation; the army commands and soldiers themselves created the chaos and confusion that led to civilian deaths. The suffering of innocents, the most tragic element of the conflict, continued, as one side's atrocities begat the other's (plate 6).

In some cases, reports of atrocities were purposely censored by UNC military officials. Reporting from Tokyo, Canadian Japanologist and Head of Mission E.H. Norman, told Canadian authorities that the US Commanding General in charge of the Eighth Army and all ROK troops, Walton Walker, had convinced newspaper correspondents not to write a story about South Korean abuses of North Korean troops which the correspondents had witnessed first hand behind allied lines in Pusan. Similarly, Colonel Alfred Katzin, the UN representative of Secretary General Trygve Lie, convinced UN representatives to delete from a report meant for the UN General Assembly, certain critical comments they had written about the southern regime's police force [*Doc. 18*].

Casualties were high on both sides. By mid-August, the ROK Army had lost 70,000 of its soldiers to death and injury. American battlefield casualties numbered about 10,000 at this time. KPA casualties reached 60,000; most of the northern army's armoured vehicles were lost, and fuel, ammunition, and other supplies were frequently destroyed in transit by the US Air Force. DPRK soldiers now tended to move at night and they increasingly used animals and human transport to move military materiel. Small arms ammunition was scarce and severe shortages of both food and clothes became a major problem. By the end of the month, 'NKPA soldiers were receiving only one or two meals per day at best and were beginning to show evidence of malnutrition, resulting in a loss of stamina and impaired combat effectiveness due to inadequate rations' (Shrader, 1995: 162). MacArthur's landing at Inchon in mid-September and the subsequent US/UN offensives forced the remainder of the North Korean Army to flee northwards.

For a brief period in the fall of 1950, South Korean and other UNC troops occupied most of northern Korea. Although the Americans told Rhee that the UN did not recognize ROK political authority in areas north of the 38th parallel, unofficially, ROK police officials, tax collectors, administrators, and right-wing youth groups began to enter North Korea and to establish southern authority there as early as the second week of October. The southern occupation of the north was a bloody affair. South Korean troops and right-wing political groups were responsible for massacres of their own and upwards of several hundred thousand northerners may have been killed.

General MacArthur, with the support of US Ambassador John Muccio, had an informal plan to strengthen Rhee's political position by holding early elections in the northern part of the country only. The idea was to move swiftly to place Rhee's candidates in a position to run for the 100 seats designated for the ROK National Assembly. MacArthur planned as late as mid-November to call for elections by the end of December 1950. His headquarters in Tokyo had not made any preparations for civil affairs teams to move into the north, and the United Nations Commission for the Unification and Rehabilitation of Korea (UNCURK) only landed in Seoul on 26 November, the day of the Chinese counter-attack. Despite the formal appearance of UN control over the reunification process, developments in northern Korea were moving in a direction which would have circumvented UNCURK as an agency formally responsible for overseeing the reunification of the country. Its role would have been restricted simply to rubber-stamping developments occurring on the ground.

The Chinese troops who entered the conflict in late November and December 1950 put an end to plans to unify the country. Ironically, about 50 percent of these soldiers had originally fought in the Chinese Nationalist armies. Inducted into communist units, they now used their US-supplied weapons against US and allied forces. But many had no guns at all – these troops were simply given grenades. Other deficiencies and hardships which the Chinese had to deal with included poor transportation systems, insufficient artillery guns, and US Air Force domination of the air war. By the end of December 1950, only one month into the volunteer army's second offensive, US officials estimated that 40,000 Chinese soldiers had been wounded or killed in battle.

Chinese supply lines were unable to meet the needs of the troops. Soldiers went without adequate foodstuffs, medicine, and protective winter clothing. Some Chinese volunteers who were captured during the conflict had not eaten for three days. To warm their bodies some took boots from dead UNC soldiers. Medical treatment was rudimentary and serious injuries which might have been treatable by UNC forces resulted in losses on the communist side. One Chinese medic prisoner of war revealed to his captors that about 70 percent of all combat soldiers suffered from frostbite, and claimed that in about 5 percent of the cases, limbs had to be amputated [*Doc. 19*].

RACE AND THE KOREAN WAR: FIGHTING JIM CROW

The Korean War was the first conflict in American history in which African-American soldiers were integrated into white military units. After the Second World War, disillusionment among some Americans about the inequities and injustices of segregation led a coalition of African Americans, Caucasians, and civil rights organizations like the National Association for the Advancement of Colored People (NAACP) to continue the fight for democratic values which had been highlighted during the war. An important turning point in the postwar debate over the status of African Americans in the military occurred in late July 1948 when President Truman issued Executive Order 9981, which stated that all persons in America's military establishment shall have 'equality of treatment and opportunity ... without regard to race, color, religion, or national origin' (Mershon and Schlossman, 1998: 183).

The order was conservative and cautious in tone. In an effort to appease the southern Democrats in Congress, Truman did not openly criticize the inequities of the existing system. He made no formal reference to desegregation, and no time-frame was given for realizing the government's stated policy. But the order did provide a legal framework to start the process of undermining segregation in the military, and it established the President's Committee on Equality of Treatment and Opportunity in the Armed Services, known as the Fahy Committee, to oversee the implementation of executive policy.

There was significant opposition to the order, particularly in the Army and Marines Corps. In March 1949, Omar Bradley, the US Army Chief of Staff (he became Chairman of the Joint Chiefs of Staff in August 1949 and remained in that position for the duration of the Korean War), told the

Fahy Committee that the Army would lose the respect of the public if it moved too quickly on the desegregation issue. By that time about 12 percent of the Army was made up of black Americans.

When the Korean War broke out, 'the Army possessed almost exactly the same racially segregated organizational structure that had existed in World War II'. Segregated units like the Eighth Army's Twenty-Fourth Infantry Regiment, which had been created during the American Civil War, participated in the early wave of counter-offensives against the KPA. Racism during the war led to arbitrary criticisms of the performance of African-American soldiers, as American Major General William Kean demonstrated when he argued that the Twenty-Fourth's soldiers were 'untrustworthy and incapable of carrying out missions expected of an Infantry Regiment' (Mershon and Schlossman, 1998: 218, 220).

Complaints from African-American soldiers about Army racism led the NAACP to send civil rights activist and lawyer Thurgood Marshall to Korea in early 1951 to investigate. Marshall discovered that the Twenty-Fourth Infantry Regiment was the target of a disproportional amount of courts martial, and that the punishments meted out were much harsher than those given to non-African Americans. In his report, entitled 'Summary Justice: The Negro GI in Korea', Marshall underlined the fact that institutionalized segregation was responsible for much of the unfair treatment of black troops in Korea.

Over the course of late 1950 and 1951, African-American soldiers were placed into units which previously had been all white (plate 7). This integration of Army personnel was partly a function of the need to find replacements for fallen comrades, and partly a function of an effort by some local commanders to end racial segregation in the Army. But high-ranking and influential officials in Tokyo, such as MacArthur's Chief of Staff, Edward M. Almond, remained opposed to desegregation and ordered a reversal of the advancements that had already taken place. Almond went on to command the X Corps during the Inchon landing. After General Ridgway replaced MacArthur in the spring of 1951, however, desegregation gained momentum. Ridgway's initiatives led to the deactivation of the Twenty-Fourth and other segregated regiments in 1951, and by May 1952 the Army had completed a first basic step in integrating its forces.

The Korean War thus provided the crisis that finally pushed a reluctant Army to begin implementing policy recommendations made in Executive Order 9981. Policies which had been articulated earlier in the Cold War were now put into practice. Desegregation in the forces did not end discrimination, but it represented an important step towards greater equality for African Americans. The experiences of African-American soldiers in Korea thus benefitted from, and contributed to, the broader domestic movement for greater racial equality.

African Americans were not the only soldiers integrated into white units. In early August 1950 General MacArthur ordered his subordinates to attach Koreans to US units. The program became known as the Korean Augmentation to the US Army, or KATUSA. For the remainder of the month about 500 Korean recruits a day were incorporated into the American Army. One historian of the experiment noted that 'many of the recruits were simply dragged off the streets of Pusan and Taegu by impressment teams' (Skaggs, 1974: 53).

The *ad hoc* nature of the experiment was resented by many US soldiers, not only because of the poor military training which the Koreans received, but because of intercultural differences, racism, and jealousies associated with working with Asians who were theoretically supposed to receive equal treatment with other US soldiers. Like African-American soldiers, Koreans were often stereotyped and treated on unequal terms. As one American colonel later complained: 'These men had no idea of sanitation, let alone the more complicated activities of military life. Yet high-level policy dictated that we treat them as our equals in every respect. They were to receive the same clothing and equipment, the same treatment, the same rations. Later they even had to have chocolate bars and "comic" books ... except for menial tasks, they were a performance cipher' (Skaggs, 1974: 53–4).

In the initial stages of the war a small number of Koreans were used as interpreters; a far greater number were employed in menial tasks such as carrying heavy loads to the front, digging trenches, and acting as 'service boys'. Beginning in early 1951 the Americans provided a company of Korean Service Corps porters to UNC infantry battalions. One New Zealand soldier wrote of the Corps: 'Although not nearly so useful as mules, they are indispensable and the next best thing in this hilly country'. The Australians referred to them as the 'Noogie' train and Canadian troops called them 'Gook company' or 'rice-burners' (McGibbon, 1996: 93).

After 1951, KATUSAs were used in positions which demanded greater skills, but as the war bogged down into trench warfare, Koreans were also seen as a means of saving US soldiers from having to perform front-line duties. This strategy was adopted by the new UN Commander who replaced General Ridgway on 12 May 1952, General Mark Clark. In September 1952, Clark recommended an increase in the numbers of KATUSA troops assigned to the US Army. He outlined some of the perceived positive features of the program: 'Because the major portion of KATUSA personnel are utilized in front-line duty a saving of lives of our soldiers results. The increased rotation from front-line duties of US and UN personnel in combat units, which KATUSA permits, decreases our casualties' (Skaggs, 1974: 55). A positive spin was thus put on a policy designed to increase Korean casualties during the war. The numbers of

Koreans assigned to this program went from just over 9,000 troops in March 1952 to a wartime high of almost 24,000 just before the armistice was signed in late July 1953.

THE BRITISH COMMONWEALTH AT WAR

Although Commonwealth troops were not a major factor in the outcome of the war, they experienced some very heavy fighting, especially during the Chinese Communist offensives in early 1951. The Commonwealth presence was also politically significant, especially in showing the US Congress that America's allies were actively engaged in fighting the Cold War. Commonwealth ground forces in Korea grew from 15,723 in mid-1951 to 24,085 two years later. British troops made up more than half these figures – 8,278 and 14,198 respectively. The percentage of Commonwealth troops on the UNC side remained roughly steady during the war, and ranged from 2.8 percent of the total in 1951 to 2.5 percent in 1953.

The First Commonwealth Division was created on 28 July 1951. It brought together three infantry brigade units which already had been operating under US strategic command in the Korean theatre: the Twenty-fifth Canadian brigade group, the Twenty-ninth British brigade, and the Twenty-eighth Commonwealth brigade, which itself was an amalgamation of British, Australian and New Zealand troops with Indian medical units. Several officers from South Africa also served in British units. The Commonwealth Division was stationed around the Imjin river, north of Seoul, and formed part of the US I Corps, commanded by Lieutenant General 'Iron Mike' O'Daniel, a man who later helped coordinate America's early involvement in Vietnam. In addition to participating in front-line battles, Commonwealth soldiers guarded POWs, collected intelligence, and coordinated assaults designed to capture prisoners.

DISEASE IN THE KOREAN WAR

All soldiers in Korea faced hardships related to disease and weather. Winters were cold. Summertime threats included malaria, dysentery, encephalitis, and yellow fever. Many soldiers contracted sexually transmitted diseases. From June 1950 to December 1953 there were 115,946 cases of venereal disease (VD) among US soldiers stationed in Korea. The incidence of VD became alarmingly high after 1951, as soldiers regularly went on 'R&R' (Rest and Recuperation). In 1952, 10,535 cases of VD were reported among Commonwealth troops. The infection rate was 376 out of every 1,000 soldiers. Canadian troops had the highest infection rate: 616 per thousand. The US peak was reached in mid-1952 with a rate of almost 250 soldiers per thousand. Military efforts to stop the spread of venereal disease among soldiers were half-hearted and relied mainly on inoculation after the disease had been transmitted. Little concern was expressed for the plight of the prostitutes themselves.

To combat diseases carried by fleas (typhus), mosquitos (malaria) and flies (dysentery), UNC soldiers were commonly given aerosol cans containing the drug DDT, or dichlorodiphenyltrichloroethane, a chlorinated organic insecticide [*Doc. 20*]. The Canadian 'Handbook of Army Health, 1950', issued to its soldiers during the Korean War, noted that fleas could be easily killed with DDT. An infested soldier should use the powder on himself, and spray his living quarters with the chemical. It was also used widely on Korean towns, which were sprayed from passing aeroplanes. For years after the war, Korean civilians – even school children – were encouraged to use DDT on themselves to prevent the spread of lice and disease. In 1972, the US Environmental Protection Agency listed the drug as a probable carcinogen, and banned all uses of it. Although many veterans complained of illness associated with their combat experiences, none of the UNC governments has accepted that DDT was responsible for sickness.

WARTIME CULTURE: UNC TROOP MORALE AND LIFESTYLE BEYOND THE TRENCHES

In the aftermath of the Chinese offensive in late 1950, numerous efforts were made to escape life on the frontline and to create a feeling of 'normalcy' among UNC soldiers. This essentially meant trying to replicate a version of the troops' domestic cultures in Korea. Popular events included movies, celebrity entertainment shows, and participation in competitive sports events. The Far Eastern Command's Motion Picture Service distributed the latest domestic releases. Live shows were organized by the United Service Organization. Stars who performed in Korea included Bob Hope, Jack Benny, Danny Kaye, Joe DiMaggio and Marilyn Monroe. Monroe, who performed ten shows in February 1954 later remembered that going to Korea 'was the best thing that ever happened to me'. Her interactions with the soldiers temporarily enabled her to lift her own suffering and to accept herself. 'I never felt like a star before in my heart', she continued. 'It was so wonderful to look down and see a fellow smiling at me' (US National Portrait Gallery, 2000, website).

'Mobile Exchanges' involved the conversion of buses into gift shops, which then toured forward corps areas. Eighteen of these began service in October 1952, and soldiers used their accumulated earnings to purchase gifts to send back home. The exchanges were particularly popular in the Christmas season of 1952. Mobile Education centres provided reading materials to the troops, and correspondence courses were offered by the University of California. The US military also had its own self-teaching

courses. In September 1953, 77,000 US troops wrote examinations for a
wide range of educational programs offered by the military.

The most popular escape from front-line duties was 'R&R' in Japan.
'R&R' began as a five-day program in December 1950, and about 6,000
men participated in its first month of operation. By the time the armistice
negotiations began in the summer of 1951, about 15,000 troops per month
were temporarily relieved from their military duties. As one US enlisted
man later recalled: 'That was something everyone looked forward to;
getting back to civilisation was everybody's ambition. Living conditions
that were inviting, relaxation, and women – they were the things we all
wanted and R&R afforded us a chance to enjoy them even for a short time'
(United States Army Center of Military History, 1950: reel 8). The program
encouraged the growth of prostitution in Japan and was responsible for
about 60 percent of the venereal disease cases which were reported by US
troops in Korea during the war.

The presence of large numbers of American troops also began to
acculturate Koreans to elements of American popular culture. Koreans
serving with American and UNC troops soon picked up Western slang, and
some began to adopt social attitudes expressed by the soldiers. Black markets involving the sale of American and Western goods such as cigarettes
also boomed. Even though Koreans working for the US Army were better
fed than ROK conscripts, they were paid very low wages. In some cases
Korean soldiers stole commodities from the Americans in order to sustain
their families.

WOMEN AND THE KOREAN WAR

Most service women on the UNC side performed traditional roles associated with nurturing, entertainment, or secretarial duties. About 7,000 of
the 22,000 women on active duty in the US military at the outbreak of the
war worked as nurses or health providers. Army nurses were sent to Korea
almost immediately; by late July 1950 there were about 100 American
nurses in the ROK, many in Mobile Army Surgical Hospital (MASH) units.
Over the course of the next year about 600 women from the Army Nurse
Corps served in Korea. Most were Second World War veterans. Other UNC
forces provided health workers as well. Nurses from Australia, Canada and
Britain worked in two British Commonwealth hospitals, one in Kure,
Japan, and another in Seoul. The International Red Cross sent women to
Korea to work as counsellors, entertainers and health providers. Acting as
surrogate mothers, the women provided psychological support for the
soldiers. Some wrote letters for disabled troops and others worked in Red
Cross clubs which supplied coffee, doughnuts, games and books to those
who visited. After the armistice was signed in July 1953, a few women were

recruited as social workers by the Red Cross to boost morale on the front lines [*Doc. 21*].

Women were also recruited to provide secretarial and supply services such as typing, stenography, and basic accounting. Although the US Army had agreed to integrate some women from the Women's Army Corps (WAC) into its regular forces before the Korean War, gender discrimination and segregation continued to exist. By 1951 there were 6,000 WACs working in low-paying jobs for the Far Eastern Command, mostly in Japan. This represented a fourfold increase from the year before. About a dozen were sent to Korea to work in secretarial and low-level administrative positions.

In the United States, poor pay, competition for good jobs in the civilian and private sectors, and the decline in public support for the war after 1951, hurt recruiting efforts. The military maintained a double standard for its female soldiers, who were required to meet higher educational standards and more rigorous entry-level investigations than enlisted men. As military historian Jeanne Holm has argued, the military establishment 'saw no real need for women except as nurses. In the absence of any compelling reason to do otherwise, the services were happy to keep the women's role small. ... Women represented a token force and nothing more' (Holm, 1992: 160).

Although women from UNC forces were prohibited from combat duty, some women from North Korea were actively involved with the guerrilla forces which followed the KPA into southern Korea. According to one first-hand account from the summer of 1950, women soldiers 'with short cropped hair were observed ... and residents stated there were a good number of them. ... Female soldiers are not necessarily aid women, but are used as front line troops' (US Army Center of Military History, 1950: reel 1). Female guerrilla fighters were said to have visited local markets later in the war to purchase medical supplies for wounded guerrillas living in the mountains. There were also North Korean women POWs among the 'civilian' prisoners held by the UNC. Some of these were family members of bureaucrats who moved south as part of the DPRK's occupation policies in 1950, but others were guerrillas captured during the war (plate 8).

SOLDIER, CIVILIAN: THE TWO KOREAS

The average ROK soldier, like most of Korean society, faced significant hardships. His wages were lower than family living requirements. The attrition rate in the ROK Army was extremely high – some 36 percent between April 1951 and April 1953 alone. Casualties and deaths averaged 250,000 per year during this period. Nutritional levels in the ROK Army were also very poor. In 1953 a US economic survey mission to Korea estimated that daily consumption of foodstuffs amounted to less than 1,500 calories; 2,200 was said to be the required amount per day.

The war had both a tragic and transforming impact on Korea. Millions of Koreans were left homeless by the conflict, factories were destroyed, refugees were left without food, families were permanently separated, and millions of others died or were injured. The South Korean government estimated that up to August 1951 war damage in its area alone amounted to over $3 billion. The south was primarily, though not exclusively, an agricultural society, and in the short term South Korea suffered severe economic stress as a consequence of destruction caused by the war. Government spending on defence was consistently higher than the total value of goods and services produced in the country. This exacerbated the high rates of inflation in the economy, already present because of insufficient supplies of basic requirements like foodstuffs. From June 1950 through to February 1953 retail prices in the southern city of Pusan rose 26-fold.

Reconstruction and relief efforts were undertaken largely under the auspices of the US Army and the United Nations. On 31 July 1950 the Security Council passed a resolution which gave the UNC responsibility for civilian relief. In December 1950 the UNC established a formal UN Civil Assistance Command for Korea (UNCACK) under the auspices of the Eighth Army. Between 1950 and 1953 some $400 million in relief was disbursed by UNCACK. Additional reconstruction work was undertaken by the UN Korean Reconstruction Agency (UNKRA) which operated into the late 1950s, providing advice and support in the areas of education, social welfare, industry and infrastructure. UNKRA sometimes worked with missionaries and the ROK Ministry of Health and Social Affairs to provide orphanages and shelter for the many homeless children and widows. Some widows also participated in technical programs designed to help them become more economically independent. After 1953 Korean orphans began to be adopted by overseas families. Since then, about 200,000 orphans have left Korea; about half have gone to families in the United States.

In the longer term, the war affected the traditional relationship between peasants and landlords by accelerating the destruction of the traditional rural base of South Korean society: a revolution in social relations, a product of the 1949 land reform and the conflict itself, facilitated the country's rapid modernization, urbanization and industrialization drive in the 1960s and 1970s. The war also had a long-term transformative impact on the role of women in South Korea, as, in the wake of the destruction, more women began to enter into the workforce. Many women and children took low-paying menial or factory work, especially in textiles, the main industry of South Korea's industrial revolution. The 1953 US-ROK Mutual Defense Treaty, which permitted the United States to retain its troops on the peninsula, ensured that prostitution would continue to thrive around US bases.

While South Korea had some opportunity to begin its economic reconstruction after 1951, North Korea continued to bear the brunt of American
aerial bombing. For the first time in modern warfare, American Air Force
pilots dropped napalm – 32,357 tons of the flammable liquid – on civilians
and soldiers alike. Hydro installations, ports, factories, towns and dams
were bombed as part of a strategy of destroying and punishing an entire
society for the war that was launched by the northern government. Between
1950 and 1953 the North Korean civilian population declined by almost
two million people, from about 9 million to roughly 7 million.

By 1952 the widespread destruction created acute shortages of consumer goods, food, and housing in the north. Many people were forced to
seek refuge in caves, underground, or to live in shanties. A situation of near
starvation existed during the winter of 1951–52, and over the course of
1952 foodstuffs were reduced by up to 50 percent in many areas of the
DPRK. In some cases crops were damaged by flooding because of US
bombing of dams. Labour shortages, a lack of animals for plowing, and the
destruction of factories which had previously produced fertilizer, all
contributed to the food crisis. Much of the country's fishing fleet had also
been destroyed or captured by enemy forces.

To deal with the emergency, 40 percent of government officials were
released from their regular duties and redeployed as workers on collective
farms which were set up jointly by the KPA and the Ministry of Railroads.
Initial efforts to relieve the food shortage were centred on the military front
– suggesting that the foodstuffs were intended for the North Korean Army.
Taxes on the peasantry were cut back or eliminated altogether. In March
1952, fishermen were ordered not to venture beyond coastal waters so as to
prevent further losses of manpower and equipment. The fishing catch in
May was 85 percent less than prewar levels.

International relief came from the DPRK's communist allies. The
country's East European allies provided economic relief and helped to
reconstruct the economy. Grains were shipped from Mongolia, China and
the Soviet Union. At the same time, the regime admitted its own incapacity
to deal with the scale of human suffering which the war had engendered. In
line with the ideology which later became known as 'Juche', or self-reliance,
the North Korean government warned the citizenry not to become
dependent on either governmental or international aid for tasks which they
themselves might be able to carry out. The inability of the state to mobilize
sufficient resources to feed, clothe, and shelter the population meant that
much of the onus for relief activity was placed on local people.

According to US intelligence sources, the disruption in the DPRK's
transportation and communication systems significantly impaired the
regime's propaganda networks, at least for a time. To strengthen internal
security the regime recruited women to fill basic policing services. The

North Korean police force was also supported by small groups of Chinese soldiers who performed local duties in towns and villages across the Korean countryside [*Doc. 22*].

Early in 1952 the communists began a major propaganda campaign to demonstrate that the United States was actively engaged in an illegal and immoral program of bacteriological and chemical warfare in North Korea. The communists reported that Chinese and DPRK soldiers began to succumb to serious illnesses in the early winter of 1952. The worst cases occurred along the communist battle lines. Witnesses also claimed to have seen odd objects falling from American planes – live insects, feathers, and leaves – or to have seen in the snow, after bombing raids, insects not normally associated with winter conditions. Some were found not to be indigenous to North Korea, and communist authorities issued statements condemning America for conducting germ warfare. North Korean propaganda tended to link its bacteriological warfare accusations with the broader character of the US aerial bombing, which did involve chemical warfare (napalm) and the mass destruction of cities. America's use of biological weapons was thus portrayed as part of a larger campaign of atrocities conducted against the North Korean people [*Doc. 23*].

There is no direct proof from American or allied sources that bacteriological warfare took place in Korea during the war. Many records of covert operations remain classified. The United States had inherited Japan's infamous 'Unit 731' Second World War germ warfare programs, and during the Korean War it did carry out experiments with bacteriological agents in Japan and the United States. A recent book on the subject concluded that there is 'a trail of documented circumstantial evidence that the CIA was closely involved in operational planning for the covert use of biological weapons during the Korean War, and that it had access to an extensive covert structure to implement these plans' (Endicott and Hagerman, 1998: 142).

THE CHINESE HOMEFRONT

In China, the Korean War and the threat of invasion were used to reinforce the domestic power of the newly victorious Chinese communists. The central government intensified its propaganda efforts and made a greater effort to mobilize the population around various war-related patriotic campaigns. The fighting received fairly extensive coverage in local newspapers, study groups were formed to discuss the conflict, and in some cases people were encouraged to organize or attend plays, operas and skits which celebrated heroic themes associated with the war. Urban populations were asked to make 'patriotic contributions' to the war effort; in some cases poorer city-dwellers demonstrated their patriotism by performing community work or doing their best to conserve resources.

In late 1950 the communists launched a nationwide 'Resist America and Aid Korea' campaign, a slogan which had some popular appeal. Other related movements included peace petitions, victory bond campaigns, and efforts to sever Chinese links with Western businessmen and missionaries. America's intervention in Korea increased Chinese insecurity about potential domestic enemies, and attempts were made by the government to organize 'thought reform' groups at various levels of the society. The object was to effect inner transformations of people's thoughts and to strengthen their collective sense of the challenges facing the New China. More ominously, the war also provided a context for the regime to rid itself of old enemies. In early 1951, Mao issued a decree for the 'suppression of counter-revolutionaries' which was soon used to repress opposition and dissent in the countryside. Former Kuomintang supporters, secret societies, Christians, and even members of the Communist Party, were persecuted under these terms. Soviet technicians sometimes supervised the imposition of this repression. All told, during the Korean War, almost a million people were victims of various forms of state retribution, which included public executions, imprisonment, detention, and various lesser penalties.

THE RED SCARE AND THE EMERGENCE OF THE US NATIONAL SECURITY STATE

The domestic American 'red scare' was rooted in the early postwar period. The Truman administration's efforts to convince the public to support the Marshall Plan and its newly-formed containment policy, and Congressional investigations of the House Un-American Activities Committee (HUAC) designed to weed out 'disloyal' citizens, had fostered an atmosphere of fear in the United States. The bitter anti-communist assaults of Republican Senator Joseph McCarthy originated in America's pre-Korean War political culture. But the Korean conflict at once intensified the ongoing hysteria and institutionalized America's national security state.

An important symbol of the new national security apparatus was the Internal Security Act of 1950. Senator Richard Nixon of California had been an early co-sponsor of the legislation, but its future was uncertain before the war in Korea. After the North Korean invasion, the bill was taken up by Senator Pat McCarran, a prominent supporter of the staunchly pro-Nationalist 'China bloc'. Although Truman vetoed the Congressional bill, the act was passed over his veto by the Congress. The legislation reflected the excesses which underpinned the domestic Cold War consensus by the fall of 1950. It required communist groups to register with the federal government, excluded immigrants who were members of 'totalitarian' political parties, prohibited communists from working in defence-related industries, and provided for the internment of undesirable radicals during a period of national crisis.

The worst elements of the domestic red scare – blacklisting, loyalty investigations, charges of conspiracy, and false accusations and insinuations – permeated into popular American culture from 1950 to 1953. By 1952, the media had stopped employing people whose names had appeared in a book entitled *Red Channels: The Report of Communist Influence in Radio and Television*. The book, which had received financial backing from Alfred Kohlberg, a leading supporter of Senator McCarthy and Chiang Kai-shek, attacked 151 'subversive' members of the entertainment industry. That year Hollywood produced a dozen movies which portrayed the evils of communism. In September, even British actor Charlie Chaplin was falsely accused of being a communist sympathizer and denied an entry permit into the United States.

AMERICAN PUBLIC OPINION AND THE KOREAN WAR

Public support for the Truman administration's foreign policies remained high during the initial months of the conflict. China's intervention in the war marked a turning point in public opinion, as support for the conflict declined significantly in its aftermath. Truman's popularity was also weakened by scandals, by charges of corruption, and by his administration's decision to implement wage and price controls in early 1951. Opinion surveys carried out from 1951 to 1953 showed that the American public had become divided over the US commitment in Korea. While 37 to 60 percent of the population continued to support US involvement in the war, between 36 and 50 percent of the population believed that the United States had been wrong in sending troops to the peninsula (Mueller, 1973: 229, 45–7).

Ironically, what had been a source of Truman's popularity – his image as a people's President – now began to hurt him. In early December 1950, amidst the Chinese assault in Korea, Truman wrote a stinging letter attacking the Washington *Post*'s music critic for writing a harsh review of his daughter's public singing performance: 'I've just read your lousy review of Margaret's concert', Truman exclaimed. 'I've come to the conclusion that you are an "eight ulcer man on four ulcer pay". ... Some day I hope to meet you. When that happens you'll need a new nose, a lot of beefsteak for black eyes, and perhaps a supporter below!' The letter reinforced a public image of the President as an incompetent and vindictive small-town politician. Many letters soon turned up at the White House from families who had lost family members in Korea. One letter from Connecticut came enclosed with a Purple Heart, an award of military merit. 'As you have been directly responsible for the loss of our son's life in Korea', the letter read, 'you might just as well keep this emblem on display in your trophy room, as a memory of one of your historic deeds. One major regret at this time is that your daughter was not there to receive the same treatment as our son received in Korea' (McCullough, 1992: 829, 831). Truman was personally hurt by these comments, but the incident dramatized the change in public mood in late 1950.

The President's decision in April 1951 to relieve MacArthur of his command further weakened his public support. In Congress, Senator Nixon led the wave of public protest. Only hours after reading of Truman's decision he wrote that the 'happiest group' celebrating MacArthur's removal were 'the Communists and their stooges'. Nixon publicly called for an expansion of the conflict and a US victory: 'the great weight of American public opinion [should] be brought in favor of the policies of MacArthur which will bring victory in the Pacific' (Ambrose, 1987: 238–9).

Partisan attacks on the Democratic administration grew more intense. Senator Joseph McCarthy moved to the forefront of the offensive against the administration's 'no win' policies. He was supported by prominent public figures like Senator Robert Taft who announced his candidacy for the Republican nomination for President in the fall of 1951. By early 1952 it appeared as though some of the foundations of Truman's postwar foreign policy might be in jeopardy.

Republican 'nationalists' like Taft were unable to take full advantage of the Truman administration's unpopularity. Dwight D. Eisenhower – commander of the famous D-day invasion of Normandy in 1944, Truman's former Chairman of the Joint Chiefs of Staff and, after December 1950, NATO's first Supreme Commander – successfully challenged Taft for the Republican nomination in mid-1952. Eisenhower was known as an 'internationalist' in foreign policy matters, and he seemed to be popular among the more moderate wing of the Republican Party. Even so, Ike failed to criticize McCarthy, and during the 1952 campaign he publicly shook hands with the man most closely associated with the term 'paranoid politics'. Indeed, some of Eisenhower's speeches sounded like they were taken right out of McCarthy's book. In September 1952 the Republican nominee for President claimed that American troops were in Korea because the Truman administration had 'lost' China to the communists.

Eisenhower's most important public declaration about Korea came in late October, during a speech in Detroit. 'I shall go to Korea', he promised. Although foreign policy issues in the 1952 campaign were generally less important to voters than domestic ones, Eisenhower's apparent commitment to find a solution to the Korean War strengthened his November election victory. He won a clear majority, taking 55 percent of the popular vote. As historian Burton Kaufman has pointed out, 'neither Eisenhower nor the Republican Party had a concrete program for ending the war' (Kaufman, 1997: 173). When the visit to Korea materialized in December,

Ike admitted he had 'no panaceas, no tricks' for bringing the war to an end (Hermes, 1966: 367). The public simply thought that Eisenhower the soldier would be able to find a way to conclude an 'honourable' end to the conflict in the 'Far East'.

POW LIFE: THE UNC PRISONERS

The majority of POWs held by the communists were members of the ROK armed forces. Of the 13,444 POWs who were eventually repatriated by the communists in the spring and summer of 1953, 8,333 had served the South Korean military. Another 3,746 were American POWs. 948 British POWs, 244 Turks, 41 Filipinos, 32 Canadians, and smaller numbers of other UNC troops were also repatriated.

Although neither the United States nor North Korea had formally signed the 1949 Geneva Convention governing treatment of war prisoners, both sides had indicated publicly that they would abide by its terms. In both cases these promises were broken. The treatment accorded to UNC POWs depended on local circumstances and on the temperament of the captors. There were a few cases where soldiers were released at the front soon after capture and told to return to their army. More commonly, prisoners were beaten or murdered. The radical changes in the momentum of the war and the armistice discussions also deeply affected the prisoners' experiences in captivity.

The North Koreans began to take prisoners soon after their initial offensive in the summer of 1950. In addition to holding American and Korean soldiers, the North Koreans rounded up clergy, foreign teachers, diplomatic representatives, and aid workers. After the Inchon landing, the POWs were forced northwards. When the Chinese 'volunteers' entered the battle, more American and Korean soldiers were taken prisoner. This chaotic period of the war was particularly harsh on the POWs and civilian internees, who were forced to march from one detention area to the next, without proper food, water, clothing, or medical attention. Prisoners continued to be arbitrarily beaten or shot, and those who received the harshest treatment tended to be those who refused to participate in communist propaganda efforts or who, labelled 'reactionaries', were reluctant to follow the orders of their captors. More than 50 percent of those who fell into communist hands between November 1950 and May 1951 did not survive the ordeal.

The first permanent camps for the POWs were built in northwest Korea, along the Yalu river, in early 1951. Several more were constructed near Pyongyang. These included the infamous 'Pak's Palace' and Camp 12, which provided comfort for those who were willing to collaborate with the enemy's propaganda program. Once the armistice negotiations got under-

1   President Harry Truman shakes hands with NATO Supreme Commander
Dwight D. Eisenhower in 1951. Eisenhower became President in 1953. US National
Archives, 306-PS-A, 51-20. *Source:* State/O'Donnell Original Negative. Photograph
© Archival Research International/Double Delta Industries Inc. and Pike Military
Research.

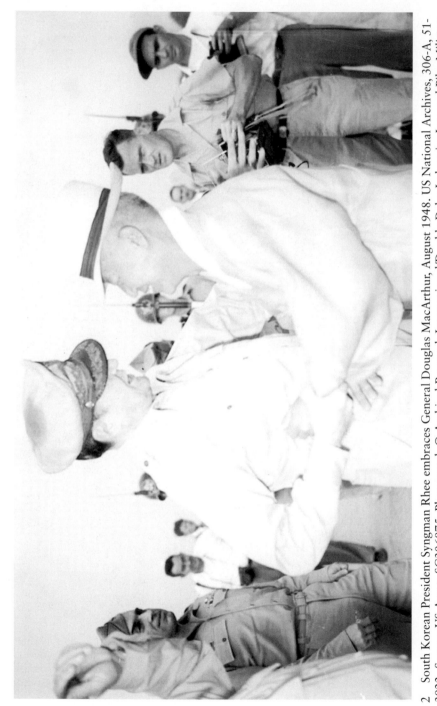

2 South Korean President Syngman Rhee embraces General Douglas MacArthur, August 1948. US National Archives, 306-A, 51-3922. *Source:* US Army, SC306875. Photograph © Archival Research International/Double Delta Industries Inc. and Pike Military Research.

3　Reception in Pyongyang during the visit of Chinese communist intellectual and activist Guo Moro (3rd from left), August 1950. Left to right: Kim Tu-bong, a prominent member of the Yanan faction of the North Korean political coalition and a member of the DPRK Politburo, 1949–56; North Korean Premier Kim Il Sung; Guo Moro; and Soviet Ambassador Terentii Shtykov. Note the Soviet-made tank emerging out of the map of southern Korea. US National Archives, 306-PS-C, 54-5250. *Source:* Eastfoto CH-91. Photograph © Archival Research International/ Double Delta Industries Inc. and Pike Military Research.

4 Premier Kim Il Sung (right) in Beijing, 12 November 1953. China's Foreign Minister Zhou Enlai is walking next to Kim. US National Archives, 306-PS-E, 51-4448. *Source:* Unknown. Photograph © Archival Research International/Double Delta Industries Inc. and Pike Military Research.

5 Korean refugees flee the fighting. US National Archives, 306-PS-E, 51-4448. *Source:* Unknown. Photograph © Archival Research International/Double Delta Industries Inc. and Pike Military Research.

6 Two civilians killed in crossfire. US tanks are in the background. February 1951. US National Archives, 111-SC-357383. Photograph © Archival Research International/Double Delta Industries Inc. and Pike Military Research.

7 Integrated South Korean and US troops advance north just before the Chinese intervention, 20 November 1950. US National Archives, 111-SC-353466. US Army Photo. Photograph © Archival Research International/Double Delta Industries Inc. and Pike Military Research.

8 North Korean female POWS board a train in August 1953 on their way from Koje Do to the POW exchange at Panmunjom during 'Operation Big Switch'. US National Archives, 111-SC-432769. US Army Photo. Photograph © Archival Research International/Double Delta Industries Inc. and Pike Military Research.

way, prisoners received better treatment. The quantity of food improved, medical treatment got better, and though the International Red Cross was refused access to the camps, in general the prisoners were much less susceptible to death caused by malnutrition or sickness. The camps simply became survivable. Of the 7,140 American soldiers in the prison camps, 2,701 died in captivity – an appalling 38 percent. The vast majority died before the armistice negotiations got underway. Between July 1951 and September 1953, twenty-four died in the camps. Except for one American general who was retained by the North Koreans, the KPA transferred all their POWs to Chinese care in late 1951.

Troops were segregated in various camps according to such designations as rank, political belief, and nationality. The communists did not use prisoners as slave labour. Rather, from the start of the armistice negotiations through to May 1952, POWs were subject to intensive indoctrination campaigns within the camps. The object of such campaigns was reminiscent of the 'thought reform' programs in mainland China. Formally, captives were treated as 'war criminals', not prisoners of war. These 'criminals' could redeem themselves through a process of indoctrination and re-education. A POW who accepted communist ideology would be given a 'lenient' treatment.

Participation in re-education programs was compulsory, and some courses took up as much as eight hours a day. A typical course dwelt on the idea that '[t]he strength of the democratic camp, led by the great Soviet Union, is incomparably greater than that of the imperialistic camp, led by the American imperialists' (O'Neill, 1985: 539). Most prisoners were unmoved by the propaganda effort, though twenty-three refused repatriation at the end of the conflict. With such meagre results, the indoctrination effort was abandoned in the summer of 1952.

Following Stalin's death in early March 1953, conditions in the camps again improved. More cigarettes, sugar and rice were provided, and some of the restrictions on religious worship were lifted. Along the Yalu, the prisoners were permitted to organize a POW olympic event, and additional food was provided for the participants. There was thus some effort to raise the physical and mental health of the POWs just before their release to the UNC side.

LIFE AND DEATH IN UNC POW CAMPS

Before the Inchon landing, the UNC held relatively few North Korean prisoners. In August 1950, less than 1,000 North Koreans were held in UNC stockades around Pusan. As we have seen, North Korean POWS were also treated with great violence by their South Korean captors. The Inchon landing in September and the subsequent UNC offensive towards the Yalu netted another 130,000 POWs. Up to this time, little thought had been given to the POWs' welfare.

In January 1951, the UNC decided to relocate prisoners to an island south of the mainland, called Koje Do (map 3). Only the sick and wounded, and those who claimed to have been forcibly inducted into the North Korean Army, were not sent to the island. At this time the UNC estimated that it held 130,000 North Koreans and 20,000 Chinese. Another 100,000 people were classified as civilians and refugees. These included DPRK functionaries who had participated in the occupation of the south, guerrillas, and family members.

The Koje Do camp was far from being a safe place to live out the war. Adequate medical facilities were only improvised late in the conflict and by the end of 1951 more than 6,000 POWs had died of illnesses such as dysentery, malaria, tuberculosis and pneumonia. Reports drawn up by UNC members and the International Committee for the Red Cross painted a picture of unsanitary conditions, poor heating and lodging, and overcrowding. Originally designed to hold only about 40,000 prisoners, even after more construction was completed to house the bulging number of prisoners, the compounds were packed with people.

The prisoners were divided along ideological lines, between pro- and anti-communists; in some compounds, former Chinese Nationalist soldiers who had been inducted into the communist 'volunteer' army were given authority over the distribution of food, clothes, and medical facilities. Security was appalling. The system encouraged outbreaks of violence and fighting among the various political factions in the camps. The extensive use of ROK guards exacerbated conflict, and violent acts of retribution were common.

The result was protracted bloodshed and violence. Homemade clubs and weapons were used with deadly force. Eighteen prisoners were killed in September 1951; in December another fourteen were killed and twenty-four were injured in rock fights and riots between various compounds. In February 1952, Compound 62's civilian internees refused to allow the UNC and ROK teams to enter, and four companies of troops were mobilized to subdue the compound. Up to 1,500 internees attacked the advancing UNC troops, and seventy-seven of these were killed when UNC troops fired on the prisoners. One American was killed and another thirty-eight were wounded. In mid-March another deadly engagement occurred between the ROK guards and communist POWs. This time the guards fired on their own, without receiving orders from their superiors. Twelve POWs died and another twenty-six were wounded.

Only after more riots and killings in May and June 1952 did the UNC decide to relocate some of the POWs to new sites on Koje Do or to two other islands to the south – Pongam Do and Cheju Do. Even then the violence continued. Further protests on both islands led to fifty-one deaths in Cheju in October and eighty-five fatalities in Pongam in December 1952. In both cases, the communist propagandists in China and the DPRK used the riots and their suppression as evidence of the failure of the UNC to provide adequate care for communist prisoners. Some have suggested that the communists ordered soldiers to surrender to the UNC in order to incite the camps' inmates. But the camps' conditions and poor security were fundamentally responsible for the violence and death.

The UNC had an indoctrination program which paralleled that of the communists, but attendance was not compulsory. Classes emphasized the superiority of 'free world' democracy over totalitarian communism. Reading materials included US Information Service news reports, and prisoners were subjected to radio broadcasts from the ROK, the Voice of America, and Radio Free Asia. The goal of the program, according to the US Psychological Operations Board, was to indoctrinate the prisoners so that they would 'serve U.S. psychological objectives after their return to Communist jurisdiction' (Foot, 1990: 115). The effort to indoctrinate the communists exacerbated tensions in the camp and it was abandoned in mid-1952; however, efforts to convince the anti-communist prisoners of the benefits of democracy continued until the end of the fighting. As Rosemary Foot (1990) has pointed out, the fundamental goal of such 'programming' was to ensure that as many prisoners as possible would not want to return home at the end of the fighting.

By using POWs to attain their own political ends in the propaganda war, the UNC and communists subjected prisoners to extended periods of needless pain and suffering. Although propaganda on both sides of the iron curtain attempted to prove that the other side was responsible for the most grievous of moral injustices, neither side examined its own inadequacies and human rights violations during the course of the conflict. The failure to do this made the legacies of the war more difficult to deal with in the longer term.

CHAPTER FIVE

FIGHTING AND NEGOTIATING: THE WAR AND THE ARMISTICE, 1951–54

KAESONG AND PANMUNJOM, JULY 1951–MAY 1952

After the failed spring 1951 offensive by the Chinese and North Korean troops, the Chinese and Americans seemed prepared to accept the fact that a stalemate had been reached. The PRC had been unable to evict UNC forces from Korea and the US leadership was also not now willing to expend the human or material resources required to unify the peninsula. The costs of an expanded war were deemed too great. Major gains in territory would require the use of weapons of mass destruction, and a decision to employ them would escalate the conflict, something neither superpower desired.

By the end of June 1951, the Soviet Union had made it clear that it was prepared to negotiate a military armistice and that territorial and political issues would not be considered at the talks. In proposing the terms in this manner, the Soviet Union limited the discussions to issues relating to Korea only. Other important matters such as seating the PRC in the United Nations, recognition of the PRC, withdrawal of foreign troops from Korea, and the return of Formosa, all of which had been integral to the debate over a Korean settlement, were now excluded.

Although the United States was receptive to the communist side's diplomatic initiative, ROK President Rhee immediately made clear to Washington his government's opposition to another negotiated division of the two Koreas. On 30 June the Korean Ambassador in the United States, Yang You Chan, forwarded a diplomatic note to Secretary Acheson outlining the terms that the ROK would accept in any negotiations with the communists. These amounted to a virtual surrender of Chinese and DPRK military forces in North Korea [*Doc. 24*]. The implication of the note was that if ROK terms were not met, the UN should vigorously prosecute the war with its Korean allies.

This was a position for which some top-ranking US military officials had sympathy. On 28 June UN Commander General Ridgway informed Washington that the UNC should only agree to a cease-fire after a final deal

82

was struck. He cited as his reason the 'uniform pattern of communist duplicity and faithlessness'. Later that summer he called the communist side a group of 'treacherous savages' who had come to power 'through murderous conspiracy'. To negotiate with such people 'and deal with them as with representatives of an enlightened and civilized people is to deride one's own dignity and to invite the disaster their treachery will inevitably bring upon us'. Ridgway's mindset, more comfortable fighting than talking, was indicative of the contradictions the United States faced as it began to negotiate an armistice with the communists (US Department of State, 1983: 586, 787–8).

Although American officials were largely in control of the course of the negotiations and the fighting, consultation among the allies did occur. In Washington, from late 1950, Ambassadors of those countries with forces in Korea were periodically invited to briefing sessions about the course of the conflict. The ROK was not asked to join these proceedings until June 1951, a reflection of the relatively limited consultation that took place between the Koreans and UN states during the course of the war. The Western allies also received information about US policy on Korea through day-to-day contact with American military and diplomatic officials, at NATO meetings, at the UN, and from liaison representatives at the UNC in Tokyo. With limited degrees of success, these venues were used to influence and shape American policy during the conflict.

Less is known about the communist deliberation process, but it appears that Stalin wanted to decentralize the consultation, making China responsible for coordinating policy with the Koreans, while the Soviet Union maintained a guiding hand in the formulation of the overall communist position. In late June, when it became clear that the United States was prepared to enter into armistice discussions, Kim Il Sung sent a letter to Mao Zedong in which he asked how he should approach the American proposals. In turn, Mao wrote to Stalin suggesting that the negotiations could begin as early as 15 July. Although Mao had asked Stalin to inform Kim of the Soviet position and to take the lead in the negotiations from Moscow, Stalin wrote 'it's up to you to lead. ... The most we can give is advice on various questions' (Hershberg, 1995–96: 65). Mao was told to maintain regular contact with Kim since it was not possible to do this from Moscow.

Following Stalin's suggestions, the Chinese and Koreans responded positively to Ridgway's message and formal armistice negotiations began on 10 July at Kaesong, a town located between the trenches of the combatants just south of the 38th parallel, northwest of Seoul (map 4). Ridgway appointed Vice-Admiral Charles Turner Joy to represent the UNC, General Xie Fang spoke for the PRC and General Nam Il, a Soviet-Korean, represented the DPRK.

In Kaesong, the negotiators approved the following five-item agenda at their tenth meeting on 26 July: approval of the agenda, item 1; establishment of a military demarcation line and a demilitarized zone (DMZ), item 2; cease-fire and inspection arrangements, item 3; disposition of prisoners of war (POWs), item 4; and recommendations to the governments of both sides, item 5.

Over the next five months the two sides concentrated their discussions on item 2. The Chinese and North Koreans proposed the 38th parallel as the demarcation line, a suggestion which Soviet official Jacob Malik had offered in his 23 June speech, but one which was for the most part south of the existing battle locations, known to American soldiers as the Kansas–Wyoming line. For negotiating purposes Admiral Joy was ordered to demand a line well north of Kansas–Wyoming, a position defended by the argument that UNC air and naval superiority should be taken into account in deciding the demarcation line.

There was no progress for several weeks and at the end of August the communists suspended negotiations, claiming that bombs had been dropped on the neutral meeting zone of Kaesong by the UN side. The UNC argued the communist charges had been fabricated, but it seems that a ROK plane, acting with covert instructions, did drop the bombs. The suspension of talks lasted until 25 October when they resumed at a new site, Panmunjom, located about 5 miles east of Kaesong (map 4).

The Panmunjom truce talks initially made better progress. Between late October 1951 and early May 1952, agreement was reached on a number of important issues: on 26 November, the communists accepted the UNC position that the provisional cease-fire line would be along the existing battle line, and the next day both sides agreed to a DMZ four kilometers in width (item 2); on 19 February 1952 an agreement was reached to hold a conference to discuss political issues, including the withdrawal of foreign soldiers from Korea and a peaceful solution to the Korean issue within 90 days of signing an armistice (item 5). This became the basis for the Geneva Conference on Korea. By 2 May 1952 both sides had also agreed to appoint representatives from Sweden, Switzerland, Poland and Czechoslovakia to a Neutral Nations Supervisory Commission (NNSC) which would oversee the implementation of a final armistice agreement (item 3).

DELAY AND DEADLOCK: THE POW ISSUE, ITEM 4

After mid-1951, the PRC felt an armistice would help bolster its international and domestic prestige, but Mao was not prepared to sign an agreement which he felt took advantage of his government's willingness to negotiate. In a message to Stalin on 14 November 1951, Mao concluded that military operations could cease by the end of the year. 'Achieving peace as a result of the negotiations is advantageous for us', Mao wrote, 'but we are also not afraid of dragging out the negotiations'. The Chinese side was prepared for a longer war, but 'victory' was defined in terms of holding the present military positions and inflicting manpower losses on the enemy. By 1952 a peaceful settlement to the conflict also seems to have been on the mind of the North Koreans. On 8 February DPRK Foreign Minister Pak Hon Yong told Peng Dehuai, the commander of the Chinese volunteers in Korea, that 'the Korean people throughout the country demand peace and do not want to continue the war'. Ten percent of the population was suffering from hunger, and most of the peasantry had subsistence food only until the spring (Hershberg, 1995–96: 71, 75).

Still, no armistice was forthcoming and the negotiations dragged on for another year and a half. Why? One reason was that both sides employed military officials as negotiators, soldiers who were more used to ordering others into battle than negotiating peaceful solutions to major conflicts. Another was that the US negotiating position began to harden and American policy towards the PRC became more aggressive. These changes in US strategy towards China were embodied in a major re-statement of American policies towards East Asia, known as NSC 48/5, approved by the President in May 1951, even before the armistice negotiations got under-way. According to the document, the Korean War presented the United States with an opportunity to weaken the power and prestige of the communists, and to limit the possibility of Chinese troops intervening in other areas of Asia such as Indochina. While recognizing that the likelihood of reunifying Korea had passed with China's military intervention, the NSC paper concluded that UN forces 'can continue to inflict heavy losses on the Chinese'. A settlement, on the other hand, would 'permit the withdrawal of Chinese forces from Korea for use elsewhere and will put an end to Chinese losses in Korea' (US Department of State, 1983: 441).

The American negotiating position was also subject to external pressures which curtailed the possibilities of making concessions to the communist side. US Congressional opinion, particularly from the Republican right, influenced the American position. In late 1951 and 1952, Senator Robert Taft criticized the Truman administration for disregarding MacArthur's recommendations to bomb air fields in Manchuria and to use Chinese Nationalist troops in Korea and south China. Partly as a result of this public pressure the Truman administration continued to formulate more aggressive policies towards the communists in the winter and spring of 1952.

Additional pressure to escalate the conflict came from South Korean officials who criticized the armistice negotiations and tried to get the United States to launch a major UN offensive which would defeat the communist forces. President Rhee felt betrayed by the UNC decision to negotiate with the communists. The UN policy reminded him of great power diplomacy towards Korea in the pre-1945 era [*Doc. 25*]. In a memo written in December 1951 and addressed to John Chang, the Head of South Korea's UN delegation to the General Assembly, Rhee bitterly criticized the Korean policies of Secretary Acheson, saying that it looked as though Korea were surrounded by 'political nincompoops!' (ROK National History Compilation Committee, 1996, vol. 30: 366).

Acheson's main concern at this time was to build up South Korea's army as a defence force to underpin America's own global containment policy. Voices advocating rollback, especially ones from the developing world, received short shrift from the Secretary, but Rhee's voice added to the chorus of those who demanded harsher penalties against the communist side.

The key issue over which the armistice negotiations bogged down was the treatment of POWs. The initial US position was to demand a one-for-one prisoner exchange until all UN POWs returned. The UNC would then release the rest of the communist prisoners to the other side. This policy coincided with the spirit of article IV of the 1949 Geneva Convention on POWs which required all prisoners to be 'forcibly' returned to their homeland following the end of hostilities. The United States and its allies soon rejected this strategy, however, opting in favour of a position which would allow the prisoners themselves to decide whether or not they would be sent back to their home countries. The new policy would support the West's anti-communist propaganda campaign, since it was believed that many communist soldiers would not opt to return home. The UNC thus adopted a position favouring 'non-forcible' or voluntary repatriation of POWs.

At the start of the armistice negotiations the communist side did not foresee the difficulties which the POW issue would soon present them with. 'I think it will not be difficult to reach agreement on this question', Mao declared in his letter to Stalin on 14 November 1951 (Hershberg, 1995–96: 71).

The change in the American position on POWs began as early as July 1951 when the chief of psychological warfare of the US Army suggested that for humanitarian and propaganda reasons the United States should not return those prisoners who did not wish to be repatriated. President Harry Truman supported the idea, arguing that a full exchange of POWS should occur only if the United States received a major concession from the other side. In late December 1951 Admiral Joy was ordered to table a position for non-forcible repatriation of all POWs. By this time the two sides had exchanged some preliminary and informal information on their prisoners. The communists claimed they held 7,142 South Korean troops and 4,417 UN soldiers, numbers disputed as being far too low by the United States and South Koreans who argued that many South Korean POWs had been forcibly incorporated into the North Korean Army. After re-screening and re-classifying their prisoners, the UNC estimated they held 132,000 POWs and 37,000 civilian internees. On 2 January 1952 Admiral Joy presented the UNC position that only those prisoners who requested repatriation would be sent home, a proposal the communists immediately rejected.

America's allies generally supported the idea of non-forcible repatriation, and Western public opinion appeared favourable to the idea; these developments reinforced the US bargaining stance and the UNC refused to compromise on its new position.

On 1 April 1952 the UNC informed the communist side that about 116,000 of their 132,000 soldiers would be returned. On this basis, it appeared that a solution to the POW issue could be worked out. The communists had previously seemed willing to let North Korean POWs decide their own fates, and if many of the Chinese POWs were returned, a deal might be possible.

The communist negotiators asked the UNC to check their POW lists and a formal screening process soon began. This investigation showed that the original estimates had been very wide of the mark and that only some 70,000 POWs wanted to be sent to their homelands. The key problem was that 16,000 of the 21,000 Chinese POWs had apparently said they did not want to be repatriated. When the communist side learned of the new figures they flatly rejected UNC plans for repatriation.

In Washington, Tokyo and other allied capitals, military and civilian officials alike were surprised by the new findings. But the numbers simply reflected the chaos and intimidation tactics that were widespread in the POW camps. Some of the prisoners had been former Chinese Nationalist soldiers; now, used as guards, they physically intimidated many of the PRC prisoners. General Ridgway recognized this and suggested that a re-screening take place, particularly for the Chinese POWs, but it was not done, partly because of the difficulties associated with accessing the communist prisoners who refused to be re-screened. The United States and UN stuck to their position and negotiations dragged on for over another year.

THE BOMBING CAMPAIGN ESCALATES

In the summer of 1952 the United States significantly escalated air attacks on North Korea in an effort to put pressure on the communist side to accept the UNC negotiating position. This strategy was supported by General Mark Clark, a soldier known for his earlier endorsement of General MacArthur's ideas for ending the war in Korea. In June, much to the dismay and alarm of America's allies, the United States bombed a dam and power station on the Yalu river on the edge of the North Korean–Chinese border. In another raid on 11 July, US, ROK, Australian and British bomber pilots flew 1,254 sorties against Pyongyang, dropping bombs and 23,000 gallons of napalm on the inhabitants. After two more major bombing campaigns against the city in August the Americans decided that there were too few targets left to justify a continuation of the bombardment. General Clark and the US Department of Defense believed that the bombing improved UNC prospects at the bargaining table and in late September President Truman cabled Clark saying that it was essential to maintain the pressure on the communists.

US officials were incorrect in their assessments that increased military pressure helped their negotiating stance. In fact, the opposite was the case: the extended bombing campaigns hardened communist resolve to fight and further prolonged the war for the POWs, civilians, and armed forces of all sides. Five days after the 11 July raid on Pyongyang, Mao sent Kim Il Sung a telegram which he also forwarded to Stalin in Moscow a few days later. Mao told Kim that the Chinese had concluded that 'at present, when the enemy is subjecting us to furious bombardment, accepting a provocative and fraudulent proposal from the enemy, which does not signify in fact any kind of concession, is highly disadvantageous for us'. If the UNC continued to refuse to make concessions, or if it broke off negotiations, 'then we must continue military operations so as to find in the course of the war ... a means for changing the present situation' (Hershberg, 1995–96: 78).

Once the armistice negotiations bogged down in 1952, Stalin and Mao seemed to have altered their strategic calculations. They appear to have calculated that continuing the war now strengthened their collective security. Stalin in particular believed that the way the United States prosecuted the war reflected American military weakness and that the US/UN side would eventually have to come to terms and negotiate the armistice. The Soviet Premier remarked to Mao that the Nazis had occupied France in twenty days but the Americans had been unable to subdue 'little Korea' after two years. Although the United States wanted to 'subjugate the world' they 'didn't know how to fight'. They were dependent on the atomic bomb, but 'one cannot win a war with that'. Stalin's disdainful comments also reflected his disregard for the tremendous suffering which had occurred during the war [*Doc. 26*].

THE INDIAN RESOLUTION

In the fall of 1952 several states made an effort in the United Nations to break the deadlock at Panmunjom by formulating resolutions which would encourage greater flexibility on all sides. The most significant of these initiatives came from the Indian delegation, led by India's representative in the UN, Krishna Menon. Menon's initial intent, in late October and early November, was to downplay the non-forcible repatriation aspects of America's position on POWs, and to suggest that the final disposition of POWs could be dealt with by a Neutral Nations Repatriation Commission (NNRC), made up of the same four states that had been recommended to serve on the Commission overseeing the implementation of the armistice agreements.

But Menon was under heavy US and allied pressure to alter his draft resolution; Britain's Foreign Minister, Anthony Eden, and Canada's External Affairs Minister, Lester Pearson, worked together to alter the original Indian Resolution to make it more attractive to American officials. Their initial efforts were not successful at convincing Acheson to accept it, and his obstinacy led to significant personal antagonism within the Anglo-American camp. The worst came one evening in mid-November, a few weeks after Eisenhower's election victory. Acheson had been drinking steadily over a number of hours and had dropped by Eden's hotel room. The 'lame duck' Secretary told Eden that unless Britain stopped supporting the Indian Resolution 'there would be no NATO, no Anglo-American friendship'. He then referred to Pearson as 'an empty glass of water' and called Menon a 'Swami' (Shuckburgh, 1986: 53–4).

Despite the apparent disunity, by late November the original Indian Resolution had been significantly revised, and now embodied references to the principle of non-forcible repatriation in its main body and preface. Still, only after the draft resolution was condemned by Soviet representative Andrei Vyshinsky did Acheson begin to support it. After further compromises by Menon, the General Assembly voted to adopt the resolution on 3 December. Since the communists had already turned their backs on it, the resolution proved of limited value in the short term when it came to resolving the deadlock in the armistice negotiations. The fate of the initial proposal also demonstrated the limitations of diplomatic coordination between the 'new' Commonwealth made up of recently decolonized countries such as India and the 'older' Commonwealth. Eden himself had told Secretary Acheson that if it came down to an 'either–or' choice between the American and Indian Resolution, Britain would side with the United States.

THE EISENHOWER ADMINISTRATION

Between 1951 and early 1953, US terms for negotiating a Korean settlement had hardened considerably. President Truman was partly responsible for this; on a number of occasions in 1952 he privately suggested that the United States should threaten the communists with a significant expansion of the conflict, involving the destruction of China and Siberia, possibly even global war, if they did not agree to end the war on US terms. In mid-May

1952 Truman wrote in his diary that unless the Soviets changed their foreign policies, war would mean that 'Moscow, St Petersburg, Mukden, Vladivostok, Pekin[g], Shanghai, Port Arthur, Dairen, Odessa, Stalingrad and every manufacturing plant in China and the Soviet Union will be eliminated' (Foot, 1985: 176).

Others in the administration seemed to share the spirit of these sentiments. UN Commander Mark Clark drew up a plan in the summer of 1952 for military operations involving air and sea attacks on China and Korea which would result in a UN drive to the 'waist' of Korea, about three-quarters up the length of the peninsula, 120 miles south of the Yalu river. In November 1952 Secretary of Defense Robert Lovett told Canadian and British officials that there was no tradition in the United States to fight for a stalemate; if the communists refused to compromise on American terms, there was a 'strong probability that the US would seek a military con-clusion' to the conflict (US Department of State, 1984: 644).

The momentum of these plans and perceptions affected the incoming Eisenhower administration, which soon developed plans of its own for achieving a limited 'victory' in Korea. An early sign of the Republicans' more aggressive stance towards Asia occurred in February 1953, when the new President announced in his State of the Union address that the American Seventh Fleet would no longer 'shield' the PRC from attacks and raids originating from Taiwan. Military planning *vis-à-vis* the Soviet Union also seemed to justify adopting a more offensive containment plan. American policymakers believed that the Soviet Union would be reluctant fully to support China militarily except in the most dire of strategic circum-stances. Paul Nitze, one of the primary authors of NSC 68, now believed that the Soviets would be willing to let the Chinese suffer a 'lot of punishment' before coming to their aid (Foot, 1985: 198). The Sino-Soviet alliance had a limited impact in deterring the Eisenhower administration from considering more aggressive containment policies.

Officials believed that if the United States threatened to escalate military pressure in the Northeast Asian theatre, fractures might develop in the Chinese-Soviet relationship. There was some talk about even over-throwing or replacing the Chinese government. In April 1953 Secretary of State John Foster Dulles suggested that an efficient containment policy might link the Korean and Taiwanese theatre of operations. Later in the year the Joint Chiefs of Staff suggested that the ultimate object of US policy should be the replacement of the PRC with a regime not hostile to the United States.

While America was prepared to export counter-revolution to the developing world, there were significant limits to the degree that it could affect the situation on the Chinese mainland. It was easier to apply pressure on China through its periphery, as in Korea. The atomic bomb was a means by which that coercion could be applied. This thinking dovetailed with the Eisenhower administration's willingness to view the bomb as 'just another weapon' and to consider its use in diplomatic as well as strategic contexts.

In the spring of 1953 Dulles believed the military conditions in Korea were ripe for utilizing American air and sea power. So did Ike. At a NSC meeting on 31 March the President told the group that 'it would be worth the cost if, through [the] use of atomic weapons, we could (1) achieve a substantial victory over the Communist forces and (2) get a line at the waist of Korea' (Lee, 1995: 177) .

A separate NSC report, NSC 147, entitled 'Analysis of Possible Courses of Action in Korea' laid out the strategic contexts in which atomic weapons could be used against continental Northeast Asia. The report noted that it was out of the question for the United States to reconsider its position on the non-forcible repatriation of POWs; the communist side, by rejecting the Indian Resolution in the late fall of 1952, had indicated that it was prepared to face maximum political pressure from the 'free world'. The issue for the NSC was whether current restrictions on military operations should be lifted. These restrictions had contributed to the 'limited' character of the Korean conflict up to that point and included the decision not to cross the Manchurian or Soviet borders except with the higher approval of Washington; agreement not to use atomic weapons except in case the UNC forces were faced with a military disaster; the consensus that Chinese Nationalists should not be employed in the Asian conflict; concurrence that 'preventive' action against the Chinese mainland not be taken except with Presidential authorization; and assent to the principle not to enforce a naval blockade against the PRC. All these positions of 'limited war' were now challenged by the highest-level American national security coordinating body.

NSC 147 laid out six possible strategies for dealing with the political-military situation in Korea and Northeast Asia, each of which required an increase in the escalatory potential of the conflict. These ranged from 'Plan A', a straightforward extension of present military operations and build-up in strength of South Korean military forces, to 'Plan F', the launching of coordinated large-scale land and air offensives against North Korea and Manchuria, resulting in a unified Korea and the 'defeat and destruction' of enemy forces. Only Plan A did not envisage the possible use of atomic weapons, though none of the contemplated courses of action envisaged the use of Nationalist Chinese troops in Korea itself [*Doc. 27*].

STALIN'S DEATH

Soviet intelligence was aware of the trend in American national security planning. Intelligence operatives informed the Kremlin in late 1952 and early 1953 that 'the U.S. joint chiefs of staff weighed the chances of using atomic bombs against North Korea and the Chinese coastline' (Zubok and Pleshakov, 1996: 154). Policy changes in the Soviet Union were forthcoming in the aftermath of Stalin's death in early March 1953, when he was replaced by a group of his subordinates, including Georgi Malenkov, an 'inner circle' technocrat who had worked closely with Stalin in intelligence and industrial development; Vyacheslav Molotov, a former Premier and Foreign Minister who had been replaced in the latter position by Andrei Vyshinsky in 1949; and Nikita Khrushchev, a blunt but talented official of peasant origins who was a firm believer in the mandate of the Russian Revolution and who would in a few years emerge as the most powerful man in the Soviet Union.

Soviet military spending had been significantly reduced even before Stalin's death, but his passing increased the momentum for a pause in the Cold War and for a negotiated settlement to several outstanding disputes between the two superpowers. On 16 March Malenkov announced that the Soviet Union had no contested issues with the United States that 'cannot be resolved by peaceful means' (Zubok and Pleshakov, 1996: 155). A few days later the Soviet Politburo worked out a plan to end the Korean War and sign the armistice. After discussions between Malenkov and Zhou Enlai, who had been in Moscow attending Stalin's funeral, the two communist allies began to devise a strategy to end the fighting.

On 30 March Zhou announced that he would agree to a previous UN proposal for both sides to exchange their sick and wounded POWs. The Chinese Foreign Minister also stated that those POWs who were unwilling to be repatriated could be handed over to a neutral state which would then determine their final disposition. These important concessions were a public sign that the communists were now prepared to compromise their previous stance on the POW issue. Several thousand sick and wounded POWs were exchanged in 'Operation Little Switch' in late April and early May 1953.

ATOMIC DIPLOMACY

US officials did not believe that the type of escalation they had planned for Korea would result in global war. Stalin's death in early March 1953 significantly encouraged US thinking in this regard. On 8 April the CIA reported that since the death of Stalin the Soviet Union had initiated a major international peace offensive. CIA Director Allen Dulles told the NSC that communist goals were to lessen the possibility of international war and to undermine the momentum for rearmament in Japan and Western Europe. The Soviets' main concern was to stem the possibility of war breaking out over Korea, and an armistice would meet their needs.

During the same meeting Secretary of State John Foster Dulles, the brother of the CIA Director, told the Council that the United States should be able to secure an armistice more amenable to American interests 'in view of our much greater power and the Soviet Union's much greater weakness currently' (US Department of State, 1984: 894). Personally, he said, he would like to tell the communists that unless they agreed to divide Korea at its waist instead of the current line of military contact, he would call off the armistice and continue the war. Eisenhower, persuaded by Dulles' reasoning, noted that the American armistice negotiators should be instructed to tell the other side that in certain circumstances, with prior notification, the armistice negotiations could be ended. The communists were well aware of the implications of such a decision: a further escalation of the war by the United States.

While the American administration threatened to escalate the Korean conflict, the communists made significant concessions in their negotiating position. On 7 May General Nam Il tabled an eight-point proposal on behalf of the communist side which called for the creation of a five-power Neutral Nations Repatriation Commission to be composed of Czechoslovakia, India, Poland, Sweden and Switzerland, which would help decide the future of those POWs who had not been repatriated. Previously, the communists had asked that all POWs be transported to a neutral state, possibly Pakistan. This new proposal adhered to an important element of the December 1952 Indian Resolution. They also agreed to limit the period that POWs could be persuaded to return home to four instead of six months. The fate of those POWs who still refused to be repatriated after four months would be discussed at the post-armistice political conference.

At this stage of the negotiations, demonstrations in South Korea against the armistice reached a peak. To maintain control over the situation UN Commander Mark Clark decided to fly from Tokyo to Seoul and visit President Rhee. It was one of the few times that the UNC consulted with Rhee in a formal way about its bargaining position. The Korean President and top-ranking members of the Korean National Assembly remained opposed to any agreement which would result in another *de facto* division of Korea. South Korean public opinion also seemed to want the war to continue. In light of President Rhee's strong feelings against a UNC proposal to allow Indian troops to handle the task of taking care of the POWs after an armistice, and his refusal to allow Koreans from either side of the border to be released to any neutral state, Clark recommended that the UNC propose that all North Korean POWs who had opted not to return home be released from their compounds as soon as the armistice became effective.

This recommendation dovetailed with the US perception that concessions could be extracted from the communists in the current international situation. The Americans put forward their new negotiating terms at

Panmunjom on 13 May. These demanded the release of all North Korean non-repatriates upon the signing of an armistice, the necessity of obtaining unanimous agreement among the members of the proposed neutral nations commission to oversee the POW imbroglio, and a specific date for the release of all POWs after the armistice was signed. The US position on North Korean POWs represented a major modification of policies that the UNC had previously accepted regarding non-forcible repatriation. The United States now would only accept a *fait accompli* for the DPRK non-repatriate prisoners. The UNC had also previously felt that decisions by the Neutral Nations Repatriation Commission should be reached by majority vote; a requirement for unanimous decisions might stalemate the commission and undermine its ability to operate.

America's allies were extremely distressed by the new bargaining terms, which were introduced at Panmunjom without prior discussion or consultation. Canadian officials felt that if the armistice negotiations broke down over these new terms the Western public would rightly believe that responsibility for the failure of discussions lay with the United States, which had abandoned principles they had accepted and voted for in the Indian Resolution the previous December. High-ranking officials in the British Foreign Office also felt the UNC position was unnecessarily provocative and British Prime Minister Churchill warned American officials that their bargaining position would not easily be accepted by the communists.

In light of allied pressure against the 13 May proposals, the Eisenhower administration decided to make some compromises. This was done only after a decision was taken in the NSC on 20 May to extend air and naval operations against China and ground operations in Korea if conditions arose on the peninsula which required more 'positive' action. In adopting this posture, the NSC reached a consensus that expanded operations would require the use of atomic weapons. In this manner the United States moved towards a possible limited nuclear war with the PRC.

On 25 May the UNC presented its final negotiating terms and Washington gave Clark permission to break off all armistice talks if the terms were rejected. The UNC dropped its demand that all North Korean non-repatriates be released upon the signing of the armistice, and accepted the principle that decisions arising from the NNRC would be based on a simple majority vote. POWs who had refused repatriation could now be screened by the other side for a period of ninety days. Over the next few days America's major allies publicly supported the UNC terms. However, they were still not prepared to support Washington's plan to escalate the war if the communist side did not accept UNC terms.

To ensure that the communist side understood the seriousness of the proposals, four days before they were introduced Secretary Dulles told Prime Minister Nehru in New Delhi that if the armistice negotiations broke down, the United States would likely increase the military pressure on the communists, and that this might very well extend the area of the conflict. Dulles told this to Nehru on the assumption that the message would be passed to the Chinese communists. On 28 May the American Ambassador in Moscow, Charles Bohlen, told Soviet Foreign Minister Vyacheslav Molotov in diplomatic language that the United States took the latest UNC proposals very seriously and that a failure of the talks would lead to a situation which the American government wanted to avoid.

It is doubtful that America's nuclear threats had a significant impact on the communist negotiators. The communist side had already made significant concessions before the final UNC position was tabled on 25 May. The Soviet officials in the Kremlin remained committed to an armistice and the Chinese were also planning on redirecting resources which had gone into the war to local production. More significant than atomic threats was the launching of China's first Five Year Plan in 1953 and the consequent economic requirement to divert resources away from military spending and towards domestic reconstruction needs. The North Korean economic situation was also in dire straits. Food shortages and inflation had seriously weakened the ability of the people to meet basic needs and these problems were exacerbated when the US Air Force accelerated its bombing attacks in 1953 on dams and railways in an effort to put pressure on the communists and to destroy the northern food supply and transportation networks.

The communist side accepted the UNC position on 4 June and by mid-June agreement on the details of the armistice agreement was complete. Only the participants' signatures remained, but on 17 June President Rhee made an effort to sabotage the negotiations by arranging, without UNC knowledge, the release of those North Korean POWs who were unwilling to be repatriated. Although the South Korean Army remained under the command of the UNC, South Korean troops obeyed a secret Presidential directive to release the prisoners. More than 24,000 escaped. The communists promptly broke off the talks and launched a limited offensive against ROK military positions on 24 June. Having successfully made the point that any unilateral ROK offensive would cost the South Koreans dearly, the communist and UN sides signed the armistice agreement on 27 July 1953. In order to get the ROK to acquiesce to the armistice agreement, the United States agreed to negotiate a Mutual Defense Treaty. However, the South Korean government refused to be a party to the armistice, and it has never signed the document, a fact which has added to the uncertainty and tensions on the Korean peninsula since 1953.

On the day the armistice was signed the United States and fifteen of its allies who had sent troops to Korea signed a Joint Policy Statement, sometimes referred to as the Greater Sanctions Statement, which warned the PRC and North Koreans that if the communist side re-initiated armed conflict on the peninsula 'such a breach of the armistice would be so grave that, in all probability, it would not be possible to confine the hostilities within the frontiers of Korea' (US Department of State, 1984: 1174). Some allies, including Canada, Britain and New Zealand, were concerned with the provocative nature of the statement, and it was not released until a few weeks after the armistice, as part of the last UNC report to the United Nations.

In August the transfer of POWs began in an exercise known as 'Operation Big Switch' (plate 8). Some 76,000 POWs were returned to the Chinese and North Koreans and another 13,000 were repatriated to the UN side through the demilitarized zone. This left more than 22,000 communist non-repatriates and 359 UN non-repatriates who were turned over to the Neutral Nations Repatriation Commission at the end of September. Of these, only about 600 of the former and ten of the latter decided to return home. At the end of January 1954 the POWs who refused to go home were released and on 1 February 1954 the NNRC voted to end its activities.

Both sides paid a high human price for dragging out the armistice. It has been estimated that about 45 percent of the deaths and battle wounds during the war occurred after the armistice negotiations began. On the UNC side alone, 125,000 soldiers were killed or wounded over the fifteen-month period that the two sides remained deadlocked over the POW issue. Over the same period the US Eighth Army conservatively estimated that almost 300,000 men from the communist side had been killed, wounded or captured.

THE GUERRILLA WAR, 1951–54

One aspect of the war which has not been given much attention is the guerrilla conflict after 1951. American soldiers helped to train South Korean guerrillas to infiltrate into the north. Since the UN controlled the seas around Korea, the southern guerrillas often used the many islands up and down the Korean peninsula as bases. On the outskirts of Pusan, the United States established an air base from which operational units were parachuted into North Korea. On occasion it would also air-drop American military personnel or a CIA agent into the north. A sabotage training school, headed by an ex-British Special Air Services (SAS) officer, was also established near Pusan. Its cover was an ROK Ministry of Fisheries research facility and the United States misleadingly claimed that the school was the Eighth Army Liaison Office for Oceanic Research.

In early 1952 the US Officer in Charge of the Guerrilla Division for the Far Eastern Command Liaison Detachment in Korea wrote a directive which became the basis for partisan efforts thereafter [*Doc. 28*]. From bases located throughout the peninsula, southern partisan guerrillas fought northern troops, conducted raids and assassinations, and destroyed police pillboxes, bridges and ammunition dumps. Children were even recruited as spies, posing as refugees to carry out intelligence-gathering work. Some unsuccessful efforts were made to develop an anti-communist partisan movement in North Korea.

The communists also were active in the guerrilla partisan war. As the northern army retreated from South Korea in 1950 and 1951, guerrillas remained behind to wage war against the UN and Korean forces. To deal with this threat to internal security, between 1951 and 1954 numerous anti-guerrilla operations were carried out by the South Korean military and police forces. These operations, variously called 'Ratkiller', 'Ferret', 'Mongoose' and 'Trample', provide an indication of the grisly nature of the guerrilla conflict. Casualties were often greater than the number of suspected partisans; American officials believed that many unfortunate civilians were caught in the crossfire, while some guerrillas escaped. Between 1951 and early 1952 the South Koreans claimed to have killed or injured some 20,000 partisans in the south. The guerrilla war carried on past the 1953 armistice agreement. As late as the spring of 1954 there were an estimated 700 'bandits' operating in the south, but by August 1954 only a handful of 'bandit' groups were left and these were conducting raids mainly for their own survival. This gruesome partisan campaign, conducted on both sides of the parallel, was an integral part of the Korean War, and one which did not end until over a year after the signing of the armistice.

CHAPTER SIX

THE GLOBAL IMPACT OF THE KOREAN WAR

IMPLEMENTING NSC 68: AMERICAN AND EUROPEAN PERSPECTIVES ON REARMAMENT

The Korean War consolidated the existing 'East–West' alliance structure which had taken shape during the momentous years from 1945 to 1950. In Europe and North America, politicians used the Korean War to implement their global rearmament policies and to mobilize the North Atlantic Treaty Organization. In this sense, the Korean conflict was an important psychological turning point in the Cold War, as Western societies were pressured to move ahead with costly militarization projects. The most sustained momentum for global rearmament came from American policymakers. In the context of the wartime emergency, the United States expanded its hegemony to all corners of the globe. Military and civilian planners now looked at the Cold War even more simplistically as an enduring confrontation between monolithic Soviet-led totalitarian societies and democratic polities associated with the Western Alliance.

To combat the Soviet system the United States created a form of a garrison state of its own, as its military spending more than quadrupled between 1950 and 1953. Before the outbreak of the war American officials anticipated annual military costs at about $13 billion, but in September 1950 the Joint Chiefs of Staff estimated that expenditures for military programs outlined in NSC 68 would total $287 billion over a five-year period – not far off from the figure of about $220 billion which was appropriated for American defence expenditures between 1951 and 1955.

Within a year of the start of the international conflict in Korea, the number of people serving in America's armed forces more than doubled to over 3.2 million; army divisions went from ten to eighteen; the Air Force went from forty-two to seventy-two wing groups; and the Navy expanded its number of ships from 600 to over 1,000. The pace of military build-up at this point exceeded that set by America when it first entered the Second World War. The bureaucracy of the Central Intelligence Agency (CIA) also mushroomed. In 1949 the CIA's Office of Policy Coordination had 302 personnel in its offices. By 1952 it had about 6,000. CIA stations in foreign countries increased from seven in 1951 to forty-seven in early 1953 (Hogan, 1998; Leffler, 1992).

Although the rearmament program substantially increased the ability of the United States to project its military power overseas, it was also designed to mobilize the collective strength of the NATO alliance, the centre of the containment and deterrence policy adopted by Western nations. Prior to the conflict, prominent US officials like Dean Rusk were concerned about neutralist public opinion in West European countries. Many Europeans had been critical of compulsory military service and rearmament; in mid-March 1950 Rusk confided to Canada's Ambassador in Washington that this 'defeatist' public sentiment might result in a repudiation of European commitments to NATO. Even allies who were supportive of the United States were wary about further defence expenditures. When Acheson told the British Foreign Secretary in May 1950 of the need to rearm in light of Soviet military power, Ernest Bevin, though sympathetic to Acheson's pleas, responded by saying that Britain was already spending as much as it could on defence. The most he could consider was a small increase of 5 to 10 percent in the defence budget.

Many West Germans also resisted rearmament. In December 1949, when Konrad Adenauer, Chancellor of the Federal Republic of Germany, advocated the creation of a West German military force, almost two-thirds of those living in the US zone opposed it. At the start of the war in Korea, West Germany still had Western occupation forces on its territory. Just over a year old, the Federal Republic lacked full sovereignty and had no army or foreign ministry of its own. For Secretary of State Dean Acheson, this state of affairs needed to be remedied, and plans were soon drawn up to enable the Germans to make a military contribution to a European military force which would also include Canadian and American contingents. Acheson believed that elites should shape public opinion rather than follow it. As he once remarked, 'if you truly had a democracy, and did what the people wanted, you'd go wrong every time' (Hunt, 1987: 180).

French, Dutch and other continental European officials were wary about US plans to create separate German armed forces. France's Defence Minister, Jules Moch, for example, had lost his son to the terror tactics of the Gestapo, and five other members of his family had been murdered in German concentration camps. It was only in December 1950, in the context of fears that the conflict in Korea might turn into a wider war, possibly engulfing Europe, that NATO leaders formally agreed to a measure of German rearmament. Germany would not have a national army or general staff but German regimental units would eventually be integrated into a NATO force or a European army controlled by European institutions. The latter option soon led to an allied project to send German troops to a new multilateral organization called the European Defence Community. At the December talks the allies also approved a more aggressive 'forward' strategy for NATO troops, who would now defend Europe as far east of the Rhine as possible.

The United States still faced significant obstacles to its rearmament plans. The war became unpopular after China's intervention, and significant opposition in Congress to an internationalist foreign policy hung like a sword of Damocles over the administration's plans. In early January 1951, just days after communist forces had taken Seoul for the second time, 'Nationalist' Republican Senator Kenneth Wherry of Nebraska introduced a resolution in the Senate which stated that that body would not support the stationing of US troops in Europe under NATO until Congress had established a policy governing the conditions under which troops would be sent. Public opinion polls showed that Americans favoured sending troops to Europe by a two-to-one margin, but they also demonstrated – by similar margins – that the public wanted Congress to play an important role in formulating those policies. After several months of debate, the Senate passed an amended resolution which permitted four US divisions to go to Europe but which precluded the sending of additional troops without Congressional approval. The 'great debate' of 1951 was thus settled largely in favour of the Democrats' internationalist policies. Even so, the administration remained on the defensive until the end of its term.

The integration of West German forces into a European Defence Community remained a fundamental Cold War objective for America over the next three years. In May 1952, the United States, France, and Britain agreed to end their joint control over the Federal Republic and to abolish the Allied High Commission, the institution which had been responsible for overseeing occupation policy. West German sovereignty was restored, though the three powers could still intervene in a time of emergency if internal or external forces threatened the West German state. The Federal Republic was also not permitted unilaterally to negotiate a peace treaty with the Soviet Union, eject Western military forces, or alter its boundaries.

These stipulations were necessary to obtain European consent to German rearmament, but they also represented the limits of German sovereignty in an age of American hegemony. Despite the effort put into the project, the European Defence Community never came to fruition. In 1954 it was defeated in the French parliament. A new plan, sponsored by British Foreign Minister Anthony Eden, emerged, and under this new scheme West Germany was formally integrated into the NATO alliance in 1955. By the middle of the decade, events set in motion by NSC 68 and the Korean War had resulted in a fundamental reorientation of NATO and European security towards a full acceptance of West Germany into the international Cold War balance of power.

GUNS AGAINST BUTTER

The costs associated with rearmament in Western Europe accelerated the decline of traditional European great powers such as Britain and France. By 1952, the Conservative government of Winston Churchill attempted to deal with Britain's decline by emphasizing the importance of the Anglo-American alliance and US aid, and by offering to negotiate a limited *détente* and *modus vivendi* with the Soviet Union. To pay for rearmament the British government also cut back significantly on social spending. Housing and the health services suffered the most. In the early 1950s the French government also faced economic hardships, including foreign exchange shortages and inflation. Officials protested the pace of rearmament and adopted exchange quotas which weakened the prospects for the emergence of a strong liberal trade regime in Europe. Maintaining an empire was now a costly proposition.

Balance of payments problems were not new to either Britain or France, and the United States significantly expanded its military assistance to help the Europeans pay for their expensive military build-up. But the wartime economy created more bottlenecks and forced European powers to allocate scarce resources – especially steel and labour – to military goods instead of to their export industries. This made their balance of payments problems worse and sharpened their sense of vulnerability to America.

Britain and France continued to search for ways to retain their great power status in the context of an economic slide exacerbated by costs associated with rearmament and the Korean War. In 1953 and early 1954 the French sought a way out of their war in Indochina, and joined the British in attempting to work out a modest *détente* with the Soviets. Their diplomacy had some limited success, and contributed to the ability of the great powers to negotiate an agreement to end the French Indochinese War in 1954 and a peace treaty with Austria in 1955.

In the United States, domestic interest groups and politicians negotiated an implicit tradeoff which favoured building up the military over increased government spending on social programs. Republican interests in Congress were successful in blocking President Truman's 1948 'Fair Deal' program which had advocated national medical insurance, increased public housing, rent controls and additional federal support for education. Because of the administration's need for Republican votes on foreign policy issues associated with rearmament, Truman backed down from his earlier promises to implement these social welfare programs. In August 1950, as part of the effort to support increased defence spending, the Senate asked the Bureau of the Budget to cut back programs unrelated to national defence by $550 million. As political scientist Benjamin Fordham has pointed out, 'virtually all of the policy initiatives of the Fair Deal disappeared after the beginning of the Korean War and were not revived again during the Truman administration' (Fordham, 1998: 126).

JAPANESE REARMAMENT

America's postwar hegemony was global in reach. When George Kennan formulated his postwar concept of containment, he wrote that it was vital that the industrial centres of world power not be allowed to fall under the influence of the Soviet bloc. Three of these centres lay in the West – in America, Britain, and Germany. The fourth was Japan. At the time of the outbreak of the war in Korea, Japan, like Germany, was an occupied state. Following Kennan's dictum, both countries' power potentials were deemed essential to the longer-term defence and economic strength of the Western Alliance. 'If the Soviet Union were able to add to itself the industrial capacity and trained manpower of Western Germany and Japan', State Department official John Foster Dulles contended in 1950, 'the world balance of power would be profoundly altered' (Leffler, 1992: 393). The United States did not tolerate neutralism in either of these countries' diplomacy; Germany and Japan had to be integrated into the alliance or the entire global strategy of containment might fail.

The crucial Japanese figure in this drama was Prime Minister Yoshida Shigeru, an influential conservative who, like Adenauer, favoured a pro-US stance in the Cold War. For domestic political reasons, the Japanese Prime Minister was wary about making concessions to the far right and moving too energetically on Japanese rearmament. After the North Korean attack, Yoshida came under heavy criticism by the socialist opposition in the Japanese Diet for allowing the United States to wage its war from American bases in Japan. When Chinese troops entered the fighting in the fall of 1950, there were calls for Japan to embrace neutralism and to distance itself from the United States. Indeed, Stalin may have had an eye on neutralist opinion in Japan when he encouraged Mao to send his volunteers into the conflict. In these circumstances, US policymakers realized that Japan's formal lack of sovereignty was being used as ammunition against the pro-American Yoshida conservatives; they now approached discussions for a peace treaty and bilateral security guarantee with a determination to complete them successfully and rapidly. The Korean War accelerated the process of negotiating a peace treaty with the Japanese.

The treaty of peace, signed in San Francisco in the fall of 1951, was relatively non-punitive and ceded to Japan sovereignty over its domestic affairs. The United States refused to invite the PRC to the proceedings; instead, it organized a separate peace treaty between Japan and Taiwan which was signed in 1952. The Soviet Union, which attended the peace conference, refused to sign the final agreement. Isolated from the treaty process, Chinese and Soviet officials emphasized in their public speeches Japan's subordinate and dependent position within the American alliance system. Communist propaganda thus attempted to drive a wedge between the two allies.

The US–Japan security treaty, which was also signed in San Francisco, restricted Japanese sovereignty in defence matters and fixed an American hegemonic presence around the islands which has lasted until today. The 1951 security treaty permitted America to station its land, sea and air forces throughout Japan, gave the United States the right to put down domestic uprisings in Japan if requested by the Japanese government, and forbade Japan from granting military base rights to any third power without the formal consent of the American government. Okinawa, which had been incorporated into the Japanese empire after the 1870s and then captured by American forces during the Pacific War, retained a semi-colonial status under US control. It was not placed under Japanese sovereignty until 1972. Okinawa today remains a major US base in the Pacific.

In the early 1950s, some Japanese conservatives felt that without a military force of its own, Japan was no better than an American protectorate. They argued that Germany was in a stronger position *vis-à-vis* US power and that Japan should have a military force of its own. In 1953 John Foster Dulles, now Secretary of State, agreed, and campaigned for a Japanese military contribution of some 350,000 troops. But article nine of the 1947 Japanese constitution required Japan to renounce war and the threat or use of force as a sovereign right, and Yoshida was unwilling to press for constitutional revision of this clause. In the immediate aftermath of the Korean War, in late 1953, the United States succeeded in getting the Japanese government to create a 'self defense force' of 180,000 troops, in return for continued US military aid.

The Korean War had an enduring impact on Japan, not only because it helped to forge the character of the postwar US–Japan security framework, but also because of its effects on the Japanese economy. Before 1950 the Japanese experienced sharp and persistent balance of payments deficits with the United States. The Japanese economy did not fully recover until the mid-1950s, but a major impetus for the growth was American procurement contracts going to Japanese businesses to produce war-related goods destined for Korea. The Toyota motor company is a case in point. Before the war its sales were declining and it lacked funds to purchase needed technology. In June 1950, the month of the attack, the company sold only 300 trucks. In July, the Americans put in an order for 1,000 trucks and within a year 5,000 were sold. Soon thereafter the company issued its first postwar dividend (Schaller, 1997).

Industries specializing in textiles, construction, motor vehicles, communications and chemicals benefitted the most from US procurement policies. In the late 1950s Japan's industrial production exceeded pre-war levels for the first time. By 1954 the Japanese defence industry earned the country $3 billion worth of goods. If Secretary of State Dean Acheson declared that the Korean War saved America, Prime Minister Yoshida is said to have greeted the war with the remark 'It's the Grace of Heaven' (Schaller, 1997: 49).

THE ROK ARMED FORCES, 1951–53

The Korean War was a watershed event for the South Korean armed forces. It initiated a massive expansion in the Korean Army, a significant strengthening of the Air Force, and inaugurated the formal emergence of the ROK Navy from what had been a coast-guard service. Mainly because of financial and technological constraints, the ROK was unable to provide for its own defence. Korea remained heavily dependent on American aid and assistance, and its force levels were largely a function of decisions taken in Washington. Syngman Rhee realized this and kept constant pressure on American officials to increase the size of his military. By mid-1951 the ROK Army comprised almost 275,000 men, or about 50 percent of total UNC forces then in Korea.

Although American policymakers were careful not to encourage the ROK to launch a unilateral offensive against the communists, by late 1951 they were anxious to expand the size of the Korean armed forces even further. Increasing the number of ROK troops was seen as the most plausible solution to dilemmas associated with high strategy, maintaining armed pressure on the communists, troop morale, and cost. President Truman, concerned about public criticism at home, supported this viewpoint. He felt that the United States should strengthen its global position, and not permit developments on the Korean peninsula to distract the United States from its overall containment stance. 'We should be ... devoting all our attention to the world situation', the President remarked in December 1951. 'That is why [I am] worried about Korea. We must not waste our position there or we may then find this country going isolationist' (US Department of State, 1983: 1295).

A National Security Council document, NSC 118/2, produced in late 1951, recommended that the United States continue to pursue a political settlement to the conflict which would provide for the gradual withdrawal of non-Korean soldiers. South Korean military strength would be rebuilt to the point where the ROK could contain or throw back a renewed attack by DPRK forces. The policy statement called for an intensification of efforts to train, equip and organize the armed forces of the ROK.

From the US point of view, Korean troops were less expensive than American ones. Given America's limited Cold War resources, Korean soldiers would also bolster America's global containment position. A survey completed in early 1953 indicated that a monthly wage for an ROK corporal was about $8 US. It cost fifteen times more to equip and send an American into battle than a Korean. If indirect benefits going to US soldiers – disability insurance, pensions, and education – were taken into account, the difference was much larger; the equivalent monthly cost for an American corporal would then amount to about $1,560 US. Although this ratio declined somewhat after 1953 because of pay increases for the poorly paid ROK recruits, significant savings were accrued by the United States in getting ROK soldiers to take up more of the regional containment burden in Northeast Asia. By the end of the war, American military aid to the ROK amounted to more than $1.5 billion annually.

As a result of continued expansion, in late July 1953 when the armistice was signed, ROK ground forces numbered almost 600,000 troops – about 63 percent of total UNC troops – while US troop strength increased to just over 300,000 men, which represented almost 33 percent of UNC forces in the ROK. In the late 1950s America introduced nuclear weapons into South Korea and withdrew many of its troops. Today, about 37,000 American soldiers are stationed in the ROK.

Using local troops to contribute to the global policy of containment was a fundamental part of American strategy in the Cold War. Indeed, the relative success of America's military strategy in Korea after 1953 led soldiers and civilian officials alike to view Korea as a kind of model for American containment policies in Asia. This was particularly true for Vietnam. But American efforts to use indigenous military forces in the war in Vietnam were much less successful, and the failure to build up local power in the former French colony eventually led the United States to take a direct military role in defeating the Vietnamese communists.

THE SINO-SOVIET ALLIANCE AND SINO-AMERICAN RELATIONS

The Korean War established the context in which the Soviet Union and China strengthened and expanded their mutual cooperation. After the Chinese intervention in late 1950, Soviet air force personnel, secretly flying MiGs from Chinese bases in Manchuria and wearing Chinese-style uniforms, helped provide cover for Chinese troops crossing the Yalu river. American leaders did not publicize this because they feared it might lead to public pressures to expand the war with the Soviet Union. Moscow continued to provide additional military supplies and advisers to China, and these helped to underpin the successes the Chinese armies had against the US and UN forces. Stalin promised to supply arms for ten Chinese divisions in 1951 and materiel for twenty divisions of troops in subsequent years. The material cost was high, and the Soviet Union experienced economic difficulties at home as a result of the cost of its rearmament effort, a precedent for its rearmament experience during the 1980s. But this aid tied down Western resources, demonstrated to the world the effectiveness of communist armies, and fomented tensions in American relations with its allies over policy towards China, all at minuscule manpower cost to the Soviet Union.

Fearful that the war might lead to an invasion of China, Chinese officials continued to view the Sino-Soviet alliance as a deterrent to the expansion of the conflict. Official Chinese propaganda downplayed tensions in the Sino-Soviet relationship and exaggerated the historical friendship between the Chinese and Russian peoples. On the first anniversary of the signing of the 1950 Sino-Soviet Treaty, Mao Zedong wrote to Stalin that the alliance had helped to reconstruct China, to defend its borders against aggression, and to promote peace and security in Asia and the world. A year later Zhou Enlai spoke of the foresight of the treaty partners in predicting the 'aggressive plans of American imperialism and its satellites' and in articulating the importance of coming to each other's aid in the event Japan or any state allied to it attacked China or the Soviet Union [*Doc. 29*].

Concern about the Japanese peace treaty, the Japanese-American alliance and the security treaty led the Soviets and Chinese to conclude an agreement which allowed Soviet troops to remain at the jointly-used naval base at Port Arthur (map 2) until the two allies entered into a formal treaty of peace with Japan. The Korean War also provided the context for the communist allies to extend mutual cooperation in the field of atomic energy: in 1955 the Chinese and Soviets signed a joint deal to mine uranium in China, and in 1956 the Soviets, Chinese, North Koreans, Mongolian and Eastern bloc countries entered into a formal agreement to create a Joint Institute for Nuclear Research in the Soviet Union.

The Korean War helped to strengthen the Sino-Soviet alliance in the short term, but tensions between two states did emerge during the conflict. These tensions contributed to the 'split' in the relationship which occurred in the late 1950s and early 1960s. Despite the underlying sense of accord in the partnership in the early 1950s, differences existed over the degree to which the Soviet Union was willing to share its nuclear secrets, over the implementation of the Soviet Union's aid program, and over Soviet military assistance. The Chinese had dedicated over two million personnel to the Korean War effort and these forces consumed huge amounts of resources, much of which could have been used for China's reconstruction effort. Discontented Chinese leaders felt that the Soviets should have provided more in the way of aid to the PRC. Although these disputes were kept well hidden from public view for most of the 1950s, by the mid-1960s the two former allies had become implacable rivals.

American diplomacy towards China hardened significantly as a result of the Korean conflict. During the war and in its aftermath the United States led an international effort to isolate the PRC, to embargo strategic materials going to communist China, and to prevent the PRC from gaining a seat in the United Nations. When John Foster Dulles met Zhou Enlai at the Geneva Conference in 1954, he refused to shake the Chinese diplomat's hand. In 1958 the United States began to station atomic weapons in Korea as part of its effort to contain the Sino-Soviet alliance. Although the UNC complained about communist violations of the armistice, the movement of these weapons into Korea broke article 13(d) of the agreement, which prohibited the introduction of reinforcing weapons and ammunition.

THE KOREAN WAR AND THE DEVELOPING WORLD

America's global containment policies which emerged from the Korean War had a dual impact on the developing world: on the one hand, they fostered new anti-communist military alliances; on the other, they accelerated trends towards 'neutralism' or non-alignment in the international system.

In the wake of the North Korean attack, Harry Truman ordered increased military and economic aid to developing countries around the Sino-Soviet periphery, including the Philippines, Vietnam, Pakistan, Iran, and Yugoslavia. Although the US administration had committed itself to supporting the French anti-communist presence in Vietnam before the outbreak of the war, it was in the aftermath of that conflict that the first American military advisers were sent into Vietnam.

Other parts of the developing world were formally integrated into existing or newly established multilateral and bilateral defence alliances. In July 1951 Dean Acheson supported the entry of Greece and Turkey into NATO and tried to get Egypt to agree to participate in a Middle East Command, a military alliance to be linked to NATO. In Asia, the United States signed separate mutual defence treaties with the Philippines (1951), Korea (1953), Taiwan (1954) and Pakistan (1954). In 1954 it created the Southeast Asian Treaty Organization (SEATO) to defend Indochina. By the middle of the decade the United States had 450 military bases in thirty-six countries located across Europe, North Africa, the Middle East, and Asia.

The Korean War also had an important impact on world leaders who were wary of Cold War rhetoric and diplomacy; it brought together many countries which adopted a neutralist stance between the two superpowers. The most prominent of these nations were India, Indonesia, and Egypt. Anita Inder Singh (1993) and Robert McMahon (1994), leading scholars on US–South Asia relations, have argued that Korea was a watershed for US ties with India and Pakistan. In the eyes of high-ranking US officials, Indian neutralism enhanced Pakistan's importance as a Cold War partner in South Asia.

Indian Prime Minister Jawaharlal Nehru criticized the North Korean invasion, calling it an act of aggression, but he refused to support US policy towards Taiwan and Indochina, and attempted to maintain Indian neutrality throughout the war. India had recognized the People's Republic of China in late 1949 and Nehru hoped the PRC could be seated in the UN. The war provided India with opportunities to enhance its non-aligned stance: it objected to the crossing of the 38th parallel in October 1950, got actively involved in negotiations for a Korean armistice, and promoted better relations with other neutralist states in Asia and Africa [*Doc. 30*]. In this way, the Korean War provided the context in which the non-aligned movement gained momentum in the 1950s.

Even so, the impact of the war should not be exaggerated. Nehru had articulated the roots of his non-aligned ideology in the early Cold War, before the Korean conflict. In December 1947, Nehru proclaimed: 'we will not attach ourselves to any particular group. ... We intend [to] co-operat[e] with the United States of America. We intend [to] co-operat[e] fully with the Soviet Union' (Government of India, 1961: 24, 28). The heightened tensions surrounding the fighting in Korea brought out themes in his philosophy which American policymakers now rejected with even greater force. As in other areas of the superpower rivalry, the war highlighted, intensified, and institutionalized, trends which were in the early stages of formation. Cold War policies underwent a deepening process during the conflict which separated their early incubation and developmental stages from their more full-blown global dynamics after 1950.

THE POLITICAL IMPACT OF THE WAR ON THE TWO KOREAS

The two Korean rulers, Syngman Rhee and Kim Il Sung, entrenched their political power during the war. In South Korea, Rhee faced down his political opposition in the spring of 1952 by declaring martial law, accusing his opponents of being communists, arresting opposition assemblymen, and using strong-arm tactics. Fearing that he could not secure enough votes in the National Assembly in upcoming Presidential elections, he ordered the Assembly to amend the constitution so that the President could be elected by the people instead of its members. Many opposition members resisted this call and a major constitutional crisis arose.

During the emergency American State and Defense Department officials considered the possibility of deposing the Korean President and setting up an interim UN government led by pro-Western Korean military officials until a modicum of political stability was re-established.

In late June, US and British officials met in Washington to discuss the Korean political situation. When British Minister of State Selwyn Lloyd inquired if the United States might overthrow Rhee, John Allison, Assistant

Secretary of State, and later Ambassador to Japan, replied that 'the situation would have to be serious' before such action were taken since there was not another Korean leader with sufficient power to run the country. He noted that 'it might be preferable to find ways of getting rid of Syngman Rhee's cronies' [Doc. 31]. In Seoul, US chargé d'affaires E. Allan Lightner campaigned for a coup against Rhee but none came, and a political compromise reached between Rhee and the National Assembly resulted in a victory for the President who was soon elected for another term.

Rhee continued to serve as President until 1960, when, in the aftermath of a rigged Presidential election, US disillusionment with the authoritarian leader hit a low point; his government collapsed in the face of nationwide student demonstrations and American diplomatic pressure to hold new elections.

In the DPRK, Kim Il Sung used the wartime emergency to consolidate his hold on power and to cultivate his 'mass line' policies with the North Korean people. In December 1950, in the wake of the northern regime's failure to unify the country, Kim openly criticized many of his top officials for mismanaging the war. Mu Chong, the Korean military commander who had served with Mao in the Long March, was expelled from the party on the grounds that he had caused the fall of Pyongyang. Mu fled the country and returned to China an exile, reportedly dying in 1951.

In line with Kim's strategy of building up his local power base, the number of party members increased rapidly after 1953. By 1956 the party claimed to have a membership of 12 percent of the entire population, the highest portion in the communist world. Half these members were recruited after July 1953.

The figure who had the most to lose from the failure to unify the country was Pak Hon Yong, the Vice-Premier and Foreign Minister of the Kim regime and former leader of the southern Communist Party. Pak was a well-known 'domestic' communist who felt Kim was too subordinate to the Soviets and lacked the necessary legitimacy to lead the Korean communist movement. Pak's supporters apparently planned a coup against the regime in 1952, but it was discovered and the plotters executed. Kim blamed Pak for the failure to reunify the country in 1950, declared Pak a traitor, and had him executed in December 1955. The charges against Pak were summarized in a speech by Kim Il Sung in February 1953, when he called Pak 'a spy on the payroll of the American scoundrels' [Doc. 32]. Pak was replaced as Foreign Minister by Nam Il, a Soviet Korean who survived the purges of the 1950s.

By the end of the Korean conflict Kim had consolidated his hold on power and he was well on his way to establishing his 'leadership' following. He died in 1994, the world's longest-lived Stalinist, revered to the last as the country's 'Great Leader'. His official biographer Baik Bong described Kim as a 'peerless patriot', an 'ever-victorious, iron-willed brilliant commander', a depiction which appears to be genuinely believed by the people in North Korea today, who view the senior Kim as a true patriot and leader of their country (Baik, 1970: 1).

CHAPTER SEVEN

THE GENEVA CONFERENCE, 1954

PRELUDE: THE US–ROK MUTUAL DEFENSE TREATY

Official South Korean opposition to the armistice in the spring of 1953 was designed in part to put pressure on the United States to negotiate a mutual security pact. President Rhee felt that the failure to negotiate such a treaty before 1950 had encouraged the communist attack.

The main stumbling block to a treaty from the American perspective was that President Rhee wanted to use the pact to support his own unification policies: if South Korean troops unilaterally attacked the north, a formal military pact might commit the United States to come to the aid of the ROK and to unify the peninsula in a conflict begun by the south. But the Americans also realized that if the terms of the treaty were carefully laid out, they might be able to inhibit Rhee from initiating a unilateral military offensive. At the end of May 1953, just days after delivering the final negotiating position to the communists, the Eisenhower administration authorized UN Commander Mark Clark and US Ambassador to Korea, Ellis Briggs, to begin negotiations with the Koreans for a mutual defence treaty. The United States made it clear that discussions would only occur if the ROK agreed to refrain from attacking the armistice and to allow the American-led UNC to retain operational control of ROK forces.

The treaty was negotiated in Seoul in July and August 1953 and signed in Washington on 1 October 1953. Article 3 stipulated that an attack on either of the parties in the Pacific or on territories under their respective administrative control would be a threat to both: each party would act to meet the common threat in accordance with its constitutional processes. Under Article 4, the ROK permitted the United States to negotiate land, air and sea bases on South Korean territory. The treaty was similar to other Mutual Defense Treaties that the United States signed with Pacific powers, including the Philippines, Taiwan, and Australia and New Zealand.

On 26 January 1954 the US Senate ratified the treaty, but added an additional written understanding which stated that the United States had no obligation to come to the aid of the ROK unless it was subject to an external armed attack. The Senate was careful not to approve a treaty that might be construed by President Rhee as giving a signal for a unilateral South Korean offensive against the north. South Korea agreed to this additional understanding and ratified the treaty on 29 January 1954. One week later President Eisenhower confirmed it as well. The formal exchange of the ratifications of the treaty was scheduled for 18 March 1954. The treaty would come into effect only after this exchange was completed.

THE ROAD TO GENEVA

Not long after Eisenhower signed the treaty, representatives of the United States, Britain, France, and the Soviet Union, meeting in Berlin, agreed to convene an international conference on Korean political issues. Article IV of the armistice agreement had called for the holding of such a conference which would have as one of its goals the peaceful settlement of the Korean question. The armistice agreement had stipulated that such a conference would be held within three months of the signing of the document. That deadline had passed, but the great powers had now come to an agreement, not only for a conference on Korea but also for one to discuss the deteriorating military and political situation which the French faced in their colony of Vietnam. Korea would thus be the first of two consecutive conferences which would attempt to negotiate permanent settlements for the two East Asian conflicts.

The South Korean government was alarmed by the Berlin agreement, which it felt had been made behind its back without proper consultation. From President Rhee's point of view, the proposed conference raised many vexing questions: would Rhee continue as President of a unified Korea if some agreement were worked out? On whose terms would Korea be unified? How would elections be carried out? Would the South Korean government be forced to compromise its constitution? Did South Korea have the right to veto any great power agreement?

At first the President refused to attend the conference. Then, on 11 March 1954, he wrote to President Eisenhower suggesting that Korea would attend the conference only if the United States secretly agreed to back an ROK military offensive against the north. To get the ROK President to change his mind the Americans announced on 16 March that it was necessary to postpone the exchange of ratifications of the Mutual Defense Treaty. This was a major blow to Rhee's diplomatic agenda. A few days later Eisenhower reminded Rhee that the UNC would not permit the South Korean military to attack the north, and that any effort unilaterally to unify the country would fail. This approach worked, and Rhee soon agreed to hold preparatory discussions with the United States.

In mid-April, Eisenhower sent his carrot: a letter to Rhee saying that

General James Van Fleet, a former Commander of the UNC, would be sent to Seoul to discuss with Rhee and other military officials the size and character of the ROK armed forces. Rhee happily complied, and agreed to send his representatives to Geneva.

EUROPE AND THE COMMONWEALTH APPROACH GENEVA

European and Commonwealth nations approached the conference with somewhat different objectives from those of the United States and ROK. For them, Geneva represented an opportunity to stem international conflict and to establish a *modus vivendi* with the communists in Asia. France viewed the situation in Northeast Asia from the perspective of its colonial position in Vietnam. The French government had about 500,000 of its empire troops engaged in the costly conflict with the communists led by Ho Chi Minh, and officials were looking for ways to extricate France from the war. It was thus important that the Geneva Conference on Korea not exacerbate international tensions which might hurt the chances for a settlement in Southeast Asia.

The British, concerned with their economy at home, wanted to spend less money on defence and hoped to redirect resources into the domestic private economy. The United Kingdom recognized that its power was overextended and Prime Minister Churchill sought improved relations with the Soviet Union in order to free some monies away from military expenditure. A negotiated peace to conflicts in East Asia would help them achieve this goal.

Britain did not support the ROK position on unification; rather, British officials called for new Presidential and legislative elections for the entire country. The UN was not seen as an appropriate institution to oversee these elections since the Korean and Chinese communists could not be expected to allow an institution which had led the war against them to determine the political outcome of a united Korea. National elections would best be supervised by an international commission made up of neutral states. But the British did not want the communists to win elections in Korea so they proposed that elections be held on the basis of proportional representation, a policy which would give the advantage to South Korea in the peninsular struggle since it held about two-thirds of the combined population of the two Koreas.

In the context of the realities of the relationship between the two Koreas in 1954, this 'balanced' approach to unification was unrealistic. Viewed in the framework of the legacies of the 1948–53 era and the heavily militarized peninsula in the mid-1950s this plan was naive, for it could do little to affect the position of the two Korean armies. Were they expected to sit back and passively participate in 'free' elections? If implemented, the plan could have eventually led to another conflict between the two Koreas. Most observers, however, believed that none of the plans suggested at Geneva would obtain communist approval. European and Commonwealth proposals were primarily designed not to unify the two Koreas but as a means of indicating to the other side that they were prepared to accept the *status quo* on the peninsula and to work out a *modus vivendi* with the communists. The British were also very concerned about the impact the conflict in Indochina might have on their own colonial interests in the region. As Foreign Office official John Addis wrote in June 1954, 'if we have in effect sacrificed our poor little Korean baby to attain a settlement in Indo-China, it will have been worthwhile' (Lowe, 1997b: 261). The Canadians and New Zealanders tended to support the British position on unification, though Australia, a more prominent 'Asian' containment partner of the United States, tended to support proposals more overtly favourable to the ROK.

COMMUNIST NEGOTIATING STRATEGY

After Stalin's death, the new Soviet Premier, Georgi Malenkov, and others in leadership positions sought to lessen international tensions. The new Kremlin strategy was later referred to as 'peaceful coexistence', though historian Vojtech Mastny (1996) has argued that Soviet policy in these years was characterized more by retrenchment than *détente* with the West. Still, retrenchment required more peaceful relationships, at least in the short term, with the Western powers.

Soviet rhetoric during 1953–54 continued to emphasize the need for 'peaceful coexistence' between the superpowers. In August 1953 Malenkov reiterated his objectives during a national radio broadcast when he proclaimed: 'we consider there [are] no objective grounds for a collision between the United States and the USSR' (Zubok and Pleshakov 1996: 164). Malenkov had also defended the importance of placing greater emphasis on agricultural and consumer sectors of the Soviet economy while ending the Soviet obsession with military production. On foreign policy issues he pushed for increased flexibility in Soviet policy *vis-à-vis* Austria, and a few years later, under the guidance of Nikita Khrushchev, the Soviets agreed to end their joint occupation of that state and establish a non-threatening neutralized country.

Soviet policies influenced and coincided with those emerging in China and North Korea. Unlike South Korea, the north embraced the Geneva Conference, insisting publicly that the Soviet Union was now consistently taking the lead in searching for negotiated settlements to international and Asian problems. Korean and Chinese propaganda called for peaceful settlements of conflicts in Korea and Vietnam.

This emphasis on negotiated settlements coincided with Chinese and North Korean efforts to rebuild their wartime economies over the course of late 1953 and early 1954. Like China, North Korea was moving forward with its first multi-year economic plan. In early August 1953, just days after signing the armistice agreement, the North Korean Workers' Party retroactively adopted a Six Month Economic Plan (July–December 1953). During the course of this mini-plan, the DPRK signed economic aid agreements with both the Soviet Union and the PRC. In September, Kim Il Sung visited Moscow where he obtained an aid agreement under which the Soviet Union agreed to provide $250 million over the next two years. In November, Kim concluded an agreement in Beijing (plate 4) which provided another $320 million of aid over a four-year period. The Chinese also agreed to forego payment for all aid given to the north between 25 June 1950 and 31 December 1953. Western officials believed that the communist aid programs were coordinated and that they indicated the communist side did not seriously believe that unification would come about soon.

That may have been true, but DPRK officials viewed the aid programs as an integral part of their unification strategy at Geneva. The North Korean people were asked to sacrifice themselves and to attain the economic targets set by the country's new Three Year Plan, introduced in January 1954, so as to build a strong economy which could overwhelm the southern 'puppet' government and guarantee the peaceful unification of the two Koreas. By mobilizing the entire population in this objective, North Korea made substantial economic progress – ahead of the ROK – throughout the 1950s and 1960s.

THE UNITED STATES AND THE GENEVA CONFERENCE

The Americans initially approached the conference with some hope that a deal could be struck with the communists. In 1953 Secretary Dulles believed that the US–ROK Mutual Defense Treaty might be used as a major diplomatic card to get the other side to agree to a neutralized Korea. He and other State Department officials felt that the Chinese might be willing to remove US bases from areas contiguous to the mainland and that they might agree to a neutralized Korea. This hope petered out early in 1954 as the conference approached. Furthermore, as discussions at Geneva progressed over the course of May, US officials became less willing to work out a negotiated settlement for the two Koreas.

Leading into the conference, the United States formulated three related plans for Korean unity. 'Plan A' was the closest to the ROK position. It called for the withdrawal of Chinese troops within a year of accepting the unification proposal, but envisaged that US/UN troops could stay for up to one year after the establishment of a unified Korean government. South

Korea's constitutional authority would simply be extended to cover the entire peninsula: new elections, overseen by the UN, would be held in the north alone, with Rhee remaining President. Although US forces would withdraw from the peninsula after the elections, the US–ROK Mutual Defense Treaty would be extended to cover the newly united peninsula and the United Nations would be responsible for the economic rehabilitation of the country.

'Plan C' went in the other direction, away from the ROK position, and towards the strategies adopted by many of America's Western allies. It called for the creation of a new Korean constitution and government with elections for the entire country. It did not specifically call for the use of the UN to supervise elections and implied that a neutral commission might replace the international agency.

'Plan B', the position the United States wanted to work towards, represented a compromise between the other two. Under this scheme the ROK would retain its constitution in the unification process, but a new national assembly would be elected according to the principle of proportional representation, and voting would also be held for the position of President. The elections in this plan, as in Plan A, would be overseen by the United Nations, and the US–ROK Mutual Defense Treaty would also encompass the new political entity.

In all likelihood, such a plan would elect a national anti-communist government. The Western allies were willing to accept this scheme, but the requirement for elections in the south threatened to weaken the power base of President Rhee, and he refused to agree to it. His real fear was that the bloc of northern voters might align themselves with anti-Rhee supporters in the south to create a coalition in the National Assembly which would change the constitution and overthrow his Presidency.

The key stipulation in all US plans for unifying the two Koreas was that the constitution of the ROK would remain intact, acting as the political umbrella which would absorb the two Koreas. The American bargaining strategy was to begin the conference with a bid representing Plan A and then to get both the ROK and the other allies to agree to the essentials of Plan B. Plan C would come into play only if the communist side showed serious signs of wanting to negotiate an independent and free Korea on terms acceptable to the West.

THE GENEVA CONFERENCE ON KOREA

The Conference formally got underway on 26 April 1954. The next day, South Korean Foreign Minister Pyun Yong-T'ae reiterated the ROK's long-held view that unification of the peninsula required complete withdrawal of the Chinese communists from Korea. Free elections, held only in the north and under UN supervision, would result in the election of representatives to the existing (ROK) National Assembly. He also told his audience that UN troops would not leave Korea until their original 'police action' was completed.

Nam Il, the KPA general who had affixed his name to the armistice agreement the previous July, followed Pyun. On the surface, he appeared more willing to engage in genuine negotiations. His proposals required all foreign troops to withdraw from the two Koreas within six months, national elections for a new National Assembly, and the formation of a new national state. In the international propaganda war, it thus appeared that North Korea was willing to accept national elections leading to the establishment of a new Korean government. If its proposals were implemented, however, the DPRK would probably have tried to limit the participation in national elections only to those groups which it felt were qualified as 'democratic'.

Nam's presentation put the allied side on the defensive, but a momentous incident – the surrender, on 7 May, of the French stronghold in Dien Bien Phu in Vietnam to the Vietnamese communists – brought the United States a step closer to the ROK position, less willing to pressure the ROK to alter its position. The United States henceforth felt that concessions on Korea would encourage its allies and the communists to believe that a negotiated settlement might be possible for Vietnam as well – something the United States wanted to avoid since its own containment policy for Southeast Asia was premised on the notion that Vietnamese communism should be defeated militarily by a combination of Vietnamese and French imperial troops, and allied help.

In late March, while the fortifications were under siege, Secretary Dulles had publicly outlined a plan, which he called 'united action', for allied military units to attack communist positions in Dien Bien Phu, eventually defeating the communist revolution and laying the foundations for a nationwide anti-communist government. According to the Secretary, the United States would provide air cover though not ground troops in this undertaking to internationalize the war in Indochina. The French and British, hoping to come to a negotiated settlement with the communists and fearing that the intervention might provoke the People's Republic of China, were reluctant to agree to Dulles' plan.

After the French surrendered their outpost on 7 May, US policymakers feared the French government might be more willing than ever to negotiate a settlement of the Indochinese war, so the American delegation in Geneva moved with greater alacrity to undermine momentum for a peaceful settlement in Korea. Dulles wrote to one of his assistants on 10 May that, in view of America's efforts to develop powerful anti-communist allies in Indochina, there was still a chance that the United States would intervene militarily in Vietnam and that 'this might involve a clash with Communist China'. In light of this he felt it 'important that we basically follow a line which will keep the confidence of our anti-communist allies in Asia rather than seem to be working against them with a view to winning the favor of Western European countries which are not disposed to be very helpful to us in Asia' (Brands, 1987: 78). Dulles' perceptions were reinforced by reports which emphasized the significance of retaining American bases in Korea in the advent of a general war with the communists [*Doc. 33*].

Unlike its Western allies, the United States was not interested in searching for a limited *détente* with the Soviets and Asian communists. The policies pursued by the Europeans and the Commonwealth at Geneva threatened to weaken the more aggressive and offensive-minded containment policies which the United States was then trying to enforce. The Americans sought ways to weaken the momentum for a negotiated settlement to the Asian wars; they remained determined to thwart allied policies which might lead to 'appeasement' of the enemy.

The fall of Dien Bien Phu and communist negotiating tactics had eliminated Plan C from the American bargaining agenda. The essentials of Plan A had been introduced by the ROK. The United States now made an effort to get the Koreans to alter their initial proposals and to move closer to the spirit of Plan B. American diplomats in Seoul, Geneva and Washington also continued to press Rhee to make concessions on his terms for Korean unification; their efforts centred on getting the South Koreans to accept elections for both North and South Korea.

On 20 May, without President Rhee's formal approval, Foreign Minister Pyun tabled a compromise position which allowed for elections in the south consistent with the constitutional processes of the ROK. Though the allies hoped the ROK could make additional concessions, US officials now decided to terminate the conference discussions. The UN, they argued, had fought since 1950 to uphold the principle of 'collective security' and only a group of nations acceptable to that international body could oversee national elections leading to the reunification of the country.

America's European allies at this time were prepared to go along with the United States. British Foreign Secretary Anthony Eden said he was ready to support the US position on ending the conference, and Georges Bidault, France's Minister of Foreign Affairs, agreed to yield to American leadership. The Canadians were more concerned about the unsatisfactory nature of the ROK compromise proposal of 20 May and felt more should be done. However, they too recognized the importance that the United States attached to ending the conference soon, and did not delay moves to close the proceedings. But the allies were less willing than the United States to emphasize the UN principle as the reason to end the meeting. Bedell Smith pointed out that many of the sixteen nations which had sent ground troops to Korea 'now take the view that the UN itself is actually a belligerent, regardless of the form and purpose of the resolution which made it so' (US Department of State, 1981: 347–8).

On 5 June the communist delegations at Geneva pressed their propaganda advantage. Nam Il and Zhou Enlai reiterated their previous positions but Soviet Foreign Minister Vyacheslav Molotov suggested that further concessions might be forthcoming on the issue of the composition and duties of the communists' 'all-Korean body' which would decide the framework for national Korean elections. This communist initiative probably represented an effort to incite dissension within the allied delegations at Geneva and to convince international public opinion that the communists adopted more flexible negotiating tactics than the West at the conference.

Anxious to end the discussions, the allies argued that Molotov's speech did not make any fundamental concessions and they refused to allow any further closed sessions. The communists continued to press for further negotiations and criticized the allied decision to terminate discussions on Korea [*Doc. 34*]. The allied nations rejected a last-minute effort by Zhou Enlai on 15 June to agree to resume negotiations for a unified Korea at a time to be decided by the various states involved. The allies then issued a joint declaration outlining their reasons for ending the conference [*Doc. 35*].

In essence, both sides recognized that there was little opportunity to create a unified Korea in 1954. The two sides talked past each other, often in an effort to achieve goals that went beyond the two Koreas themselves. The major failure of the conference was not Korean unification but the establishment of human and economic ties which might have made living together on the same peninsula more amenable to both Koreas. Syngman Rhee was unwilling to sacrifice his political power and felt the country was too weak economically to accept communist offers for joint cooperative efforts in this direction. The conference did help to consolidate the armistice, though the President mentioned to the Americans afterwards that he now considered the armistice to be null and void. He told Ambassador Briggs that he would not attempt a unilateral offensive immediately, but he continued – unsuccessfully – to engage the United States in his plans to unify the peninsula through military force.

The Geneva Conference on Korea ultimately represented an implicit agreement by the great powers to maintain a divided Korea in their respective spheres of interest. The great powers disagreed over unification but prevented both Koreas from going to war with the other once again. The centre of Asian conflict was now moving to Southeast Asia, in Indochina and Vietnam in particular. Geneva helped to eliminate Korea as an area where the great powers and their proxy allies fought each other, and it reinforced an uncertain peace for more than four decades.

CHAPTER EIGHT

REASSESSING 'THE LONG PEACE'

The years since the end of the Second World War have been referred to as the era of 'the long peace' (Gaddis, 1987). During this period, historians have argued, international conflict was stemmed as a result of the super-power stalemate in Europe and the emergence of a continental 'balance of power'. Western rearmament in the wake of the North Korean attack in June 1950 is implicitly said to have contributed to this 'long peace'. But as events in Korea also remind us, this European-centred vision of world order after 1945 needs to be put in the larger context of extra-European developments. While Western leaders successfully laid the foundations for several decades of peaceful economic development and growth in the West, civil and regional conflicts proliferated in the developing world after 1945, in the aftermath of what was often a politically destabilizing experience with decolonization.

The Second World War, a struggle for global dominance among the traditional and newly-emerged great powers, is often misconstrued primarily as a war for world freedom and liberty. Democracy did not come easily to the developing world; its processes were often complicated or thwarted by the aspirations of the two new superpowers who extended their potent tentacles into the political vacuum caused by the war. In the United States, stability, not liberty, became the key word for its policies towards many developing countries. The Soviet Union and its allies consolidated their power through authoritarian methods and strict controls over their populations. Korea was part of these international trends. The Korean War emerged in the shadow of Korea's precipitate decolonization from the Japanese empire. In 1945 the two new superpowers divided the peninsula into their own spheres of influence with the sleight of an American hand. With the traditional European powers in decline, the United States and Soviet Union were able to influence the international system in ways unmatched in world history.

This was particularly true for the United States, which came out of the war with the globe's most dynamic economy. In the context of the emerging

Cold War with the Soviet Union, a rivalry to which events in Korea contributed, American policymakers became increasingly insecure about their ability to maintain their newly-found power and influence in the world. In early 1950, at a time when a kind of paranoid politics of fear came increasingly to define America's political scene, the Truman administration formulated plans, in the grave Cold War document known as NSC 68, for a massive expansion of its military power. The United States implemented this program against the backdrop of its participation in the Korean War. America's allies recognized the significance of Washington's new-found commitment to global containment and overcame their initial reluctance to send ground troops to the United Nations' 'police action' against DPRK soldiers.

Overall, the significant mobilization for global struggle which occurred in the West in the wake of the conflict did not match the level of manpower dedicated to fighting the battle itself. Although the war expanded to include many UN countries and China, unlike some previous wars of the twentieth century, the Korean conflict remained 'limited'. Global nuclear war was a frightening possibility in most Western policymakers' minds. But on the peninsula itself, the war absorbed all the human power and resources of the two Koreas. The distinction between limited and global war, useful from a comparative viewpoint when looking at the totality of the twentieth century's massive scale of warfare, should be used with caution and a firm understanding of the impact of this war on the two Koreas. Up to four million Koreans died in the conflict, including over one million southern civilians and soldiers, two million DPRK civilians, and half a million DPRK soldiers. For Koreans, the division of the country and the ensuing war were traumatic, defining events of the century, comparable in their revolutionary impact not to the First or Second World Wars but to the experience of being subjected to Japanese colonial rule for thirty-five years.

The war was not a watershed in the twentieth century, but it was a formative event in the history of the Cold War. The cost of rearmament accelerated the decline of the traditional European great powers, while it propelled the United States to the very height of its global might. In its wake, both Germany and Japan marshalled their military and 'self-defence' forces on the side of the West. Japan's economy may have benefitted the most from this international war-economy footing, and many important industries were revived as a result of American procurement programs for Korea.

Korea was the first major battlefield of the international rivalry between the two superpowers. But it also accelerated the emergence of the neutralist world, and gave countries like India, Egypt, and Indonesia opportunities to develop foreign policies which attempted to define a range of manoeuverability which escaped the long arm of superpower influence, at least in the short term. During the Korean War, India attempted most vigorously to fulfil this role, acting as both a neutral nation and a mediator between the two sides. Its diplomacy met with limited success. Indian warnings prior to China's intervention went unheeded, and efforts to bring an earlier end to the conflict in late 1952 failed to bring the two sides closer on the prisoners-of-war issue. Although other Commonwealth nations, like Britain and Canada, reserved some sympathy for Indian initiatives, when faced with a choice between their South Asian allies and the United States, the 'old' Commonwealth usually favoured the Western Alliance. American diplomats tended purposefully to marginalize the Indians and to limit their influence on diplomatic discussions involving Korea. South Korean leader Syngman Rhee was also very suspicious of Prime Minister Nehru and Indian diplomacy in general; he attempted to exclude India from the Neutral Nations Supervisory Commission, and to prevent India from having any influence on the peace settlement which he vigorously tried to subvert.

In North Korea, while allied counter-offensives devastated factories and villages, Kim Il Sung consolidated his authoritarian rule over the country through a series of purges. It appears that the DPRK, unlike South Korea, was ready for a negotiated peace by 1952, but the Soviet Union and China thought otherwise. Stalin's death brought forth significant changes in the Sino-Soviet negotiating stance and the three communist allies entered the Geneva Conference in 1954 with proposals meant to support their wider objective of lowering international tensions and consolidating spheres of influence. In the aftermath of the armistice agreement, both the Soviet Union and the PRC signed important economic reconstruction agreements with the DPRK. Chinese troops remained in the north until 1958, performing important reconstruction tasks with other Eastern bloc nationals.

If Stalin's goal in supporting the North Korean invasion was to distract the allied powers from Europe, his diplomacy must be judged as a failure in the long term. Although the Soviet Union lost very few soldiers in the conflict, the rearmament of the Soviet bloc proved very costly. Only in the aftermath of Stalin's death were Soviet officials able to reallocate resources into the domestic civilian economy. Furthermore, although the conflict solidified Soviet–PRC relations in the short term, it also laid the bases for increased tensions over the longer term. Many of the debates between the Soviets and Chinese – especially the Soviet Union's limited support for its allies and the failure by the Chinese to gain access to nuclear technologies – emerged from Sino-Soviet experiences during the Korean War. The Soviet role in North Korea declined after 1950 and was eclipsed by that of the PRC. Not until mid-1961 – and in the context of Sino-Soviet rivalry for influence in the international arena – did the Soviet Union sign a treaty of friendship, cooperation and mutual assistance with the DPRK. Article 1 of the agreement stated that if either party came under attack by any state or coalition of states, the other party would immediately extend military and other types of assistance to the other by all means at its disposal.

For China, the conflict demonstrated its ability first to push back and later to stall the most modern army in the world, but this occurred at a tremendous cost to its own military forces. As many as one million PRC soldiers were killed and wounded during the war. The war also prevented the PRC from implementing its post-revolution economic reconstruction tasks and from completing the conquest of Chiang Kai-shek's armies in Taiwan. Indeed, Chiang emerged as an unscathed beneficiary of the war, with his economy and armies strengthened and a mutual defence treaty signed with the United States in 1954.

The United States also moved to consolidate the power of the southern regime after 1953. American military and State Department officials recognized that it was strategically and economically advantageous to expand the Korean Army, and planning for this was carried out in 1953 and 1954. Although President Rhee wanted a larger and more potent attacking force, American policymakers kept the Korean leader within their own containment framework for Northeast Asia and thwarted Rhee's efforts to obtain US backing for an offensive against the north. To placate Rhee the United States agreed to negotiate a mutual defence treaty. The treaty came into effect after much difficult bargaining in November 1954, several months after the end of the Geneva Conference.

The events of 1950–54 set the framework for much of the postwar history of the two Koreas in the international system. The US–ROK Mutual Defense Treaty continues to define the South Korean–American bilateral military relationship. Many sanctions imposed upon the DPRK in the 1950s remain in place. The normalization of relations between the West and the PRC in the 1970s and 1980s did not affect in a significant way Western diplomacy towards the DPRK.

Since the early 1990s, however, important changes have occurred in the international system, which have overturned some of the earlier legacies of the war. Amidst major political changes sweeping Russia, in the fall of 1990 the ROK normalized diplomatic relations with its historical enemy. In 1991 the two Koreas simultaneously entered the United Nations; formal diplomatic ties between the ROK and PRC began in the summer of 1992. Since that date bilateral trade between the two states has increased tremendously. In 1994 the DPRK rejected the 1953 armistice agreement and since late 1997 the PRC, the United States and the two Koreas have held periodic negotiations aimed at promoting a more secure and peaceful environment in Northeast Asia.

The success or failure of these discussions will also shape how we will view the legacies of the early Cold War. Currently, North Korea and the

United States remain deadlocked in their discussions to normalize diplomatic relations, while South Korea has promised to respect the legitimacy of the northern regime. Despite changes in international outlook, the legacies of the war years continue to influence the way Korean, American, and Chinese policymakers, and indeed the international community as a whole, approach their international and domestic agendas. The international system's early Cold War inheritance has not played itself out yet, and the final chapter of this book has yet to be written. The participants in the Korean War have yet to produce a peace treaty and until that occurs there cannot be an era of long peace, either for the two Koreas or for the international community.

PART FIVE   DOCUMENTS

Unless otherwise stated, the place of publication is New York. Where a source also appears in the bibliography an abbreviated citation is used.

DOCUMENT 1   BRITISH AUTHOR DAVID REES ON KOREA'S
'LIMITED WAR'

This influential interpretation of the war, published in 1964, downplayed the domestic causes of the Korean War and the tremendous loss of life suffered by the Koreans and Chinese. Especially for Koreans, the Korean War was total war.

In spite of its nominal adherence to containment the pre-Korean War defence policy of the Truman Administration was in fact largely based on air-atomic striking power. In improvising a containment policy in the Far East by meeting the Communist challenge by conventional forces the Administration through its military advisers, the Joint Chiefs of Staff, limited not only military action to the area of Korea, but ... limited its objectives after the Chinese intervention to a restoration of the *status quo ante bellum*. In emphasizing their North Atlantic foreign policy Truman and Acheson were also attempting to limit popular participation in the Korean War. Resources that could be spared for Korea were also limited, as well as the weapons systems and target systems which were used inside the peninsula. Not only were atomic weapons not used, but the important North Korean port of Rashin, for example, near the sensitive Soviet border, was partly restricted to UNC air attack.

David Rees (1964) *Korea: The Limited War* (St Martin's Press), p. xiii.

DOCUMENT 2   US PRESIDENT HARRY S. TRUMAN RECALLS HIS
DECISION TO SEND TROOPS TO KOREA

In this excerpt from his memoirs, observe how the President's decision was influenced by his own interpretation of the history of war in the twentieth century. America in 1950 was near the height of its global power, and the President interpreted history in global terms, which made it easier to legitimize his decision to order troops to fight in Northeast Asia.

In my generation, this was not the first occasion when the strong had attacked the weak. I recalled some earlier instances: Manchuria, Ethiopia, Austria. I remembered how each time that the democracies failed to act it had encouraged the aggressors to keep going ahead. Communism was acting in Korea just as Hitler, Mussolini, and the Japanese had acted ten, fifteen and twenty years earlier. I felt certain that if South Korea was allowed to fall Communist leaders would be emboldened to override nations close to our own shores. If the Communists were permitted to force their way into the Republic of Korea without opposition from the free world, no small nation would have the courage to resist threats and aggression by stronger Communist neighbors. If this was allowed to go unchallenged it would mean a third world war, just as similar incidents had brought on the second world war. It was also clear to me that the foundations and the principles of the United Nations were at stake unless this unprovoked attack on Korea could be stopped. ...

Our allies and friends abroad were informed through our diplomatic representatives that it was our feeling that it was essential to the maintenance of peace that this armed aggression against a free nation be met firmly. We let it be known that we considered the Korean situation vital as a symbol of the strength and determination of the West. ... Not only in Asia but in Europe, the Middle East, and elsewhere the confidence of peoples in countries adjacent to Soviet Union would be adversely affected, in our judgment, if we failed to take action to protect a country established under our auspices and confirmed in its freedom by action of the United Nations. If, however, the threat to South Korea was met firmly and successfully, it would add to our successes in Iran, Berlin, and Greece, a fourth success in opposition to the aggressive moves of the Communists. And each success, we suggested to our allies, was likely to add to the caution of the Soviets in undertaking new efforts of this kind. Thus the safety and prospects for peace of the free world would be increased.

Harry Truman (1965) *Years of Trial and Hope, Memoirs by Harry S. Truman* (Doubleday),
pp. 378–9, 386–7.

DOCUMENT 3   **THE DEMOCRATIC PEOPLE'S REPUBLIC OF KOREA (NORTH KOREA) AND THE KOREAN WAR**

North Korean Foreign Minister Pak Hon Yong sent this statement to the President of the United Nations on 28 September 1950 to protest at the American and United Nations intervention in the Korean conflict.

American intervention and the civil war started by American imperialists and their running dogs headed by Rhee Syngman have inflicted tremendous calamities and hardships upon the Korean people, for which the U.S. government is solely responsible.

Through its official representatives, the United States government supplied the traitorous bandits of Rhee Syngman with political, military and economic aid, and directed in the building and training of Rhee Syngman's army and in working out the aggressive plan for the invasion of North Korea. Such encouragement and aid spurred the Syngman Rhee clique to start a civil war in Korea. ...

The government of the Democratic People's Republic of Korea had long since known of the aggressive anti-people's plans of the Rhee Syngman clique and strove to avoid a fratricidal civil war and took all measures it could to achieve the peaceful unification of our fatherland. ... As far back as May, 1950, [our] government ... received reliable information to the effect that the Rhee Syngman clique had scheduled the attack on North Korea for mid-June, 1950. This enabled [our] government ... to take timely measures for repulsing the attack of the Rhee Syngman troops.

Democratic People's Republic of Korea, Ministry of Foreign Affairs (1950) *Documents and Materials Exposing the Instigators of the Civil War in Korea: Documentation from the Archives of the Rhee Syngman Government* (Pyongyang), pp. 1, 12–13.

DOCUMENT 4   **US SECRETARY OF STATE DEAN ACHESON OFFERS AN EXPLANATION FOR THE NORTH KOREAN OFFENSIVE OF 25 JUNE 1950**

Compare Acheson's interpretation to those offered in Documents 1 , 2 and 3, and note Acheson's emphasis on the importance of protecting Japan. Concern for Japan's future heavily influenced his reaction to the northern invasion.

It seemed close to certain that the [North Korean] attack had been mounted, supplied, and instigated by the Soviet Union and that it would not be stopped by anything short of force. If Korean force proved unequal to the job, as seemed probable, only American military intervention could do it. Troops from other sources would be helpful politically and psychologically but unimportant militarily. ...

Plainly, this attack did not amount to a *causus belli* against the Soviet Union. Equally plainly, it was an open, undisguised challenge to our internationally accepted position as the protector of South Korea, an area of great importance to the security of American-occupied Japan. To back away from this challenge, in view of our capacity for meeting it, would be highly destructive of the power and prestige of the United States. By prestige I mean the shadow cast by power, which is of great deterrent importance. Therefore, we should not accept the conquest of this important area by a Soviet puppet under the very guns of our defensive perimeter with no more resistance than words and gestures in the Security Council. It looked as though we must steel ourselves for the use of force. That did not mean, in words used later by General Mark Clark, that we must be prepared 'to shoot the works for victory,' but rather to see that the attack failed.

Dean Acheson (1969) *Present at the Creation: My Years in the State Department* (Norton), p. 405.

DOCUMENT 5   THE STRENGTH OF THE KOREAN COMMUNIST
PARTY (KCP) IN SOUTHERN KOREA, 1945–47

Historian Chong-sik Lee and political scientist Robert Scalapino describe the strength of the KCP in southern Korea in the early postwar era. The key to communist and leftist power lay in their superior organizational and mobilizational abilities among the general population, as compared to the more traditional elitist political ethos of Korean conservatives. The 'strenuous events' referred to below were the arrest of many communists and the passing of laws aimed at debilitating the party's organizational base.

What was the size of the party in the south in this initial period, and what were the sources of strength upon which it could draw? To the first question, there is no precise answer available. In early September [1945], shortly after their arrival, American occupation authorities estimated that the KCP had approximately 3,000 members in the area south of the 38th parallel. As of January 1946, the estimated figure had risen to between 20,000 and 30,000. ... By the late spring of 1946, KCP leaders were asserting that Party membership had reached 200,000. The figures compiled by American and South Korean authorities were considerably less – generally in the order of 40,000 to 60,000. A year later, in September 1947, after some strenuous events, Party membership was estimated by the Military Government as 'probably' between 30,000 and 40,000 – and the Party's fortunes were soon to decline.

Robert Scalapino and Chong-Sik Lee (1972) *Communism in Korea Part I: The Movement* (University of California Press, Berkeley), pp. 256–7.

DOCUMENT 6   CHOE YONG-GON AND THE KOREAN
REVOLUTION, MAY 1947

Choe Yong-Gon fought in Manchuria in the Northeast Anti-Japanese United Army in the 1930s, joining Kim Il Sung's forces in 1938. In the excerpt below, taken from a US intelligence source, he emphasized the importance of the Chinese Revolution as a training ground for Korean soldiers. In 1948 Choe became North Korea's first Minister of Defence.

Korea will soon be ours. At present there is not a single unit in the [communist] United Democratic Forces now driving the Kuomintang from Manchuria that does not have my troops in it. At the end of the Manchurian campaign these troops will be seasoned, trained veterans. When the Americans and the Russians withdraw, we will be able to liberate Korea immediately.

Bruce Cumings (1990) *The Origins of the Korean War*, p. 359.

DOCUMENT 7   PRESIDENT RHEE'S WAR PLANS, 8 FEBRUARY 1949

This memo was produced by US Secretary of the Army Kenneth Royall during a visit to Seoul. In this conversation between Royall, the American Ambassador to Korea John Muccio and Rhee, the President's mind was preoccupied with the deteriorating military situation in China and the implications the Chinese Revolution had for Korea.

[President Rhee] stated he would like the police to have enough rifles to keep 18–20 thousand on the northern border ... [and] that, with sufficient equipment, the Southern Korean Army could be increased by 100,000 within six weeks. ... [T]he President stated ... that if North Korea were invaded by South Korea, a large proportion of the North Korean Army would desert to the South Korean Army. ...

He said he would like to increase the Army, provide equipment and arms for it, and then in a short time move north into North Korea. ... He saw nothing could be gained by waiting. ... One of the principal difficulties of the entire Korean situation was the vacillation of the U.S. State Department, which vacillation he thought that had played a strong part in the loss of China, and might be seriously harmful in Korea. ...

US Department of State (1971) *Foreign Relations of the United States, 1949: The Far East and Australasia,* vol. VII, part 2 (Government Printing Office, Washington, DC), pp. 956–8.

DOCUMENT 8   KIM IL SUNG'S APPEAL FOR SOVIET SUPPORT OF A SOUTHERN OFFENSIVE, 14 SEPTEMBER 1949

This document was transmitted by Soviet official Grigorii Tunkin in Pyongyang to the Soviet Foreign Ministry in Moscow. Tunkin had been chief of the First Far Eastern Division of the Soviet Foreign Ministry and a Soviet representative on the Joint Commission. In 1947 Tunkin told the Commission that it should not consult with those Korean organizations who opposed trusteeship. Here he relays his opinions about Kim Il Sung's military plans to take the Ongjin peninsula, based on conversations he had with Kim and Pak Hon Yong on 12 and 13 September. Like Rhee, Kim seemed to believe that a military offensive would weaken his opponents' morale.

The partial operation outlined by Kim Il Sung can and will probably turn into a civil war between north and south. ... Is it advisable to the north to begin a civil war now? We propose that this is not advisable.

The northern army is insufficiently strong to carry out successful and rapid operations against the south. Even taking into account the help which will be rendered to the northern army by the partisans and the population of South Korea it is impossible to count on a rapid victory. Moreover, a drawn-out civil war is disadvantageous for the north both militarily and politically. In the first place, a drawn-out war gives the possibility to the Americans to render corresponding aid to Syngmann Rhee [sic]. After their lack of success in China, the Americans probably will intervene in Korean affairs more decisively than they did in China and, it goes without saying, apply all their strength to save Syngmann Rhee [sic]. ... [I]t is inadvisable that the north begin a civil war now. Given the present internal and external situation a decision about an attack on the south would be correct only in such case as the northerners could count on ending the war quickly; the preconditions for it are not there.

James Hershberg (ed.) (1995) *Cold War International History Project Bulletin*, p. 7.

DOCUMENT 9   **STALIN UNDERSTANDS THE DYNAMICS OF KOREA'S 'CIVIL WAR'**

In the following excerpt from a Soviet document dated 19 January 1950, Soviet Ambassador to Pyongyang Terentii Shtykov reports to Soviet Foreign Minister Vyshinsky a conversation he had with an intoxicated Kim Il Sung on 17 January 1950. Kim is sensitive to Stalin's arguments, yet he may be hinting at a more traditional type of military offensive, using the border clashes as an excuse. Note how Kim referred to China's apparent willingness to help the Koreans as a way to put pressure on the Soviets.

Kim stated that when he was in Moscow [in March 1949], Comrade Stalin said to him that it was not necessary to attack the south, in case of an armed attack on the north of the country by the army of Rhee Syngmann [sic], then it is possible to go on the counteroffensive to the south of Korea. But since Rhee Syngmann [sic] is still not instigating an attack, it means that the liberation of the people of the southern part of the country and the unification of the country are being drawn out, that he (Kim Il Sung) thinks that he needs again to visit Comrade Stalin and receive an order and permission for the offensive action by the Peoples' Army for the purpose of the liberation of the people of southern Korea. Further Kim said that he himself cannot begin an attack, because he is a communist, a disciplined person and for him the order of Stalin is law. ... Kim underscored that Mao Zedong promised to render him assistance after the conclusion of the war in China.

James Hershberg (ed.) (1995) *Cold War International History Project Bulletin*, p. 8.

DOCUMENT 10   STALIN TO THE SOVIET AMBASSADOR IN PYON-
             GYANG, TERENTII SHTYKOV, 30 JANUARY 1950

This message was the first indication Kim Il Sung had that Stalin was willing to support his military offensive. It came on the heels of a message from Shtykov (above) that Kim was asking again for Soviet support. The second paragraph was apparently the price to be paid for Stalin's authorization of additional arms. At best, Kim was treated as junior partner in the Soviet–Korean relationship.

1. I received your report. I understand the dissatisfaction of Comrade Kim Il Sung, but he must understand that such a large matter in regard to South Korea such as he wants to undertake needs large preparation. The matter must be organized so that there would not be too great a risk. If he wants to discuss this matter with me, then I will always be ready to receive him and discuss with him. Transmit all this to Kim Il Sung and tell him that I am ready to help him in this matter.

2. I have a request for Comrade Kim Il Sung. The Soviet Union is experiencing a great insufficiency in lead. We would like to receive from Korea a yearly minimum of 25,000 tons of lead. ... I hope that Kim Il Sung will not refuse us in this. It is possible that Kim Il Sung needs our technical assistance and some number of Soviet specialists. We are ready to render this assistance. Transmit this request of mine to comrade Kim Il Sung and ask him for me, to communicate to me his considerations on this matter.

James Hershberg (ed.) (1995) *Cold War International History Project Bulletin*, p. 9.

DOCUMENT 11   **MAO AND THE KOREAN REVOLUTION**

The following Soviet document reports a conversation Mao Zedong and Zhou Enlai had with North Korea's Ambassador in Beijing, Li Chou-yuan, in late April or early May 1950. The conversation was reported in a telegram dated the 12th from Shtykov to Soviet Foreign Minister Vyshinsky. On 13 May Kim Il Sung flew to Beijing to discuss his war plans with the CCP leaders. The last paragraph is based on a separate conversation Shtykov had had with Kim in Pyongyang the same day.

[T]he question of the necessity of a meeting between Kim Il Sung and Mao Zedong was discussed. ... Mao, turning toward Li as if asking when you intend to begin the unification of the country, without waiting for an answer stated that if you intend to begin military operations against the south in the near future, then they should not meet officially. In such a case the trip should be unofficial.

Mao Zedong added further that the unification of Korea by peaceful means is not possible, solely military means are required to unify Korea. As regards the Americans there is no need to be afraid of them. The Americans will not enter a third world war for such a small territory. ...

Kim Il Sung reported to me that with regard to the question of the preparation of the operation he had given all necessary orders to the chief of the general staff, who already has begun to implement them, that his wish is to begin the operation in June, but he is still not convinced that they will manage it in this period.

Hershberg, James (ed.) (1995–96) *Cold War International History Project Bulletin*, p. 39.

DOCUMENT 12   **NSC 68, 7 APRIL 1950**

The Korean War set the context in which NSC 68, part of which is extracted below, became one of the most critical of America's Cold War planning documents. President Truman formally approved the document in late September 1950, and immediately ordered a tripling of America's defence budget. In his memoirs, Secretary Acheson described the document as a blunt but effective propaganda instrument, designed to win over the minds of American officialdom.

[T]his Republic and its citizens in the ascendancy of their strength stand in their deepest peril.

The issues that face us are momentous, involving the fulfillment or destruction not only of this Republic but of civilization itself. ...

The assault on free institutions is world-wide now, and in the context of the present polarization of power a defeat of free institutions anywhere is a defeat everywhere. ...

A further increase in the number and power of our atomic weapons is necessary in order to assure the effectiveness of any U.S. retaliatory blow. ... Greatly increased general air, ground and sea strength, and increased air defence and civilian defence programs would also be necessary to provide reasonable assurance that the free world could survive an initial surprise atomic attack ... and still permit the free world to go on to the eventual attainment of its objectives. ...

A program for rapidly building up strength and improving political and economic conditions will place heavy demands on our courage and intelligence; it will be costly; it will be dangerous. But half-measures will be more costly and more dangerous, for they will be inadequate to prevent and may actually invite war. Budgetary considerations will need to be subordinated to the stark fact that our very independence as a nation may be at stake.

Michael Hunt (1996) *Crises in U.S. Foreign Policy: An International History Reader*, pp. 165–7.

DOCUMENT 13   CHINESE AND INDIAN DIPLOMACY

This document provides a glimpse of Chinese and Indian diplomacy during a dangerous phase of the Korean War. In this telegram, the British Minister in Beijing reports on a conversation Zhou Enlai had with Indian Ambassador Panikkar on 3 October. Zhou underlined a statement made by Indian Prime Minister Jawaharlal Nehru a few days earlier that every effort should be made to settle the Korean conflict peacefully and that UN forces should not cross the parallel until every means of seeking such a solution were vigorously explored.

Chou En-lai [Zhou Enlai] sent for the Indian Ambassador ... and informed him that if 'American' armed forces crossed [the] 38th Parallel the People's Government of China would send in troops across the frontier to participate in the defence of North Korea. Chou said this action would not be taken if only South Korean troops were to cross the 38th parallel. (The Indian Ambassador said that in this context 'American' force is synonymous with United Nations troops). ...

Chou went on to say that the Chinese Government was prepared to accept the Indian Government's position regarding Korea as stated by Nehru at [his] Press Conference on September 30th ... but that China would accept no settlement of [the] Korean question to which China was not a party.

Great Britain, Foreign and Commonwealth Office (1991) *Documents on British Policy Overseas*, pp. 165–6.

DOCUMENT 14   CANADA–US RELATIONS, NATO AND THE KOREAN CONFLICT, DECEMBER 1950

The following Canadian cabinet memorandum, prepared by Secretary of State for External Affairs Lester Pearson and Minister of National Defence Brooke Claxton on 28 December 1950, demonstrates vividly, in the language of the Cold War, the Canadian government's concerns about strengthening the NATO alliance and preventing a third world war from breaking out in late 1950. Although Pearson was willing to seat the PRC in the UN at this time, and was also willing to discuss the issue of the status of Formosa with the PRC, positions the US government disagreed with, the Canadian cabinet agreed on the need to maintain the Canada–US global partnership and the NATO Alliance.

2. By their support of the Chinese intervention in Korea, the Soviet Government have shown that they are willing to run the risk of a third

world war. In such a war the Soviet Union would have, initially, and probably over the next two years, a preponderance of land and air forces in the conventional methods of warfare. Also they would probably have a small stockpile of atomic weapons. ...

4. Although we have differed with the United States on a number of issues on Far Eastern policy, there is agreement between the Canadian and United States Governments that:

(a) peace is now in jeopardy;

(b) the expansion of Soviet imperialism must be opposed;

(c) the principle of collective resistance to aggression must be maintained; and

(d) the main front which must be defended is Western Europe.

Our disagreements arise only in deciding how our agreement on these basic points should be translated into immediate policy and action. ...

5. [The West's] relative weakness is the most dangerous in Western Europe. This is ... one of the basic reasons why we have contended that all possible steps should be taken to avoid becoming embroiled in a war with communist China. ...

7. Assuming that a major war with China can be avoided, it must, nevertheless, be recognized that the defeat which the United Nations have suffered in Korea makes more likely communist attacks on other parts of Asia, the Middle East and Eastern Europe. ...

15. The defence of the West depends on continued and increased participation and assistance by the United States and this will be more likely to be forthcoming if Congress and the American people believe that their effort is being matched by a comparable effort in other countries. ...

17. It seems essential that, in common with other countries of the North Atlantic, we should re-examine our defence programme in the light of these somber developments. We will all require to press forward at a much accelerated speed if we are to attain the goal of security which is set by the North Atlantic Treaty.

Canada, Department of External Affairs and International Trade (1996) *Documents on Canadian External Relations, 1950–1954*, vols 16–20 (Canadian Communications Group, Ottawa), vol. 16, pp. 1159–62.

DOCUMENT 15   SYNGMAN RHEE ASKS HARRY TRUMAN TO EXPAND THE WAR

This message, written by President Rhee, was transmitted to President Truman by the South Korean Ambassador to the United States, John M. Chang, on 10 January 1951. In his personal communication to Truman,

Rhee recommended that the United States rollback the international borders of communism. In 1960, after Rhee's government was toppled by student unrest, Chang became Prime Minister of Korea's Second Republic. His government was overthrown by a military coup in the spring of 1961.

We pray to God for your health, for everything depends on you now more than ever. Even now you can save the situation by giving us immediate arms and ammunition for our 250,000 trained youths, and later another 250,000 now undergoing training. With these half million men fully armed, in addition to our present fighting strength to help the valiant United Nations forces, we can turn the tide. If we lose this opportunity the Chinese and northern Communists will destroy all our armed forces and most of the anti-Communist civilian population.

 ... What is still worse is the far-reaching effects of this disaster on you and other great leaders who courageously undertook to check the Communist aggression in Korea. They will all try to lay the blame on you, and the Soviets and their puppets all over the world will triumph and rejoice. The United Nations will never save either themselves or others from another world war, but only make that war more disastrous. To save the situation we must do all we can to defeat and destroy the Chinese invaders now. Give arms to the Koreans and allow them to carry on the war according to guerrilla tactics, and authorize General MacArthur to use any weapons that will check Communist aggression anywhere, even the atom bomb. A few bombs on Moscow alone will shake the Communist world.

Republic of Korea, National History Compilation Committee (1996) *Taehan Min' guksa Charyojip*, vol. 30, pp. 13–14.

DOCUMENT 16   **A SOUTH KOREAN NATIONAL ASSEMBLYMAN DESCRIBES THE NORTHERN ADVANCE**

The following excerpts from a US intelligence report were written in August 1950, as the North Korean Army was pushing southwards towards the Pusan perimeter. The report is based on a conversation which US authorities had with a 'political refugee' – an unnamed member of South Korea's National Assembly who escaped Seoul and arrived in Taegu around 9 August. The impressionistic information provides a sense of the fluid and complicated nature of the conflict and the relationship between Korean civilians and soldiers in the early stages of the war.

'The N[orth] K[orean] Army does not conduct any of its execution of undesireable [sic] civilian[s] but left this dirty work to the guerrillas to perform[.] [T]he N[orth] K[oreans] are very kind to the civil populace and are using every means to get [the] civil populace of S[outh] K[orea] on their side. ... The N[orth] K[oreans] are using [the] strafing of civilians by friendly planes as a means to sway public feeling against the Americans. Furthermore, they leave persons, especially women and children, who had died of starvation unburied and propagandize the people into believing that they were killed by American troops. N[orth] K[oreans] are using every means possible to stop the southward evacuation of S[outh] K[orean] civilians in their occupied areas. To accomplish this, they are telling the civilians that the Americans would shoot them on sight. On or about 21 Jul[y], while in Seoul, he saw news plastered on billboards claiming the seizure of PUSAN by N[orth] K[orean] troops. ... [He] was told by [a] N[orth] K[orean] soldier that they did not harm [POWS] and that they were teaching the prisoners the righteous ways of living. ... He heard N[orth] K[orean] troops mention the fact that an order was issued by Kim [Il] Sung for the capture of Japanese in the American Army but that they had not at that time been able to capture any.'

US Army Center of Military History, Historical Manuscripts Collection (1950–53), *The Korean War*, reel 1.

DOCUMENT 17   BRITISH DIPLOMAT HENRY SAWBRIDGE REPORTS FROM KOREA, 17 AUGUST 1950

In Korea at the outset of the conflict, British diplomat Henry Sawbridge reflected on the plight of southern refugees. He cynically noted that the civilians 'embarrassed' the US Air Force – that is, they had been killed by USAF strafing. He also underlined a decision by US forces to order troops to fire on the refugees trying to pass through allied lines.

[T]here is the matter of the strategic use of refugees of whom, up to a few days ago, there were upwards of 3 million in the unoccupied area. ... Although the Central and Provincial Governments, especially the latter, have done their best to cope with this vast problem, it is clearly getting beyond their control and the resources available to meet it. ... Whether or not as a matter of deliberate design, these herds of refugees have frequently served as cover for advancing enemy forces and have on numerous occasions been a great embarrassment to the air force. Among the refugees there has also been considerable guerrilla infiltration by enemy guerrilla and regular troops and agents of every description. ... On 5th August, the United States authorities felt themselves compelled to issue an order to the effect that no more refugees were to be allowed to pass through the lines and that those who attempted to do so should be fired upon.

United Kingdom Public Record Office, London, 1950, Foreign Office 371, FK1015/202.

DOCUMENT 18   E.H. NORMAN REPORTS BEHIND THE SCENES FROM JAPAN, 26 SEPTEMBER 1950

Writing to Ottawa, Norman outlined two examples of the way in which UN authorities remained complicit in their silence against injustices committed during the Korean War. The information he reports here came from his contacts with Australia's Head of Mission to Japan, Colonel W.R. Hodgson, and Colonel Alfred Katzin, the South African-born representative of UN Secretary General Trygve Lie. Katzin was sent to Korea to liaise with the UN Commission on Korea, the successor to UNTCOK which had overseen elections in the south in 1948.

While [Australian Ambassador Hodgson] was in Korea, several hundred North Korean prisoners-of-war, some of them badly wounded, were brought by train into Pusan. Awaiting them there on the station platform were a large number of Korean police who at once fell upon the prisoners and, both by heavy boots and rifle butts, gave them a most terrible beating. The particularly unfortunate part of the incident was that it took place in broad daylight with many eye-witnesses, including a large number of Allied newspapermen, some of whom took pictures of the incident. Colonel Hodgson told me that General Walker had great difficulty – and in fact held a rather stormy interview with some correspondents – in persuading the newspapermen not to make use of the material that they had seen or photographed. In this connection, Colonel Katzin also told me in confidence ... that he succeeded after a long series of arguments in persuading the Commission [UNCURK] to delete certain passages in their report to the Assembly. These passages contained unfavourable comments on this same aspect of the South Korean regime, namely, the brutality of the police and the large-scale arrest of political suspects who are then left in jail. Colonel Katzin felt that the publicizing of material like this would only play into the hands of the Russians.

Canadian National Archives, Department of External Affairs Records, file 50069–A–40.

DOCUMENT 19   A CAPTURED CHINESE DOCUMENT

The following document was captured from the 26th Chinese Army in Korea, in November 1950. It outlines some of the challenges and poor conditions under which the Chinese soldiers were required to fight in the war.

'A shortage of transportation and escort personnel makes it impossible to accomplish the mission of supplying the troops. As a result, our soldiers frequently starve. From now on, the organisation of our rear service units should be improved.

The troops were hungry. They ate cold food, and some had only a few potatoes in two days. They were unable to maintain the physical strength for combat; the wounded personnel could not be evacuated. ... The fire power of our entire army was basically inadequate. When we used our guns there were no shells and sometimes the shells were duds.'

John Gittings (1967) *The Role of the Chinese Army* (Oxford University Press, London),

pp. 133–4.

DOCUMENT 20   **AN AUSTRALIAN SOLDIER REMEMBERS LIFE IN THE TRENCHES, 1951**

This recollection of the war was written by Australian veteran Maurie Pears, who was born in Sydney in 1929. He served with the third battalion of the Royal Australian Regiment.

Holes in the ground don't make healthy homes! In the summer we were pestered with flies, mites, rashes and diarrhoea. ... Winter was just as tough. Frostbite and metal burn, especially on patrol at night, was fearsome. The cold at times would freeze a cup of coffee in the open and you had to shave in the bottom of the hutchie to prevent the water freezing on your face. ... Every time we came back into the line into new positions we faced dirty hutchies and weapon pits left over from the previous occupants. It took days to clean them up and bring them to our Battalion standard. Our first task was always a spring clean. ... If you were unlucky you would pick up lice in your head and cr[o]tch. Some of the hutchies and pits were filthy and infested with rats and had to be shoveled clean as we moved in.

The treatment for all complaints was simple, Aspirin for a pain, No9's for the trots, mistadtussim for a cough, barbasol shaving cream for a rash or frostbite and wash your head and cr[o]tch in DDT to get rid of the bities. Somehow we survived but many have suffered for years afterwards. The liver is never the same after a DDT bath. For all this the Digger received the basic soldier's wage, a bottle of beer in reserve for which he paid and a thankless return home. Years later, weary and older and a lot sicker he had to battle with a much younger bureaucracy for welfare.

Maurie Pears and Fred Kirkland (2000) 'Korea Remembered',

http://www.ffasfs.com.au/chapter10.htm

DOCUMENT 21   A CANADIAN RED CROSS WORKER IN THE DMZ

After the armistice was signed in July 1953 the Canadian Department of National Defence asked the Canadian Red Cross to send a team of women to Japan and Korea to boost the morale of the troops. Ms Dorothea Powell Wiens, of British Columbia, Canada, was one of about twenty young women who were eventually sent to Asia. The following is an excerpt from her memoir, describing her experience in Korea from late 1954 to early 1955. She had previously been stationed in Japan, and in Korea she supervised a team of four other women. Note the presence of Korean 'domestics'.

We were met in Seoul and driven sixty miles north to the [25th] Canadian Brigade Headquarters ... just south of the DMZ. ... Arriving at my destination ... I found that ... five Red Cross girls occupied one side and three Korean girls, our domestics, occupied the other. There was a kitchen, a bathroom of sorts and a breezeway in between. ...

Compared with the relative freedom of movement permitted in Japan, the Korean situation was rather like a prison. We were allowed to go no-where, except with our own jeep and driver on assignments. We were not even allowed to go for walks, since the area was still mined. We were invited to, and attended, formal military functions where we were the only women present, but we did not ... date the servicemen. ...

We did not meet the Korean people to the same extent that we met the Japanese. The area in which we were serving was considered a war zone and, except for the few employe[es] ... all Koreans had been evacuated. ... Those few Koreans we did know were friendly, laughing, happy people, covering well the heartache of lost homes, lost families, lost children and husbands listed as 'whereabouts unknown.'

All of our Red Cross work time was spent at the recreation centre where, at all times, there would be four or five of the Red Cross team present. The girls put in long hours because they loved the work and there was very little else to do. There would be about a hundred soldiers at any given time. ... Most of my time was spent dealing with low morale, uncertainties, dom-estic concerns and homesickness of young men, many of whom were not yet twenty years of age. ...

Frances Martin Day, Phyllis Spence and Barbara Ladouceur (eds), (1998) *Women Overseas: Memoirs of the Canadian Red Cross Corps* (Ronsdale Press, Vancouver), pp. 348–50.

DOCUMENT 22   **DEPARTMENT OF STATE'S OFFICE OF INTELLIGENCE RESEARCH REPORT ON NORTH KOREA, 20 NOVEMBER 1952**

The following excerpt is taken from a State Department study entitled 'Current Economic and Political Conditions in North Korea'.

A major problem facing the north Korean regime has been the serious decline in the morale of the civilian population due to severe and prolonged privation. Recent information indicates that discontent (and possibly even subversion) exists on the home front. The government has repeatedly cautioned the population against reactionary and subversive elements in rear areas who make use of 'the restless, discontented, cowardly, [and] revengeful to spy on military secrets, to spread rumors, to alienate the people from the government, and even to assassinate government leaders.'

... [D]espite weaknesses in north Korea's own internal security forces, and despite the breakdown of the propaganda machine, popular dissatisfaction and unrest have thus far been contained. This has been due primarily to the fact that Korean police forces have been supplemented and bolstered by small garrisons of Chinese troops stationed in many towns and villages throughout the country. In addition, the North Korean army, which at present mans only a small part of the fighting front, has remained reliable; its morale appears to be considerabl[y] higher than that of the civilian population. Both its reliability and morale has been [e]nsured by continuous indoctrination and surveillance and, further, by sufficient food rations and supplies.

US National Archives, OSS and State Department Numbered Intelligence Reports, 1941–1961, Report No. 6062.

DOCUMENT 23   **NORTH KOREAN CLAIMS ABOUT THE AMERICAN USE OF BACTERIOLOGICAL AGENTS IN KOREA**

In April 1953 the Acting Minister of Foreign Affairs for the DPRK, Lee Dong Hen, forwarded a report to the UN Security Council written by the 'Commission of the Central Committee of the United Democratic Fatherland Front for the Investigation of the Atrocities and Determination of the Damage Caused by the American Interventionists and the Syngman Rhee Clique'. Excerpts below are all taken from the report. The vitriolic propaganda campaign reflected both the intensity of emotion and the tremendous hardships which the North Korean side experienced during the war.

The American interventionists and the anti-democratic Syngman Rhee clique of traitors, in their furious rage against the freedom-loving Korean people, are committing more and more crimes in their endeavour to turn our country into a desert, to exterminate our people and to obliterate all memory of its culture. Concealing their criminal [sic] acts under the blue flag of the United Nations, the American aggressors are committing in Korea atrocities which the monstrous crimes of their teachers in aggression, the Hitlerite invaders, pale into insignificance. Every day the American air force is carrying out cruel and barbarous raids on peaceful Korean towns and villages, killing women, children and old people. ... Violating all accepted standards of international law and trampling upon the fundamental principles of human morality, the American interventionists are making widespread use in Korea of such barbarous and inhuman weapons of mass destruction as napalm bombs and bacterial and chemical weapons. ... From 28 January 1952 to 25 March 1952 bacterial weapons were used 400 times over the northern part of the Republic as a whole. At 0300 hours on 22 November 1952 American aircraft dropped infected insects in ... Kangwon [southeastern DPRK] province. On 21 December 1952 American aircraft bombed and brutally machine-gunned peaceful inhabited localities in ... Hwanghae [southwest DPRK] province, and then dropped insects infected with bacteria in six villages of the area. ... The use of bacterial weapons by the American interventionists for the mass destruction of the population of North Korea has been confirmed by captured American airmen ... who themselves dropped bacterial bombs on cities and villages in North Korea.

US National Archives, RG 59, Decimal Records, 1950–1954, 611.95A26/4–353

DOCUMENT 24   **SOUTH KOREA'S ARMISTICE TERMS**

This diplomatic note was sent by the South Korean Government to Secretary Dean Acheson on the eve of the Armistice negotiations. It was signed by Ambassador Yang You Chan, who succeeded Ambassador John Chang in 1951.

30 June 1951

Your Excellency;

I have the honor to invite your Excellency's attention to the following five points which the Republic of Korea considers as the basic conditions of any cease-fire arrangement that may be effected. These conditions are:

1. The Chinese must withdraw beyond the Korean traditional boundaries into Manchuria without causing any harm to the lives and property of the civilian population in North Korea.

2. The North Korean communists must be disarmed.

3. The U.N. must agree to prevent any third power from giving assistance to the North Korean communists militarily, financially or otherwise.

4. The official representatives of the Republic of Korea shall participate in any international conference or meeting which discusses or considers any phase of the Korean problem.

5. No plan or program or course of action will be considered as having any legal effect which may conflict with the administrative sovereignty or territorial integrity of Korea.

Republic of Korea, National History Compilation Committee (1996) *Taehan Min' guksa*
Charyojip, vol. 30, p. 312

DOCUMENT 25   PRESIDENT RHEE'S VIEW OF HISTORY

In this personal letter written in December 1951 to former Ambassador to the United States and now Prime Minister John Chang, who was then leading the Korean Delegation to the Sixth UN General Assembly Meeting in Paris, President Rhee reflects on Korea's past history. Compare this with Document 2, above.

[D]o your very best to make [the UN] understand we are not children. We have seen the course of history flow over our country time and again. We learned something in 1905, in 1910, in 1919, in 1931, in 1937, in 1941, in 1945 – and have been seeing the same lesson repeated over and over again ever since. Weakness and appeasement in the face of aggressive designs always leads to more and more aggression. Only those who dare to be strong deserve to be free. There is no reason why you should have to teach such elementary lessons to the statesmen of the world's greatest powers. But it appears that you do. ... If our friends and Allies now agree to our division, what hope will be left for us? Our greatest hope must always lie in our own unaided determination to resist and to fight to the death for our own liberties.

Republic of Korea, National History Compilation Committee (1996) *Taehan Min' guksa*
Charyojip, vol. 30, p. 371.

DOCUMENT 26   ZHOU ENLAI AND STALIN, 1952

This Soviet document recorded a conversation about the POW issue between top-ranking Chinese and Soviet officials in Moscow on 20 August 1952. The Chinese, apparently concerned with avoiding a major war with the West, believed that a continuation of the Korean conflict would prevent the United States from pursuing more aggressive adventures elsewhere.

Stalin, on the other hand, did not believe the United States was prepared to initiate another world war.

<u>Zhou Enlai</u> informs that Mao Zedong ... believes that one should stand firmly committed on the return of all POWs. The [North] Koreans believe that the continuation of the war is not advantageous because the daily losses are greater than the number of POWs whose return is being discussed. But ending the war would not be advantageous to the USA. Mao Zedong believes that the continuation of the war is advantageous to us, since it detracts USA from preparing for a new world war.

<u>Stalin</u>: ... The North Koreans have lost nothing, except for casualties that they suffered during the war. Americans understand that this war is not advantageous and they will have to end it, especially after it becomes clear that our troops will remain in China. ... Of course, one needs to understand Korea – they have suffered many casualties. But they need to be explained that this is an important matter. They need patience and lots of endurance. ... Americans are not capable of waging a large-scale war at all, especially after the Korean War. ... Americans are merchants. Every American soldier is a speculator, occupied with buying and selling. ... No, Americans don't know how to fight. ... They are pinning their hopes on the atom bomb and air power. But one cannot win a war with that.

James Hershberg (ed.) (1995–96) *Cold War International History Project Bulletin*,
pp. 12–13.

DOCUMENT 27   NSC 147, ANALYSIS OF POSSIBLE COURSES OF ACTION IN KOREA

This document, dated 2 April 1953, was prepared by the NSC Planning Board for an NSC meeting the following week. At that meeting it was agreed that if an acceptable political settlement was not reached 'within a reasonable time' the United States was prepared to void all armistice agreements made up to that point.

Use of Atomic Weapons
   ...
   22. *Military Advantages:*
   a. Would considerably augment capabilities of U.S.–UN forces and somewhat offset the implications of developing a conventional capability to produce equivalent military effects outside Korea.
   b. Would result in curtailment of Communist Chinese capability of continuing present hostilities, of threatening U.S.–UN security in Korea and Japan, or of initiating aggression elsewhere.

c. Might serve to increase the deterrent effect of our atomic capabilities on the USSR, as pertains to both global and limited war.

d. Threats to our military position in Korea could be eliminated more effectively, quickly and cheaply than by use of conventional weapons.

23. *Military Disadvantages:*

a. Unless the use of atomic weapons results in a decisive military victory, the deterrent effect might be reduced.

b. Any profitable strategic use requires extension of hostilities outside of Korea.

c. A precedent would be established, and UN forces and installations are, in general, better targets for atomic weapons than those of the enemy; for example, the ports of Inchon and Pusan, UN airfields and concentrations for amphibious operations.

d. Use of substantial numbers will reduce the U.S. stockpile and global atomic capabilities.

US Department of State (1984) Foreign Relations of the United States, p. 845.

DOCUMENT 28   GUERRILLA WAR DIRECTIVE, 11 APRIL 1952

This document, which originated in the Headquarters of the US Far Eastern Command Liaison Detachment (Korea) Guerrilla Section, became the basis for US–ROK partisan guerrilla operations between 1952 and 1954. It shows the gruesome reality behind the fighting in the Korean War.

Subject: Guerrilla Operations Outline ...

9. CIVILIANS: Non-guerrilla civilians will be well treated. The guerrilla will assume the role of friend of the people and attempt to assist them in their resistance to the Communist movement. ...

10. CHINESE GUERRILLAS: Efforts will be made to develop Chinese guerrillas from deserters from the C[hinese] C[ommunist] F[orces]. Reports reaching this headquarters indicate that limited numbers of former Nationalists are deserting the CCF and forming guerrilla bands. These will be supported and encouraged to enlarge their guerrilla tactics. ...

18. DEMOLITION TARGETS: Locomotives, trucks and personnel are considered the most lucrative targets for demolition. ... Our effort will be directed at targets least readily destroyed by aerial attack. ...

19. ASSASSINATION: Primary assassination targets are Korean Communist leaders. Communist or North Korean Labor Party leaders who will not render partisan assistance to our forces will be assassinated. If succeeding Communist leaders are assassinated, the ambitions of minor leaders will be dampened. This has already been demonstrated by our efforts in some sectors. ... Only selected Soviets should be assassinated ... in areas that

abound with pro-communists. This creates doubt between the Soviets and their satellite Korean followers. Korean communist leaders should be assassinated wherever found.

Ed Evanhoe (1995) *Dark Moon: Eighth Army Special Operations in the Korean War* (Naval Institute Press, Annapolis, ML), pp. 146–50.

DOCUMENT 29   **ZHOU ENLAI SPEAKS ABOUT SINO-SOVIET RELATIONS, 1952**

The following speech, delivered in Beijing by Chinese Premier and Foreign Minister Zhou Enlai, was written for the celebration of the second anniversary of the signing of the Sino-Soviet alliance, 14 February 1952.

The great Sino-Soviet Treaty of Friendship, Alliance and Mutual Assistance was built on the basis of long years of the profound friendship that has existed between the people of China and the Soviet Union. ... Facts have now shown clearly that American imperialism and its satellite states are reviving Japanese militarism, are proving hostile to China and the Soviet Union, are menacing Asia and are preparing for a new aggressive war on a still greater scale. ... Since their disastrous failure in the Korean War, the American imperialists have been shamelessly stalling the Korean armistice negotiations, while continuing to occupy Taiwan. ...

Last September, American imperialism and its satellite states signed with the Yoshida Government of Japan the unlawful, unilateral 'San Francisco Peace Treaty' and at the same time concluded a 'U.S.–Japanese Security Pact'. In December, Yoshida, Premier of the reactionary Japanese Government, 'assured' America that he would conclude a 'bilateral treaty' with the remnant Kuomintang gang on Taiwan. ... At the behest of America, the British Government in Hongkong [sic] has been allowing the remnant Kuomintang gangsters to infiltrate into China's Kwangtung Province ... for purposes of sabotage. ...

American imperialism is the most frantic enemy of the Chinese people, the Soviet people and the peace-loving people of the world. Since the Second World War, it has gone in for a mad extension of armaments in America and its satellite states and the establishment of military bases, and the rearming of Western Germany and Japan, in an attempt to encircle the Soviet Union, the Chinese People's Republic and the People's Democracies and enslave the people of Asia and the whole world. This policy of American imperialism has already driven its vassal states to bankruptcy and will inevitably give rise to a new economic crisis within America itself. ...

United Kingdom Public Record Office, London, 1950, Foreign Office 371, file 99265.

DOCUMENT 30   INDIAN PRIME MINISTER JAWAHARLAL NEHRU AND THE KOREAN CRISIS, 7 DECEMBER 1950

On the ninth anniversary of the bombing of Pearl Harbor, Prime Minister Nehru took the opportunity to give a speech to the Indian parliament. He warned of the dangers of the current crisis and embraced a peaceful and negotiated solution to the war in Korea.

Some hon. Members seem to think that I should issue an ultimatum to China, that I should warn them not to do this or that or that I should send them a letter saying that it is foolish to follow the doctrine of communism. I do not see how it is going to help anybody if I act in this way. ... The point at issue is that China is a great nation which cannot be ignored, no matter what resolution you may pass. ...

I doubt if, after the terrible disaster of a world war, democracy can survive. The democratic nations may win the war – mind you, I have little doubt that they will – but I doubt if after the disaster of a world war democracy can survive at all. I even doubt whether any high standards of living can survive. ...

I am not thinking in terms of blocs, because it does not interest me very much. ... In fact, every question that comes before us has to be seen from a hundred different viewpoints. ... We do hardly anything without consulting the countries of the Commonwealth. Of course, we are in close touch with the U.S.A. and with other countries. We have been in close contact with the countries of South-East Asia, like Burma and Indonesia. They are constantly keeping us informed of what they do. ... The very objectives for which human life and human society have stood all these years now seem to be challenged. They are challenged, sometimes, by a theory or an ideology. They are challenged by authoritarianism which crushes the individual and they are challenged even in democratic societies, not by democracy but by this growth of violence and by the mentality that war breeds. ...

Government of India, Ministry of Information and Broadcasting (1961) *India's Foreign Policy*, pp. 52–5.

DOCUMENT 31   THE 1952 POLITICAL CRISIS IN THE REPUBLIC OF KOREA

The following document records a conversation between British and American officials discussing the possibility of overthrowing the government of South Korea. The meeting was held on 23 June 1952 in Washington.

Mr. Lloyd asked whether the U.S. could conceive of a circumstance under which it would wish to depose Syngman Rhee. Mr. Allison replied that the situation would have to be serious before deposing Rhee. He asked who would be put in Rhee's place and questioned whether there was any other personality available. When ... asked whether [the UK] ... had unearthed any substitute for Rhee, Mr. Lloyd replied in the negative, saying no strong leader was available although there were various groups of people who at least could form a cabinet capable of remaining in power so long as there was available money and material from the outside. However, such a cabinet would not stand up when the Allied forces leave.

Mr. Allison commented that it might be preferable to find ways of getting rid of Syngman Rhee's cronies. ... Mr. Lloyd added that he did not think that Rhee would be deposed and doubted the advisability of formally deposing Rhee even if he could later be kept on as a 'guest of the U.S.'. Mr. Allison stated that the best approach might be to let Syngman Rhee know that we would retain him if he did certain things but that, otherwise, it would be necessary to depose him.

Harry Truman Library, Independence, Missouri, Selected Records Relating to the Korean War,
Box 13, file 47.

DOCUMENT 32   KIM IL SUNG PURGES PAK HON YONG, 1953

The following is an excerpt from a speech Kim made in Pyongyang on 8 February 1953, on the fifth anniversary of the founding of the Korean People's Army.

Pak Hon Yong, a spy on the payroll of the American scoundrels, bragged that South Korea had 200,000 [communist] party members and that in Seoul alone there were as many as 60,000. But, in reality this rascal, in league with the Yankees, totally destroyed our Party in South Korea. Although we advanced as far as the Nakdong River, no revolt broke out in South Korea. Pusan is located a stone's throw from Taegu, and even if a few thousand workers in Pusan had risen to hold a demonstration, the question would have been different. If some people in the South had revolted we would have definitely liberated Pusan and the American scoundrels would not have been able to land.

Sung Chul Yang (1994) *The North and South Korean Political Systems: A Comparative Analysis* (Westview Press, Boulder, CO), p. 366.

DOCUMENT 33   KOREA'S STRATEGIC SIGNIFICANCE

Arthur Dean, Deputy to Secretary Dulles for the Korean Political Conference, wrote this memo to Dulles on 25 May. It demonstrates how US thinking about the situation in Vietnam and Indochina affected perceptions and policy vis-à-vis *the Korean phase of the conference. The Van Fleet report, referred to below, recommended an increase in the size of Korean military forces by ten combat divisions.*

While we were negotiating the Armistice in 1953, [the] J[oint] C[hiefs] [of] S[taff] decided we no longer needed to maintain bases on the mainland of Asia and that we were quite prepared with or without [a] phased withdrawal [of] Chinese Communists to withdraw our troops in South Korea down to a corps, while at the same time strengthening [the] ROK army so it could hold in event of attack until we could return. ...

In view of our possible entry into the Indo-Chinese situation and in view of current conditions in Japan requiring [a] complete review of conditions for use of Japanese bases, and [the] inability without use of force or co-equal phased withdrawal to obtain withdrawal [of] Chinese Communist forces from North Korea, it consequently seems better to recognize, however regrettable, that North and South Korea must remain separated. We must then strengthen ROK forces or at least increase our share of military cost of ROK army operations and enter into [a] program of economic aid designed to alleviate [the] continued severance of North and South Korea. ...

Further, we should endeavour to persuade the Swiss and the Swedes to withdraw from the N[eutral] N[ations] S[upervisory] C[ommission], and give wide publicity to the futility of the NNSC, thus undercutting Communist hints that some such allegedly neutral body, rather than the UN, might be acceptable for working out all-Korean election laws, overseeing all-Korean elections, etc. Once the NNSC has been abolished, we should also explore the legal possibility, because of Communist violations, of freeing ourselves from the restrictions of the armistice, though we have no intention of resuming hostilities.

This series of moves – clean-cut breaking off of the negotiations, abolition of the NNSC, possibly freeing ourselves from the restrictions of the armistice, exchanges [of] ratification of the Mutual Defense Treaty, implementation of the Van Fleet mission report – by demonstrating a hard position in the Korean situation may help our bargaining position *vis-à-vis* Indo-China.

US Department of State (1981) *Foreign Relations of the United States*, pp. 317–19.

DOCUMENT 34   **NORTH KOREA BACKS THE COMMUNISTS' POSITION AT GENEVA**

This editorial, entitled 'Public Opinion of the World Demands the Peaceful Settlement of the Korean Question' , was printed in the North Korean newspaper Nodong Sinmun *(Workers' Daily) on 14 June, the day before the conference ended. It reflected communist efforts to maintain their 'peace' offensive against the UN side.*

The problem of perpetuating the peace in Korea attained through the armistice, and unifying divided Korea by peaceful means, is the major problem to be settled at the Geneva Conference. The amicable adjustment of the Korean question is not only in the interest of the Korean people, but is related to the peace of the Far East and the whole world. ...

As is known widely, the delegation of our Republic, the Soviet Union, and the Chinese People's Republic, reflecting the ardent aspiration of the peoples of the world, have been making all-out efforts for an amicable solution to the Korean question. ...

A majority of the delegates attending the Geneva Conference [have] consented to our proposal for all-Korea free elections on the basis of democratic principles, and recognized that the evacuation of all foreign troops from Korea is imperative for an amicable solution to the Korean issue. Now that we have basically agreed on the necessity of supervision of all-Korea elections by an international organization, we must strive to reach agreement on some controversial points by continuing negotiation. ...

However, the South Korean delegate and the Americans, who are opposed to any peaceful proposal concerning the Korean question, are trying their best to thwart the progress of the conference, and using laughable pretexts. Refusing Molotov's [5 June] proposal, American delegate Smith opposed all-Korea free elections, and advocated that the elections be carried out under the surveillance of the prejudicial United Nations. ...

The American side is called upon to give up their scheme to block the road to a peaceful solution of the Korean question as promptly as possible and [to] enter practical negotiations based on Molotov's proposal. Should the Americans and their satellites continue their efforts to break up the conference, in defiance of the wishes of the peoples of the world, they could not be free from responsibility in the just judgment of the people.

US Central Intelligence Agency, Foreign Broadcast Information Service, *Daily Reports* (Government Printing Office, Washington, DC), 16 June 1954, pp. FFF 3–4.

DOCUMENT 35   DECLARATION BY THE SIXTEEN, 15 JUNE 1954

This declaration was issued by the UN side to legitimize its decision to terminate discussions on the Korean question at Geneva. It was signed by representatives of the following countries: Australia, Belgium, Canada, Colombia, Ethiopia, France, Greece, Luxembourg, the Netherlands, New Zealand, the Philippines, the Republic of Korea, Thailand, Turkey, the United Kingdom, and the United States of America.

... [W]e, as nations who contributed military forces to the United Nations Command in Korea, have been participating in the Geneva Conference for the purpose of establishing a united and independent Korea by peaceful means. ...

We have earnestly and patiently searched for a basis of agreement which would enable us to proceed with Korean unification. ...

The Communist delegations have rejected our every effort to obtain agreement. The principal issues between us, therefore, are clear. Firstly, we accept and assert the authority of the United Nations. The Communists repudiate and reject the authority and competence of the United Nations in Korea and have labelled the United Nations itself as the tool of aggression. Were we to accept this position of the Communists, it would mean the death of the principle of collective security and of the United Nations itself. Secondly, we desire genuinely free elections. The Communists insist upon procedures which would make genuinely free elections impossible. It is clear that the Communists will not accept impartial and effective supervision of free elections. Plainly, they have shown their intention to maintain Communist control over North Korea. They have persisted in the same attitudes which have frustrated United Nations efforts to unify Korea since 1947. ...

In the circumstances we have been compelled reluctantly and regretfully to conclude that, so long as the Communist delegations reject the two fundamental principles which we consider indispensable, further consideration and examination of the Korean question by the conference would serve no useful purpose. We re-affirm our continued support for the objectives of the United Nations in Korea.

US Department of State (1981) *Foreign Relations of the United States, 1952–1954*, vol. XVI, pp. 385–6.

GLOSSARY

American Military Government (AMG)   Refers to US military rule of Korea south of the 38th parallel from September 1945 to August 1948.

Democratic People's Republic of Korea (DPRK)   Official name of North Korea. The DPRK was formally established on 9 September 1948.

Executive Order 9981   Issued by President Harry Truman on 26 July 1948 to ensure that personnel in America's armed forces would not face discrimination on the basis of 'race, color, religion or national origin'. The order established an executive committee, the President's Committee on Equality of Treatment and Opportunity in the Armed Forces, to implement the directive.

Geneva Conference (April–June 1954)   Arose out of Article IV of the 1953 military armistice. During the conference the communist side proposed inter-Korean economic and cultural exchanges but these were rejected by the American and South Korean delegates. Attendees consisted of representatives from the UNC, the People's Republic of China, the two Koreas, and the Soviet Union.

House Un-American Activities Committee (HUAC, 1937–1975)   During the early Cold War era this committee of the House of Representatives initiated a public red-scare campaign, involving the investigation of individuals accused of 'Un-American' activities, which included association with a communist organization. In the Senate, Joseph McCarthy adopted a number of HUAC's undemocratic tactics.

Inchon landing   Famous amphibious military assault on the Yellow Sea port of Inchon, 40 miles west of Seoul on 15 September 1950. The success of the attack forced the North Korean Army into retreat and fuelled demands to cross the 38th parallel and to unite Korea under UN auspices.

Joint Chiefs of Staff   A military body composed of representatives of the Army, Navy, and Air Force, which advised the US President.

Juche   A form of nationalism in North Korea associated with the adulation of the leader. Formulated under Kim Il Sung, it stresses North Korea's right to determine its own foreign and domestic policies, independent of communist or Western great power interference. Juche was articulated as a popular ideology after the mid-1950s.

Korean Augmentation to United States Army (KATUSA)   Involved the integration of Koreans into the US Army during the Korean War.

Korean People's Army (KPA)   Name of North Korea's Army. By the outset of the North Korean offensive in mid-1950 many of its soldiers had fought with Chinese communist armies in Manchuria and elsewhere in China.

Korean People's Republic (KPR)   Established in the aftermath of Japan's surrender in 1945, the KPR was not recognized as a legitimate government in the American zone of occupation. Seen as a leftist organization, the American military worked to undermine its power across the area south of the 38th parallel. In the north, the Soviet occupation force initially worked with the KPR's local people's committees.

McCarthyism   Term used to describe the anti-communist crusade in the United States associated with the Wisconsin demagogue, Senator Joseph McCarthy (1908–57). McCarthy's untruthful accusations included a statement in January 1950 that there were several hundred communists in the US State Department.

Moscow Agreement   During discussions at Moscow in December 1945 the United States and the Soviet Union agreed to establish a Joint Commission to initiate the process of creating a unified Korean provisional government. The meetings of the Joint Commission became deadlocked and the United States brought the 'Korean Question' to the UN in the fall of 1947, thus accelerating the process of creating two separate Koreas.

National Security Council 68 (NSC 68)   A critical document of the early Cold War drafted before the outbreak of the Korean War which called for a massive expansion in America's military arsenal. President Truman approved the document in the fall of 1950. The increase in national security spending which followed significantly increased US diplomatic involvement and intervention around the world.

National Security Law   A major component of South Korea's National Security State, this piece of legislation was passed by the South Korean legislature in November 1948, in the aftermath of rebellions in Cheju Do and Yosu. The law was broadly defined and was used to suppress political opposition.

Neutral Nations Repatriation Commission   A UN Commission composed of India, Sweden, Switzerland, Poland and Czechoslovakia which oversaw the process of prisoner repatriation. It allowed both sides to make appeals to those prisoners who had initially refused to go back to their home countries. All POWs were released by January 1954 and the Commission ceased its operations in February 1954.

Neutral Nations Supervisory Commission (NNSC)   Established as part of the 1953 armistice machinery the Commission was composed of representatives from Poland, Czechoslovakia, Sweden and Switzerland. It was supposed to ensure that both sides adhered to the armistice, but the United States blocked the Commission from operating in South Korea in 1956.

Non-forcible repatriation   Concept introduced by the US/UN side during the armistice negotiations in early 1952 to indicate their determination to let prisoners of war decide whether or not they would return home.

North Atlantic Treaty Organization (NATO)   The West's main military alliance. Created in April 1949, it called for a US military commitment to Europe in the event of internal or external aggression against any of the signatories.

Republic of Korea (ROK)   Formal name for South Korea which was established south of the 38th parallel on 15 August 1948.

Reverse Course   Phrase used to describe a major shift in American occupation policy for Japan over the course of 1947 and 1948. Japan was now to be re-habilitated economically and militarily as America's major Cold War ally in Asia.

38th parallel In September 1945 the United States made an offer to the Soviet Union to divide Korea at the 38th parallel. Soviet Premier Stalin accepted. In the fall of 1948 the dividing line became the *de facto* border of the two Koreas. As a result of the Korean War, the border between the two Koreas now dips just below the parallel in the west and above the parallel in the east (map 4).

Truman Doctrine The doctrine emerged out of a speech President Truman made to a Joint Session of the US Congress on 12 March 1947. Truman asked for $400 million to provide military and economic aid to Greece and Turkey in order to prevent the spread of 'totalitarianism'. It is associated with a broadening of America's anti-Soviet commitments in the Cold War.

United Nations Civil Assistance Command Korea (UNCACK) Established under the authority of the UNC in 1950 to provide relief and aid to the South Korean population. It continued to operate until 30 June 1953.

United Nations Command (UNC) Term used for the military forces on the UN side which came under the control of the UN Commander. The UNC was created by a UN Security Council resolution on 7 July 1950 and General Douglas MacArthur was appointed first Commander of these forces.

United Nations Commission for the Unification and Rehabilitation of Korea (UNCURK) Created by a UN resolution of 7 October 1950 to oversee the unification of North and South Korea. It was made up of representatives from Australia, Chile, the Netherlands, Pakistan, the Philippines, Thailand and Turkey. Its operations were curtailed by China's intervention in the war, though it continued to operate and to submit reports to the UN until 1972.

United Nations Korean Reconstruction Agency (UNKRA) Created by a UN resolution of 1 December 1950, the Agency was originally supposed to help rehabilitate a unified Korea. It continued to operate until 1960, and provided economic aid to the ROK in the areas of industry and infrastructure.

United Nations Temporary Commission on Korea (UNTCOK) After the United States brought the Korean Question to the UN in 1947, it sponsored a resolution to create a commission which would oversee elections in all of Korea. After the Soviets refused to give UNTCOK access to areas north of the 38th parallel, the Commission changed its mandate and oversaw elections for South Korea only. These elections led to the establishment of the Republic of Korea in 1948.

US–ROK Mutual Defense Treaty Negotiated by President Rhee and representatives of the United States in the spring of 1953. Rhee wanted a NATO-type arrangement which would commit US forces in the event of conflict on the peninsula, but the United States only agreed to consult with its ally in the event of war. About 37,000 US troops remain in South Korea today.

WHO'S WHO

Acheson, Dean (1893–1971) Replaced George Marshall as Secretary of State in 1949 and served in that capacity for the remainder of the Truman administration. An Atlanticist, Acheson saw the Korean War as an opportunity to expand NATO and rearm the West against the perceived global Soviet threat.

Bevin, Ernest (1881–1951) British Foreign Secretary, 1945–51. A strong proponent of the Anglo-American alliance, Bevin supported the American decision to intervene in the Korean War and to send UNC troops across the 38th parallel.

Clark, Mark (1896–1984) Replaced Matthew Ridgway as UN Commander in May 1952. He escalated the bombing of North Korea to put pressure on the communists to make concessions at the bargaining table. He was disappointed with the Eisenhower administration's failure to 'win' the war in Korea, and retired from the Army in October 1953.

Dulles, John Foster (1888–1959) Played an important role in negotiating the Japanese Peace Treaty and became President Eisenhower's Secretary of State in 1953. He is associated with the Eisenhower administration's threat in the spring of 1953 to use atomic weapons against China if UN armistice terms were not met.

Eden, Anthony (1897–1977) British Foreign Secretary, 1951–55, Eden was concerned with the UK's economic problems which had been exacerbated by the rearmament program associated with the war in Korea. His efforts to create a *modus vivendi* with the communists in Asia conflicted with his belief in the necessity of sustaining a partnership with the United States in world affairs.

Eisenhower, Dwight D. (1890–1969) US President, 1953–60. In late 1950 President Truman appointed Eisenhower Supreme Commander of NATO forces in Europe. Ike's Presidential campaign in 1952 is famous for his statement that he would go to Korea if elected. Although a fierce Cold Warrior, Ike was also concerned about the impact that military spending would have on America's economy.

Kim Il Sung (1912–94) Leader of a partisan resistance movement against the Japanese army in Manchuria in the 1930s. In 1941 he fled to the Soviet Far East, and returned to Soviet-occupied Korea in 1945. Kim became Premier of the DPRK in 1948 and obtained Soviet and Chinese support for an invasion of South Korea in the winter and spring of 1949/50. He consolidated his power during the war.

Lie, Trygve (1896–1968) Secretary General of the United Nations at the time of the North Korean offensive on 25 June 1950. Lie facilitated the US-led effort to rollback communism in Korea.

MacArthur, Douglas (1880–1964) Controversial US Army General who commanded UN forces from July 1950 to April 1951. He conceived the Inchon landing, criticized the limited war precept, and advocated the use of nuclear weapons against China. He was relieved of his command by President Truman after making a series of pronouncements which undermined the Commander-in-Chief's authority.

Mao Zedong (1893–1976)   Chinese communist leader who believed in the revolutionary power of the peasantry. During China's civil war (1946–49) his forces defeated the Chinese Nationalists under Chiang Kai-shek. He became Chairman of the People's Republic of China on 1 October 1949. In the fall of 1950 he ordered Chinese 'volunteers' into the Korean War.

McCarthy, Joseph (1908–57)   American Senator who led a paranoid anti-Soviet campaign in the United States from 1950. His accusations were shown to be falsifications and he was censured by the US Senate in 1954.

Molotov, Vyacheslav (1890–1986)   Soviet Foreign Minister, 1939–49, and after Stalin's death, from 1953 to 1956. He represented the USSR at the Geneva Conference in 1954. In 1957 he was implicated in a plot to overthrow Nikita Khrushchev and was forced to take a series of minor posts in the foreign service.

Mu Chong (1905–51)   Associated with the Yanan faction of the North Korean communist movement. Born in northern Korea, Mu Chong joined the Chinese Communist Party in 1926. He survived the Long March and left China after Korea's liberation. He commanded the North Korean II Corps during the Korean conflict. In December 1950 he was held responsible for the fall of Pyongyang and purged from government. He went to China and died soon thereafter.

Nam Il (1913–76)   A Soviet Korean, Nam Il arrived in Korea with Soviet forces in 1945. He was appointed Deputy Chief of Staff of the Korean People's Army in July 1950 and Chief of Staff in December 1950. He was chief DPRK representative at the armistice negotiations. In August 1953 Nam Il succeeded Pak Hon Yong as Foreign Minister, and he was North Korea's top-ranking representative at the Geneva Conference in 1954.

Nehru, Jawaharlal (1889–1964)   Indian Prime Minister, 1947–64. Nehru adopted a neutralist position in the Cold War. Although he agreed to send an Indian ambulance unit to Korea, he criticized the UN decision to cross the 38th parallel in the fall of 1950. Between 1951 and 1953 Nehru supported efforts to negotiate a peaceful end to the Korean War.

Nitze, Paul (1907–)   Head of the Policy Planning Staff in the Department of State, 1950–53. A Cold War hawk, Nitze was intimately involved in drafting NSC 68. In the spring of 1953 he supported the use of atomic diplomacy against the communists in order to achieve an armistice acceptable to the United States.

Pak Hon Yong (1900–55)   A member of the 'domestic' faction of the Korean communist movement during the Japanese occupation, Pak emerged as leader of the Korean communists in southern Korea after 1945. He fled the south in 1946 and became Vice-Premier and Foreign Minister of North Korea in 1948. Pak was made a scapegoat for the northern failure to unify the country during the war and was executed in 1955.

Pearson, Lester (1897–1972)   Canadian Secretary of State for External Affairs during the Korean War. Pearson supported the main thrust of US foreign policy towards Korea, though was concerned about the regional implications of US policy, especially as they related to the People's Republic of China. He criticized MacArthur's belligerent statements and supported a negotiated settlement to the war.

Pyun Yong T'ae (1892–1952)   South Korean Foreign Minister, 1951–55. Pyun supported the broad terms of Rhee's foreign policy and was the ROK's senior representative at the Geneva Conference on Korea.

Rhee, Syngman (1875–1965)   Emerged as a prominent nationalist-in-exile during the Japanese colonial period. A fierce anti-communist, in 1948 he became the first President of the Republic of Korea. After China's intervention in the Korean War, he suggested that the United States expand the conflict into China and the Soviet Union. After the armistice was signed he continued to advocate an offensive against North Korea.

Ridgway, Matthew (1895–1993)   Commander of the US Eighth Army from December 1950 to the spring of 1951, when he replaced General MacArthur as UN Commander. In 1952 Ridgway became Supreme Allied Commander in Europe after Eisenhower decided to run as a candidate for the nomination of the Republican Party.

Stalin, Joseph (1879–1953)   Soviet Premier and General Secretary of the Communist Party of the Soviet Union. Stalin was initially cool to Kim Il Sung's suggestions to launch a northern offensive against South Korea, but changed his mind in early 1950. Stalin was careful not to involve Soviet ground troops in the conflict. After his death in March 1953, the communist side moved swiftly to negotiate an armistice with the United Nations.

Truman, Harry (1884–1973)   President of the United States from April 1945 to January 1953. He ordered American troops into the Korean War but did not expand the war into China. He fired General MacArthur in April 1951 and is closely associated with the policy of non-forcible repatriation of POWs.

Vyshinsky, Andrei (1833–1954)   Soviet Foreign Minister, 1949–53. In the fall of 1950 he warned the UNC against crossing the 38th parallel. In 1952 he attacked the Indian Resolution, which had attempted to find a way out of the POW impasse. After Stalin's death he became permanent Soviet representative to the UN.

Yang You Chan (1897–1975)   South Korean Ambassador to the US, 1951–60. Yang criticized the 1953 Korean Armistice and was Foreign Minister Pyun's deputy at the 1954 Geneva Conference.

Yoshida Shigeru (1878–1967)   Japanese Prime Minister, 1948–54. A critical figure in postwar Japanese history, he negotiated the Peace Treaty and the US–Japan Mutal Security Treaty, thus establishing the basis for the postwar US–Japanese alliance. He is known for his support of Japanese economic recovery and welcomed the conflict in Korea as a means of achieving his government's economic objectives.

Zhou Enlai (1898–1976)   Premier and Foreign Minister of the People's Republic of China during and after the Korean conflict. In the fall of 1950 Zhou warned the UN not to send non-Korean troops across the 38th parallel. After Stalin's death Zhou indicated that the communists were prepared to sign an armistice agreement.

The place of publication is New York unless otherwise stated.

PRIMARY SOURCES

There are a number of very useful primary materials available for the study of the Korean War. On early twentieth-century Korean history, students should consult the fine collection of translated Korean source materials in Peter Lee, ed., *Sourcebook of Korean Civilization, Volume 2: From the Seventeenth Century to the Modern Period* (Columbia University Press, 1993). Documents pertaining to the early Korean communist movement can be found in Dae Sook Suh, *Documents on Korean Communism, 1918–1948* (Princeton, NJ: Princeton University Press, 1970). An important but neglected series on the postwar diplomacy of South Korea has been published by the ROK National History Compilation Committee, *Taehan Min'guksa Charyojip [A Collection of Historical Documents of the Republic of Korea]*, (Kwachon: National History Compilation Committee, 1987–). For the North Korean perspective on South Korea's role in starting the war, see Democratic People's Republic of Korea, Ministry of Foreign Affairs, *Documents and Materials Exposing the Instigators of the Civil War in Korea: Documentation from the Archives of the Rhee Syngman Government* (Pyongyang, 1950).

The most important primary document book series on US–South Korean diplomacy is the US Department of State's *Foreign Relations of the United States (FRUS)*. Relevant volumes, all published by the US Government Printing Office in Washington, DC, include: *The British Commonwealth and the Far East, 1945*, vol. VI (1969); *The Far East, 1946*, vol. VIII (1971); *The Far East, 1947*, vol. VI (1972); *The Far East and Australasia, 1948*, vol. VI (1974); *The Far East and Australasia, 1949*, vol. VII, part 2 (1971); *Korea, 1950*, vol. VII (1976); *Korea and China, 1951*, vol. VII, part 1 (1983); *Korea, 1952–1954*, vol. XV, parts 1–2 (1984); *The Geneva Conference, 1952–1954*, vol. XVI (1981). Scholarly Resources has produced a useful fifteen-reel microfilm series entitled *The Korean War*.

A valuable collection of materials from communist archives has been gathered together in a series published by the Woodrow Wilson International Center for Scholars. The following issues of the *Cold War International History Project Bulletin* contain materials on the Korean War. All are edited by James Hershberg: 'Cold War Crises' (Spring 1995); 'The Cold War in Asia' (Winter 1995–96); 'The Cold War in the Third World and the Collapse of Detente in the 1970s' (Winter 1996–97).

The UK and Canada have also published materials on their countries' diplomacy during the Korean War. These can be found in Canada, Department of External Affairs and International Trade, *Documents on Canadian External Relations, 1950–1954*, vols 16–20 (Ottawa: Canada Communications Group,

1990–97); and Great Britain, Foreign and Commonwealth Office, *Documents on British Policy Overseas: The Korean War*, Series II, vol. IV (London: HMSO, 1991).

The 1954 Geneva Conference on Korea is documented in *FRUS 1952–1954: The Geneva Conference*, vol. XVI (above) and in the following reprint volume: Great Britain, Secretary of State for Foreign Affairs, *The 1954 Geneva Conference, Indo-China and Korea* (with a new introduction by Kenneth Young) (Greenwood Reprint, 1968).

CHAPTER ONE

For surveys of Korean history in the late nineteenth and early twentieth centuries, students should read the relevant sections of Bruce Cumings, *Korea's Place in the Sun* (Norton, 1997); Carter Eckert et al., *Korea Old and New: A History* (Seoul: Ilchokak Publishers, 1990); and Lee Ki-baik, *A New History of Korea* (Cambridge, MA: Harvard University Press, 1984). Three fine general studies of US foreign policy are Michael Hunt, *Ideology and U.S. Foreign Policy* (New Haven, CT: Yale University Press, 1987); Thomas Paterson et. al., *American Foreign Policy: A History since 1900* (Toronto: D.C. Heath, 1988); and Walter LaFeber, *The American Age* (Alfred Knopf, 1987). The larger context of post-1945 Korean–American relations is explored in Frank Baldwin, ed., *Without Parallel: The American–Korean Relationship since 1945* (Pantheon, 1973); and Donald Stone Macdonald, *U.S.–Korean Relations from Liberation to Self-Reliance: The Twenty Year Record* (Boulder, CO: Westview Press, 1992).

Important secondary works which provide historical perspective on the domestic origins of the Korean War include Vipan Chandra, *Imperialism, Resistance, and Reform in Late Nineteenth-century Korea* (Berkeley, CA: Institute of Asian Studies, University of California, Berkeley, 1988); Robert A. Scalapino and Chong-sik Lee, *Communism in Korea Part I: The Movement* (Berkeley, CA: University of California Press, 1972); Chong-sik Lee, *The Politics of Korean Nationalism* (Berkeley, CA: University of California Press, 1965); Ramon Myers and Mark Peattie, eds, *The Japanese Colonial Empire, 1895–1945* (Princeton, NJ: Princeton University Press, 1984); Michael Robinson, *Cultural Nationalism in Colonial Korea, 1920–25* (Seattle, WA: University of Washington Press, 1988); Gi-Wook Shin, *Peasant Protest & Social Change in Colonial Korea* (Seattle, WA: University of Washington Press, 1996); and Dae Sook Suh, *The Korean Communist Movement, 1918–1948* (Princeton, NJ: Princeton University Press, 1967).

Rhee's speech writer and adviser, Robert Oliver, wrote a number of books depicting Rhee in a positive light. These include: *Syngman Rhee: The Man Behind the Myth* (Dodd Mead, 1955); and *Syngman Rhee and American Involvement in Korea, 1942–1960* (Seoul: Panmun Books, 1978). Dae Sook Suh has written an important biography, *Kim Il Sung* (Columbia University Press, 1988). For a communist interpretation, read Bong Baik's three-volume survey *Kim Il Sung* (Guardian Publishers, 1969–70).

The story of America's wartime relationship with China and the Japanese empire is examined in Xiaoyuan Liu, *A Partnership for Disorder: China, the United States, and Their Policies for the Postwar Disposition of the Japanese Empire, 1941–1945* (Cambridge: Cambridge University Press, 1996). For the history of US–Korea relations during the war, see Bruce Cumings, *The Origins of the Korean*

War: Liberation and the Emergence of Separate Regimes (Princeton, NJ: Princeton University Press, 1981); Kyu-Park Hong, 'From Pearl Harbor to Cairo: America's Korea Diplomacy, 1941–1943', *Diplomatic History*, 13 (1989), pp. 343–58; and James Matray, *The Reluctant Crusade: American Foreign Policy in Korea, 1941–1950* (Honolulu, HI: University of Hawaii Press, 1985).

CHAPTER TWO

American and Soviet foreign policy during the Cold War is discussed in John Lewis Gaddis, *Strategies of Containment: A Critical Appraisal of Post-War American National Security Policy* (London: Oxford University Press, 1982); Michael Hogan, *The Marshall Plan: America, Britain, and the Reconstruction of Western Europe, 1947–1952* (London: Cambridge University Press, 1987); Melvyn Leffler, *A Preponderance of Power: National Security, the Truman Administration and the Cold War* (Stanford, CA: Stanford University Press, 1992); Vojtech Mastny, *The Cold War and Soviet Insecurity: The Stalin Years* (London: Oxford University Press, 1996); and Vladislav Zubok and Constantine Pleshakov, *Inside the Kremlin's Cold War: From Stalin to Khrushchev* (Cambridge, MA: Harvard University Press, 1996).

For the critical 1945 to 1950 period in Korea, see Charles Armstrong, 'Surveillance and Punishment in Postliberation North Korea', *Positions: East Asian Cultures Critique*, 3 (1995), pp. 695–722; Bruce Cumings's two-volume work, *The Origins of the Korean War* (Princeton, NJ: Princeton University Press, 1981, 1990); Bruce Cumings, ed., *Child of Conflict: The Korean–American Relationship, 1943–1953* (Seattle, WA: University of Washington Press, 1983); Peter Lowe, *The Origins of the Korean War* (London: Longman, 1997a); James Matray, *The Reluctant Crusade* (1985); James Matray, 'Captive of the Cold War: The Decision to Divide Korea at the 38th Parallel', *Pacific Historical Review*, 50 (1981), pp. 145–68; and John Merrill, *Korea: The Peninsular Origins of the War* (Newark, NJ: Delaware University Press, 1989). For an interpretation of the Soviet occupation of North Korea which differs at key points with Cumings's interpretation, read Eric Van Ree, *Socialism in One Zone: Stalin's Policy in Korea, 1945–1947* (Oxford: Berg Publishing, 1989). Kim Chull Baum and James Matray, eds, *Korea and the Cold War: Division, Destruction, and Disarmament* (Claremont, CA: Regina Books, 1993) contains a number of essays which examine the origins of the war from the perspectives of the key actors.

CHAPTER THREE

The Chinese and Soviet perspectives leading up to the North Korean offensive are explored in Sergei Goncharov, John Lewis, and Xue Litai, *Uncertain Partners: Stalin, Mao and the Korean War* (Stanford, CA: Stanford University Press, 1993); Yufan Hao and Zhihai Zhai, 'China's Decision to Enter the Korean War: History Revisited', *China Quarterly*, 121 (1990), pp. 94–115; Youngho Kim, 'The Origins of the Korean War: Civil War or Stalin's Rollback?', *Diplomacy and Statecraft*, 10 (1999), pp. 186–214; Chae-Jin Lee, *China and Korea: Dynamic Relations* (Stanford, CA: Hoover Institution Press, 1996); Zhihua Shen, 'Sino-Soviet Relations and the Origins of the Korean War: Stalin's Strategic Goals in the Far East', *Journal of Cold War Studies*, 2 (2000), pp. 44–68; Kathryn Weathersby, 'The Soviet Role in the

Early Phase of the Korean War: New Documentary Evidence', *Journal of American–East Asian Relations*, 2 (1993), pp. 1–33; and Kathryn Weathersby, 'New Findings on the Korean War', *Woodrow Wilson Cold War International History Project Bulletin*, 3 (1993), pp. 14–18. See also Mastny, *The Cold War and Soviet Insecurity* (1996) and Zubok and Pleshakov, *Inside the Kremlin's Cold War* (1996).

The military dimensions of the Korean War are discussed in the following monographs: Roy Appleman, *South to the Naktong, North to the Yalu* (Washington, DC: Office of the Chief of Military History, 1961); Clay Blair, *The Forgotten War: America in Korea 1950–1953* (Times Books, 1987); Max Hastings, *The Korean War* (London: Pan Books, 1987); and Callum MacDonald, *Korea: The War before Vietnam* (London: Macmillan, 1986). In *Diasaster in Korea: The Chinese Confront MacArthur* (College Station, TX: Texas A&M University Press, 1989), Roy Appleman challenges the argument that MacArthur's decision in October 1950 to divide the Eighth Army and the X Corps was a mistake.

There are numerous studies on the diplomatic history of war. For a sampling, consult Burton Kaufman, *The Korean War: Challenges in Crisis, Credibility and Command* (Philadelphia, PA: Temple University Press, 1997); and William Stueck, *The Korean War: An International History* (Princeton, NJ: Princeton University Press, 1995).

The background to China's intervention in the conflict is covered in Jian Chen, *China's Road to the Korean War: The Making of the Sino-American Confrontation* (Columbia University Press, 1994); Michael Hunt, *The Genesis of Chinese Communist Foreign Policy* (New York: Columbia University Press, 1996); and Michael Sheng, 'Beijing's Decision to Enter the Korean War', *Korea and World Affairs*, 19 (1995), pp. 294–313. China's Cold War rivalry with the United States is explored by Thomas J. Christensen, *Useful Adversaries: Grand Strategy, Domestic Mobilization, and Sino-American Conflict* (Princeton, NJ: Princeton University Press, 1996); Shunguang Zhang, *Deterrence and Strategic Culture: Chinese–American Confrontations, 1949–1958* (Ithaca, NY: Cornell University Press, 1992); and Qiang Zhai, *The Dragon, the Lion, and the Eagle: Chinese–British–American Relations, 1949–1958* (Kent, OH: Kent State University Press, 1994). For Taiwan, see Robert Accinelli, *Crisis and Commitment: United States Policy toward Taiwan, 1950–1955* (Chapel Hill, NC: University of North Carolina Press, 1996).

Anglo-American policies towards Korea and Asia during the war are the subject of a number of books and articles. These include Rosemary Foot, 'Anglo-American Relations in the Korean Crisis: The British Effort to Avert an Expanded War, December 1950–January 1951', *Diplomatic History*, 10 (1986), pp. 43–57; Rosemary Foot, *The Wrong War: American Policy and the Dimensions of the Korean Conflict, 1950–1953* (Ithaca, NY: Cornell University Press, 1985); Steven Hugh Lee, *Outposts of Empire: Korea, Vietnam and the Origins of the Cold War in Asia, 1949–1954* (Montreal: McGill-Queen's University Press, 1995); Peter Lowe, *Containing the Cold War in East Asia: British Policies towards Japan, China and Korea, 1948–1953* (Manchester: Manchester University Press, 1997b); and William Stueck, 'The Limits of Influence: British Policy and American Expansion of the War in Korea', *Pacific Historical Review*, 55 (1986), pp. 65–95.

MacArthur's role in planning the Inchon landing and the northern offensive, his relations with President Truman, and his dismissal occupy an important place in the historiography of the war. See Laura Belmonte, 'Anglo-American Relations and the

Dismissal of MacArthur', *Diplomatic History*, 19 (1995), pp. 641–67; D. Clayon James, *The Years of MacArthur: Triumph and Disaster* (Boston, MA: Houghton Mifflin, 1985); and Michael Schaller, *Douglas MacArthur: The Far Eastern General* (Oxford University Press, 1989). Lester Pearson's views of the General are an important sub-theme of an article by George Egerton, 'Lester Pearson and the Korean War: Dilemmas of Collective Security and International Enforcement in Canadian Foreign Policy, 1950–1953', *International Peacekeeping*, 4 (1997), pp. 51–74. For more on Canada, refer to Lee, *Outposts of Empire* (1995); Lester Pearson, *Mike: The Memoirs of the Right Honorable Lester B. Pearson*, vol. 2 (Toronto: University of Toronto Press, 1973); and Denis Stairs, *The Diplomacy of Constraint: Canada, the Korean War, and the United States* (Toronto: University of Toronto Press, 1974).

CHAPTER FOUR

The history of desegregation in the American military is described by Richard Dalfiume, *Desegregation of the U.S. Armed Forces: Fighting on Two Fronts, 1939–1953* (Columbia, MO: University of Missouri Press, 1969); and Sherie Mershon and Steven Schlossman, *Foxholes & Color Lines: Desegregating the U.S. Armed Forces* (Baltimore, MA: The Johns Hopkins University Press, 1998). A very good recent study of the relationship between American foreign policy and race is Thomas Borstelmann, 'Jim Crow's Coming Out: Race Relations and American Foreign Policy in the Truman Years', *Presidential Studies Quarterly*, 29 (1999), pp. 549–70. David Skaggs examines 'The KATUSA Experiment: The Integration of Korean Nationals into the U.S. Army, 1950–1965', *Military Affairs*, 38 (1974), pp. 53–8.

There are a number of studies of British Commonwealth troops in Korea. Consult David Bercuson, *Blood on the Hills: The Canadian Army in the Korean War* (Toronto: University of Toronto Press, 1999); Anthony Farrar-Hockley, *The British Part in the Korean War, Volume II: An Honourable Discharge* (London: HMSO 1995); Jeffrey Grey, *The Commonwealth Armies and the Korean War* (Manchester: Manchester University Press, 1988); Ian McGibbon, *New Zealand and the Korean War, Volume II: Combat Operations* (Oxford: Oxford University Press, 1996); and Robert O'Neill, *Australia in the Korean War, 1950–1953; Volume II: Combat Operations* (Canberra: Australian Government Publication Service, 1985).

The role of women in the war can be gleaned from Frances Martin Day, Phyllis Spence and Barbara Ladouceur, eds, *Women Overseas: Memoirs of the Canadian Red Cross Corps* (Vancouver, BC: Ronsdale Press, 1998); Jeanne Holm, *Women in the Military: An Unfinished Revolution* (Novato, CA: Presido Press, 1998); and Peter Soderbergh, *Women Marines in the Korean War Era* (Westport, CT: Praeger, 1994).

Material on the Chinese homefront can be found in Kenneth Lieberthal, *Revolution and Tradition in Tientsin, 1949–1952* (Stanford, CA: Stanford University Press, 1980); Maurice Meisner, *Mao's China and After: A History of the People's Republic* (The Free Press, 1999); and William Rosenberg and Marilyn Young, *Transforming Russia and China: Revolutionary Struggle in the Twentieth Century* (Oxford: Oxford University Press, 1982). For the Chinese volunteers' experience, see John Gittings, *The Role of the Chinese Army* (London: Oxford

University Press, 1967); Samuel Griffith, *The Chinese People's Liberation Army* (McGraw-Hill, 1967); and Charles Shrader, *Communist Logistics in the Korean War* (Westport, CT: Greenwood Press, 1995).

For analyses of the social aspects of the war in the two Koreas, refer to Bruce Cumings, *The Origins of the Korean War* (1990); B.C. Koh, 'The War's Impact on the Korean Peninsula', *The Journal of American-East Asian Relations*, 2 (1993), pp. 57–76; and Chapters 1 and 2 of John Lee's, *Han Unbound: The Political Economy of South Korea* (Stanford, CA: Stanford University Press, 1998). Katherine Moon explores the role of prostitution in Korean-American relations in *Sex among Allies: Military Prostitution in US–Korea Relations* (Columbia University Press, 1998). Korea's postwar industrialization is a major theme of works by Robert Spencer, *Yogong: Factory Girl* (Seoul: Seoul Computer Press, 1988); and Jung-en Woo, *Race to the Swift: State and Finance in Korean Industrialization* (Columbia University Press, 1991). There are a few memoirs in English of the Korean perspective on the fighting. See Sun Yup Paik, *Wartime Memoirs of the Republic of Korea's First Four-Star General* (Dulles, VA: Brassey's, 1992); and Donald K. Chung, *The Three Day Promise: A Korean Soldier's Memoir* (Tallahassee, FL: Father and Son Publishing, 1990). The latter book tells the story of a North Korean who served in both the North and South Korean armies. A sensitive account of the experiences of a MASH surgeon can be found in Dorothy G. Horitz, ed., *We Will Not Be Strangers: Korean War Letters Between a M.A.S.H. Surgeon and His Wife* (Chicago, IL: University of Illinois Press, 1997). For the debate over bacteriological warfare, see Stephen Endicott and Edward Hagerman, *The United States and Biological Warfare* (Bloomington, IN: Indiana University Press, 1998). John Ellis van Courtland Moon critiques the book in 'Dubious Allegations, the United States and Biological Warfare: Secrets from the Early Cold War and Korea', *Bulletin of the Atomic Scientists*, 55 (1999), pp. 70–3.

Cold War culture in America is explored by Paul Pierpaoli, Jr, *Truman and Korea: The Political Culture of the Early Cold War* (Columbia, MO: Missouri University Press, 1999); and by Stephen Whitfield, *The Culture of the Cold War* (Baltimore, MD: The Johns Hopkins University Press, 1996). On the origins and growth of America's national security state and McCarthyism, see Richard Freeland, *The Truman Doctrine and the Origins of McCarthyism: Foreign Policy, Domestic Politics, and Internal Security, 1946–1948* (New York University Press, 1985); Benjamin O. Fordham, *Building the Cold War Consensus: The Political Economy of U.S. National Security, 1949–51* (Ann Arbor, MI: The University of Michigan Press, 1998); Michael Hogan, *A Cross of Iron: Harry S. Truman and the Origins of the National Security State 1945–1954* (Harvard, MA: Cambridge University Press, 1998); and Richard Rovere, *Senator Joe McCarthy* (Harper & Row, 1959). There are numerous biographies of US political figures from this era. Stephen Ambrose has written *Nixon: The Education of a Politician 1913–1962* (Simon and Schuster, 1987); and *Eisenhower: Soldier and President* (Simon and Schuster, 1990). On Truman, see David McCullough, *Truman* (Touchstone, 1992). For an exploration of the domestic American context of the war read John E. Mueller, *War, Presidents and Public Opinion* (John Wiley & Sons, 1973); and Ronald Caridi, *The Korean War and American Politics: The Republican Party as a Case Study* (Philadelphia, PA: University of Pennsylvania Press, 1968).

CHAPTER FIVE

The armistice negotiations are covered in a number of texts, including Rosemary Foot, *A Substitute for Victory: The Politics of Peacemaking at the Korean Armistice Talks* (Ithaca, NY: Cornell University Press, 1990); Walter Hermes, *Truce Tent and Fighting Front* (Washington, DC: GPO, 1966); and O'Neill, *Australia in the Korean War* (1985), above (Chapter Four). For a Chinese communist perspective, consult Peng Dehuai, *The Memoirs of a Chinese Marshal* (Beijing: People's Publishing House, 1984). For a memoir written by one of the top UNC negotiators, see C. Turner Joy, *How Communists Negotiate* (Macmillan, 1955). Joy's diary has been edited by Allen Goodman, *Negotiating While Fighting: The Diary of Admiral C. Turner Joy at the Korean Armistice Conference* (Stanford, CA: Hoover Institute Press, 1978).

Presidential attitudes towards nuclear weapons are discussed in Barton Bernstein, 'Truman's Secret Thoughts on Ending the Korean War', *Foreign Service Journal*, 57 (1980), pp. 31–2; Dwight D. Eisenhower, *Mandate for Change, 1953–1956* (Garden City, NY: Doubleday, 1963); Rosemary Foot, 'Nuclear Coercion and the Ending of the Korean Conflict', *International Security*, 13 (1988–89), pp. 92–112; Edward Keefer, 'President Dwight D. Eisenhower and the End of the Korean War', *Diplomatic History*, 10 (1986), pp. 267–89; and Lee, *Outposts of Empire* (1995). Foot's article should be compared with Roger Dingman, 'Atomic Diplomacy during the Korean War', *International Security*, 13 (1988–89), pp. 50–91.

Foot, *A Substitute for Victory* (1990); Lowe, *The Origins of the Korean War* (1997a) and *Containing the Cold War in East Asia* (1997b); and Kaufman, *The Korean War* (1997) describe UN diplomacy over the Indian Resolution. Evelyn Shuckburgh, *Descent to Suez: Diaries 1951–1956* (Norton, 1986) provides a first-hand account of the meeting between Acheson and Eden in Eden's hotel room. For an account of the US–ROK secret partisan war against the north, read Ed Evanhoe, *Dark Moon: Eighth Army Special Operations in the Korean War* (Annapolis, ML: Naval Institute Press, 1995).

CHAPTER SIX

For an examination of the world disarmament movement and European attitudes towards rearmament, consult Lawrence S. Wittner, *One World or None: A History of the World Nuclear Disarmament Movement through 1953* (Stanford, CA: Stanford University Press, 1993). American and European rearmament issues are also explored in Rosemary Foot's 'Pax Americana: Setting the Global Agenda after the Korean War', in William J. Williams, ed., *A Revolutionary War: Korea and the Transformation of the Postwar World* (Chicago, IL: Imprint Publications, 1993); in Leffler, *A Preponderance of Power* (1992) and Hogan, *A Cross of Iron* (1998).

Studies on the relationships between Japan, the American occupation and the war include Roger Dingman, 'The Dagger and the Gift: The Impact of the Korean War on Japan', in William J. Williams, ed., *A Revolutionary War* (1993), cited above; two books and an article by John Dower, *Empire and Aftermath: Yoshida Shigeru and the Japanese Experience, 1868–1954* (Cambridge, MA: Harvard University Press, 1979); *Embracing Defeat: Japan in the Wake of World War II* (Norton, 1999); and 'Peace and Democracy in Two Systems: External Policy and

Internal Conflict', in Andrew Gordon, ed., *Postwar Japan as History* (Berkeley, CA: University of California Press, 1993); and two books by Michael Schaller, *The American Occupation of Japan: The Origins of the Cold War in Asia* (London: Oxford University Press, 1985); and *Altered States: The United States and Japan since the Occupation* (London: Oxford University Press, 1997). On Japanese economic history more generally, see Takafusa Nakamura, *The Postwar Japanese Economy: Its Development and Structure, 1937–1994* (Tokyo: University of Tokyo Press, 1995).

Sino-Soviet and Sino-American relationships are examined in Gordon Chang, *Friends and Enemies: The United States, China and the Soviet Union, 1948–1972* (Stanford, CA: Stanford University Press, 1990); Odd Arne Westad, ed., *Brothers in Arms: The Rise and Fall of the Sino-Soviet Alliance 1945–1963* (Washington, DC: Woodrow Wilson Center Press, 1998); Goncharov et al., *Uncertain Partners* (1993); and Meisner, *Mao's China and After* (1999).

For the South Asian context of the Cold War consult Robert McMahon, *Cold War on the Periphery: The United States, India and Pakistan* (Columbia University Press, 1994); and Anita Inder Singh, *The Limits of British Influence: South Asia and the Anglo-American Relationship, 1947–1956* (St Martin's Press, 1993). A selection of Nehru's speeches has been compiled by the Government of India, Ministry of Information and Broadcasting, *India's Foreign Policy: Selected Speeches of Jawaharlal Nehru, September 1946–April 1961* (Delhi: Commercial Printing Press, 1961).

The political systems of the two Koreas are analyzed by Sung Chul Yang, *The North and South Korean Political Systems: A Comparative Analysis* (Boulder, CO: Westview Press, 1994). Several articles have been written on the 1952 political dispute. See Jong Yil Ra, 'Political Crisis in Korea, 1952: The Administration, Legislature, Military and Foreign Powers', *Journal of Contemporary History*, 27 (1992), pp. 301–18; and Edward Keefer, 'The Truman Administration and the South Korean Political Crisis of 1952: Democracy's Failure?', *Pacific Historical Review*, 60 (1991), pp. 145–68.

CHAPTER SEVEN

A good article on American objectives at the Geneva Conference on Korea has been published by Henry Brands, 'The Dwight D. Eisenhower Administration, Syngman Rhee and the "Other" Geneva Conference of 1954', *Pacific Historical Review*, 56 (1987), pp. 78–99. See also Hakjoon Kim, *Unification Policies of South and North Korea, 1945–1991: A Comparative Study* (Seoul: Seoul National University Press, 1992); Steven Hugh Lee, 'Negotiating the Cold War: The United States and the Two Koreas', *Journal of American–East Asian Relations*, 2000 (forthcoming); Robert O'Neill, *Australia in the Korean War, 1950–1953, Volume I: Strategy and Diplomacy* (Canberra: Australian Government Publication Service, 1981); and J.Y. Ra, 'The Politics of Conference: The Political Conference on Korea, 26 April–15 June 1954', *Journal of Contemporary History*, 34 (1999), pp. 399–416.

WEBSITES

There are numerous websites on Korea, US diplomacy, and the international history of the Korean War. Several useful ones are listed below.

http://www.army.mil/cmh-pg/ is the site for the US Army Center of Military History. The site contains web versions of several official histories of the Korean conflict.

http://www.ffasfs.com.au/chapter10.htm is Maurie Pears and Fred Kirkland, 'Korea Remembered', An Australian soldier's memoirs.

http://www.koreanwar.org/ is a Korean War website catering to US veterans. It is interesting for understanding the contemporary memory and culture of the war.

http://www.npg.si.edu/exh/marilyn/korea5.htm is the US National Portrait Gallery 2000 website where there is a collection of recently discovered photos of Marilyn Monroe in Korea, 1954.

http://www.people.fas.harvard.edu/~hoffmann/ is one of the best links to Korean Studies material.

http://www.seas.gwu.edu is the website for the Cold War International History Project. The site has articles and translated primary source material from communist sources dealing with various aspects of the Korean War.

http://www2.hawaii.edu/korea/bibliography/biblio.htm provides a comprehensive bibliographical listing of secondary materials dealing with Korean themes, including the Korean War.

http://www2.h-net.msu.edu/~diplo/ is the major website for discussions and resources dealing with US foreign policy.

BIBLIOGRAPHY

The place of publication is New York unless otherwise stated.

Ambrose, Stephen. (1987) *Nixon: The Education of a Politician 1913–1962.* Simon and Schuster.

Appleman, Roy. (1961) *United States Army in the Korean War: South to the Naktong, North to the Yalu, June–November 1950.* Washington, DC: GPO.

Baik, Bong. (1970) *Kim Il Sung: From Building Democratic Korea to Chullima Flight.* Guardian Publishers.

Brands, Henry. (1987) 'The Dwight D. Eisenhower Administration, Syngman Rhee and the "Other" Geneva Conference of 1954', *Pacific Historical Review*, 56, pp. 78–99.

Chen, Jian. (1994) *China's Road to the Korean War: The Making of the Sino-American Confrontation.* Columbia University Press.

Cumings, Bruce. (1981) *The Origins of the Korean War: Liberation and the Emergence of Separate Regimes.* Princeton, NJ: Princeton University Press.

Cumings, Bruce. (1990) *The Origins of the Korean War: The Roaring of the Cataract 1947–1950.* Princeton NJ: Princeton University Press.

Cumings, Bruce. (1997) *Korea's Place in the Sun.* Norton.

Eckert, Carter, Ki-baik Lee, Young Ick Lew, Michael Robinson and Edward Wagner. (1990) *Korea Old and New: A History.* Seoul: Ilchokak Publishers.

Egerton, George. (1997) 'Lester Pearson and the Korean War: Dilemmas of Collective Security and International Enforcement in Canadian Foreign Policy, 1950–1953', *International Peacekeeping*, 4, pp. 51–74.

Endicott, Stephen and Edward Hagerman. (1998) *The United States and Biological Warfare: Secrets of the Early Cold War and Korea.* Bloomington, IN: Indiana University Press.

Engelhardt, Tom. (1995) *The End of Victory Culture: Cold War America and the Disillusioning of a Generation.* Basic Books.

Foot, Rosemary. (1985) *The Wrong War: American Policy and the Dimensions of the Korean Conflict, 1950–1953.* Ithaca, NY: Cornell University Press.

Foot, Rosemary. (1990) *A Substitute for Victory: The Politics of Peacemaking at the Korean Armistice Talks.* Ithaca, NY: Cornell University Press.

Fordham, Benjamin. (1998) *Building the Cold War Consensus: The Political Economy of US National Security Policy, 1949–51.* Ann Arbor, MI: University of Michigan Press.

Gaddis, John Lewis (1987) *The Long Peace: Inquiries into the History of the Cold War.* Oxford: Oxford University Press.

Goncharov, Sergei, John Lewis and Xue Litai. (1993) *Uncertain Partners: Stalin, Mao and the Korean War.* Stanford, CA: Stanford University Press.

Government of India, Ministry of Information and Broadcasting. (1961) *India's Foreign Policy, Selected Speeches of Jawaharlal Nehru, September 1946– April 1961*. Bombay: Commercial Printing Press.

Great Britain, Foreign and Commonwealth Office. (1991) *Documents on British Policy Overseas: The Korean War*, Series II, vol. IV, London: HMSO.

Hermes, Walter. (1996) *Truce Tent and Fighting Front*. Washington, DC: GPO.

Hershberg, James. (ed.) (1995) *Cold War International History Project Bulletin*. 'Cold War Crises'. Washington, DC: Woodrow Wilson International Center for Scholars.

Hershberg, James. (ed.) (1995–96) *Cold War International History Project Bulletin*. 'The Cold War in Asia'. Washington, DC: Woodrow Wilson International Center for Scholars.

Hershberg, James. (ed.) (1996–97) *Cold War International History Project Bulletin*. 'The Cold War in the Third World and the Collapse of Detente in the 1970s'. Washington, DC: Woodrow Wilson International Center for Scholars.

Hogan, Michael. (1998) *A Cross of Iron: Harry S. Truman and the Origins of the National Security State 1945–1954*. Cambridge: Cambridge University Press.

Holm, Jeanne. (1992) *Women in the Military: An Unfinished Revolution*. Novato, CA: Presido Press.

Hunt, Michael. (1987) *Ideology and U.S. Foreign Policy*. New Haven, CT: Yale University Press.

Hunt, Michael. (1992) 'Beijing and the Korean Crisis, June 1950–June 1951', *Political Science Quarterly*, 107, pp. 453–78.

Hunt, Michael. (1996) *Crises in U.S. Foreign Policy: An International History Reader*. New Haven, CT: Yale University Press.

Kaufman, Burton. (1997) *The Korean War: Challenges in Crisis, Credibility and Command*. Philadelphia, PA: Temple University Press.

Lee, Steven Hugh. (1995) *Outposts of Empire: Korea, Vietnam, and the Origins of the Cold War in Asia, 1949–1954*. Montreal: McGill-Queen's University Press.

Leffler, Melvyn. (1992) *A Preponderance of Power: National Security, the Truman Administration and the Cold War*. Stanford, CA: Stanford University Press.

Lowe, Peter. (1997a) *The Origins of the Korean War*. Longman.

Lowe, Peter. (1997b) *Containing the Cold War in East Asia: British Policies towards Japan, China and Korea, 1948–1953*. Manchester: Manchester University Press.

Mastny, Vojtech. (1996) *The Cold War and Soviet Insecurity: The Stalin Years*. London: Oxford University Press.

Matray, James. (1981) 'Captive of the Cold War: The Decision to Divide Korea at the 38th Parallel', *Pacific Historical Review*, 50, pp. 145–68.

Matray, James. (2000) 'The Acheson Speech Re-examined', paper delivered to the Society for Historians of American Foreign Relations (SHAFR) Conference, Toronto, Canada, 22 June, 2000.

McCullough, David. (1992) *Truman*. Touchstone.

McGibbon, Ian. (1996) *New Zealand and the Korean War*. London: Oxford University Press.

McMahon, Robert. (1994) *Cold War on the Periphery: The United States, India and Pakistan*. Columbia University Press.

Mershon, Sherie and Steven Schlossman. (1998) *Foxholes & Color Lines: Desegregating the US Armed Forces*. Baltimore, MA: The Johns Hopkins University Press.

Mueller, John. (1973) *War, Presidents and Public Opinion.* John Wiley Sons.

O'Neill, Robert. (1985) *Australia in the Korean War, 1950–1953, Volume II: Combat Operations.* Canberra: Australian Government Publication Service.

Paterson, Thomas, J. Garry Clifford and Kenneth Hagan. (1988) *American Foreign Policy: A History since 1900.* Toronto, ON: D.C. Heath.

Republic of Korea, National History Compilation Committee. (1987–) *Taehan Min'guksa Charyojip (A Collection of Historical Documents of the Republic of Korea).* Kwachon: National History Compilation Committee.

Rhodes, Richard. (1995) *Dark Sun: The Making of the Hydrogen Bomb.* Touchstone.

Schaller, Michael. (1997) *Altered States: The United States and Japan since the Occupation.* London: Oxford University Press.

Shrader, Charles. (1995) *Communist Logistics in the Korean War.* Westport, CN: Greenwood Press.

Shuckburgh, Evelyn. (1986) *Descent to Suez: Diaries 1951–1956.* Norton.

Singh, Anita Inder. (1993) *The Limits of British Influence: South Asia and the Anglo-American Relationship, 1947–1956.* St Martin's Press.

Skaggs, David. (1974) 'The KATUSA Experiment: The Integration of Korean Nationals into the US Army, 1950–1965', *Military Affairs,* 38, pp. 53–8.

Stueck, William. (1996) *The Korean War: An International History.* Princeton, NJ: Princeton University Press.

United States Army Center of Military History, Historical Manuscripts Collection. (1950–53) *The Korean War.* Wilmingdon, DE: Scholarly Resources Microfilm, 15 reels.

United States, Congress. (1953) *The United States and the Korean Problem, Documents 1943–1953.* Washington, DC: GPO.

United States, Department of State. (1969) *Foreign Relations of the United States, 1945: The British Commonwealth and the Far East,* vol. VI. Washington, DC: GPO.

United States, Department of State. (1976) *Foreign Relations of the United States, 1950: Korea,* vol. VII. Washington, DC: GPO.

United States, Department of State. (1981) *Foreign Relations of the United States, 1952–1954: The Geneva Conference,* vol. XVI. Washington, DC: GPO.

United States, Department of State. (1983) *Foreign Relations of the United States, 1951: Korea and China,* vol. VII, part 1. Washington: GPO.

United States, Department of State. (1984) *Foreign Relations of the United States, 1952–1954: Korea,* vol. XV, parts 1–2. Washington, DC: GPO.

Weathersby, Kathryn. (1998) 'Stalin, Mao, and the End of the Korean War', in Odd Arne Westad (ed.), *Brothers in Arms: The Rise and Fall of the Sino-Soviet Alliance 1945–1963.* Washington, DC: Woodrow Wilson Center Press.

Zubok, Vladislav and Constantine Pleshakov. (1996) *Inside the Kremlin's War: From Stalin to Khrushchev.* Cambridge, MA: Harvard University Press.

INDEX

SEMINAR STUDIES IN HISTORY

General Editors: Clive Emsley & Gordon Martel

The series was founded by Patrick Richardson in 1966. Between 1980 and 1996 Roger Lockyer edited the series before handing over to Clive Emsley (Professor of History at the Open University) and Gordon Martel (Professor of International History at the University of Northern British Columbia, Canada and Senior Research Fellow at De Montfort University).

STUART BRITAIN

Social Change and Continuity: England 1550–1750 (Second edition)
Barry Coward   0 582 29442 8

James I (Second edition)
S J Houston   0 582 20911 0

The English Civil War 1640–1649
Martyn Bennett   0 582 35392 0

Charles I, 1625–1640
Brian Quintrell   0 582 00354 7

The English Republic 1649–1660 (Second edition)
Toby Barnard   0 582 08003 7

Radical Puritans in England 1550–1660
R J Acheson   0 582 35515 X

The Restoration and the England of Charles II (Second edition)
John Miller   0 582 29223 9

The Glorious Revolution (Second edition)
John Miller   0 582 29222 0

EARLY MODERN EUROPE

The Renaissance (Second edition)
Alison Brown   0 582 30781 3

The Emperor Charles V
Martyn Rady   0 582 35475 7

French Renaissance Monarchy: Francis I and Henry II (Second edition)
Robert Knecht   0 582 28707 3

The Protestant Reformation in Europe
Andrew Johnston   0 582 07020 1

The French Wars of Religion 1559–1598 (Second edition)
Robert Knecht   0 582 28533 X

Phillip II
Geoffrey Woodward   0 582 07232 8

The Thirty Years' War
Peter Limm   0 582 35373 4

Louis XIV
Peter Campbell   0 582 01770 X

Spain in the Seventeenth Century
Graham Darby   0 582 07234 4

Peter the Great
William Marshall   0 582 00355 5

EUROPE 1789–1918

Britain and the French Revolution
Clive Emsley   0 582 36961 4

Revolution and Terror in France 1789–1795 (Second edition)
D G Wright   0 582 00379 2

Napoleon and Europe
D G Wright   0 582 35457 9

Nineteenth-Century Russia: Opposition to Autocracy
Derek Offord   0 582 35767 5

The Constitutional Monarchy in France 1814–48
Pamela Pilbeam   0 582 31210 8

The 1848 Revolutions (Second edition)
Peter Jones   0 582 06106 7

The Italian Risorgimento
M Clark   0 582 00353 9

Bismark & Germany 1862–1890 (Second edition)
D G Williamson   0 582 29321 9

Imperial Germany 1890–1918
Ian Porter, Ian Armour and Roger Lockyer   0 582 03496 5

The Dissolution of the Austro-Hungarian Empire 1867–1918 (Second edition)
John W Mason   0 582 29466 5

Second Empire and Commune: France 1848–1871 (Second edition)
William H C Smith   0 582 28705 7

France 1870–1914 (Second edition)
Robert Gildea   0 582 29221 2

The Scramble for Africa (Second edition)
M E Chamberlain   0 582 36881 2

Late Imperial Russia 1890–1917
John F Hutchinson   0 582 32721 0

The First World War
Stuart Robson   0 582 31556 5

EUROPE SINCE 1918

The Russian Revolution (Second edition)
Anthony Wood   0 582 35559 1

Lenin's Revolution: Russia, 1917–1921
David Marples   0 582 31917 X

Stalin and Stalinism (Second edition)
Martin McCauley   0 582 27658 6

The Weimar Republic (Second edition)
John Hiden   0 582 28706 5

The Inter-War Crisis 1919–1939
Richard Overy   0 582 35379 3

Fascism and the Right in Europe, 1919–1945
Martin Blinkhorn   0 582 07021 X

Spain's Civil War (Second edition)
Harry Browne   0 582 28988 2

The Third Reich (Second edition)
D G Williamson   0 582 20914 5

The Origins of the Second World War (Second edition)
R J Overy   0 582 29085 6

The Second World War in Europe
Paul MacKenzie   0 582 32692 3

Anti-Semitism before the Holocaust
Albert S Lindemann   0 582 36964 9

The Holocaust: The Third Reich and the Jews
David Engel   0 582 32720 2

Germany from Defeat to Partition, 1945–1963
D G Williamson   0 582 29218 2

Britain and Europe since 1945
Alex May   0 582 30778 3

Eastern Europe 1945–1969: From Stalinism to Stagnation
Ben Fowkes   0 582 32693 1

Eastern Europe since 1970
Bülent Gökay   0 582 32858 6

The Khrushchev Era, 1953–1964
Martin McCauley   0 582 27776 0

NINETEENTH-CENTURY BRITAIN

Britain before the Reform Acts: Politics and Society 1815–1832
Eric J Evans   0 582 00265 6

Parliamentary Reform in Britain c. 1770–1918
Eric J Evans   0 582 29467 3

Democracy and Reform 1815–1885
D G Wright   0 582 31400 3

Poverty and Poor Law Reform in Nineteenth-Century Britain, 1834–1914:
From Chadwick to Booth
David Englander   0 582 31554 9

The Birth of Industrial Britain: Economic Change, 1750–1850
Kenneth Morgan   0 582 29833 4

Chartism (Third edition)
Edward Royle   0 582 29080 5

Peel and the Conservative Party 1830–1850
Paul Adelman   0 582 35557 5

Gladstone, Disraeli and later Victorian Politics (Third edition)
Paul Adelman   0 582 29322 7

Britain and Ireland: From Home Rule to Independence
Jeremy Smith   0 582 30193 9

TWENTIETH-CENTURY BRITAIN

The Rise of the Labour Party 1880–1945 (Third edition)
Paul Adelman   0 582 29210 7

The Conservative Party and British Politics 1902–1951
Stuart Ball   0 582 08002 9

The Decline of the Liberal Party 1910–1931 (Second edition)
Paul Adelman   0 582 27733 7

The British Women's Suffrage Campaign 1866–1928
Harold L Smith   0 582 29811 3

War & Society in Britain 1899–1948
Rex Pope   0 582 03531 7

The British Economy since 1914: A Study in Decline?
Rex Pope   0 582 30194 7

Unemployment in Britain between the Wars
Stephen Constantine   0 582 35232 0

The Attlee Governments 1945–1951
Kevin Jefferys   0 582 06105 9

The Conservative Governments 1951–1964
Andrew Boxer   0 582 20913 7

Britain under Thatcher
Anthony Seldon and Daniel Collings   0 582 31714 2

INTERNATIONAL HISTORY

The Eastern Question 1774–1923 (Second edition)
A L Macfie   0 582 29195 X

The Origins of the First World War (Second edition)
Gordon Martel   0 582 28697 2

The United States and the First World War
Jennifer D Keene   0 582 35620 2

Anti-Semitism before the Holocaust
Albert S Lindemann   0 582 36964 9

The Origins of the Cold War, 1941–1949 (Second edition)
Martin McCauley   0 582 27659 4

Russia, America and the Cold War, 1949–1991
Martin McCauley   0 582 27936 4

The Arab–Israeli Conflict
Kirsten E Schulze   0 582 31646 4

The United Nations since 1945: Peacekeeping and the Cold War
Norrie MacQueen   0 582 35673 3

Decolonisation: The British Experience since 1945
Nicholas J White   0 582 29087 2

The Origins of the Vietnam War
Fredrik Logevall   0 582 31918 8

The Vietnam War
Mitchell Hall   0 582 32859 4

WORLD HISTORY

China in Transformation 1900–1949
Colin Mackerras   0 582 31209 4

Japan faces the World, 1925–1952
Mary L Hanneman   0 582 36898 7

Japan in Transformation, 1952–2000
Jeff Kingston   0 582 41875 5

US HISTORY

American Abolitionists
Stanley Harrold   0 582 35738 1

The American Civil War, 1861–1865
Reid Mitchell   0 582 31973 0

America in the Progressive Era, 1890–1914
Lewis L Gould   0 582 35671 7

The United States and the First World War
Jennifer D Keene   0 582 35620 2

The Truman Years, 1945–1953
Mark S Byrnes   0 582 32904 3

The Korean War
Steven Hugh Lee   0 582 31988 9

The Origins of the Vietnam War
Fredrik Logevall   0 582 31918 8

The Vietnam War
Mitchell Hall   0 582 32859 4